The Persuasion Industry

John Pearson & Graham Turner

THE
PERSUASION
INDUSTRY

Readers Union Eyre & Spottiswoode 1966

This RU edition was produced in 1966 for sale to its members only by Readers Union Ltd at Aldine House, 10-13 Bedford Street, London W.C.2 and at Letchworth Garden City, Herts. Full details of membership may be obtained from our London address.

The book is set in 9-pt Georgian and has been reprinted by the Northumberland Press Ltd, Gateshead. It was first published by Eyre & Spottiswoode (Publishers) Ltd

Contents

Introduction

No industry has a more noticeable face than advertising, yet none is more faceless. We all know the advertisements and we all react to them in one way or another; but few of us really know the men behind them or the inside story of the way they work.

Because of this, the more heated the controversy about advertising, the more nebulous it seems to become. For without understanding something of the men behind the advertisements and why they operate the way they do any discussion about advertising must inevitably remain academic. The target is too impersonal. No advertisement produces itself.

The further we went into the advertising business, the more surprises we got. We found it crazier, gentler, more varied and yet in a curious way more sinister than either its critics or its defenders had led us to expect. It seemed a lonely, rather ingrown world, strangely cut off from the society it spends so much time and money attempting to reach.

This was even more so in the case of public relations – and since public relations, whether the advertising men like it or not, is a part of the total persuasion industry, we decided that we had to deal with them together.

This is a reporters' book about the way that the industry works in Britain today. It sets out to explain the men behind the advertisements and P.R. campaigns and the character of the different agencies where they work. It does not pretend to cover *every* agency or firm – that would clearly be impossible – but even though selective it does seek to put a face to persuasion.

Most of our work was done from 1962 to the end of 1964 and in an industry as volatile as this, there may well be changes of detail by the time we go to press – campaigns that have already died, copywriters who have moved on to other agencies.

The list of acknowledgments for a book like this, which depends on pressing people for information which it is not always in their interest (nor more powerfully, in those of their clients) to divulge, could be endless. Most of them are mentioned in the course of the book – for not the least pleasant of the surprises this bizarre industry had in store for us was the frankness and kindness with which we were almost invariably received.

J.P.
G.T.
January 1965

PART 1. ADVERTISING

1. The Fight for the Ford Account

On September 27th, 1960, six men gathered in the board-room of their first floor offices at the Fleet Street end of the Strand. They were the directors of an advertising agency called Rumble, Crowther and Nicholas, and before they sat down they knew they were about to take the most crucial decision any board can face.

The issue before them was whether they were to keep their biggest client – the Ford Motor Company of Great Britain.

No advertising agency likes giving up business, and especially business like this. The Ford account is one of the plums of the advertising world. RCN were spending an average of £547,000 a year on Ford's behalf (it was £890,000 by 1961), almost all of it in newspaper advertising, and in return they received 15 per cent – £82,050 – the standard commission which national newspapers pay to agencies which take space in their pages.[1]

It was particularly odd that a firm like Rumble, Crowther and Nicholas should even consider resigning their largest account. They were not a big company and Ford provided no less than 40 per cent of their income. Every year the account put a fat bonus into each of the six directors' pockets.

Their £2 million business was tiny compared with the £15½ million which J. Walter Thompson, the largest American-owned agency in

[1] Some provincial weekly papers pay only 10 per cent commission, but the majority of provincial dailies offer 15 per cent. The commercial television companies, cinemas and most poster firms, on the other hand, give standard 15 per cent rates.

Britain, then handled. The London Press Exchange, the largest British-owned agency, was seven times as big and even the fourteenth largest agency, McCann-Erickson, was twice R C N's size.[2]

Rumble, Crowther and Nicholas, moreover, had been doing Ford's advertising for fourteen years, a long time by agency standards. They had helped launch a score of new models – Consuls, Zephyrs, Zodiacs, Anglias – and for all that time they had shown the devoted deference due from every agency to the source of its prosperity, the client.

Yet there was surprisingly little discussion in the board-room that Wednesday morning. Ernest Walker, a shortish, stocky man who had previously been Managing Director of R C N for three years and had now become Chairman, said they could shelve the issue no longer; the time had come to resign. Oddly enough, nobody disagreed and the vote was unanimous.

The motives behind this mysterious episode have never been fully explained. There was, of course, the official obituary notice from R C N which said in the vaguest possible terms that they had disagreed with Ford on 'certain technical aspects' of the work. This, it got about later, meant that (in R C N's view) Ford had been making too many last-minute changes in their advertisements, getting the agency a bad name in Fleet Street and causing the quality of their work to suffer.

To the more cynical, this seemed an unlikely explanation. Their evidence suggested that R C N had realized Ford were tiring of them – as clients are periodically apt to do – and in fact were already looking round for another agency. Being none too happy themselves, they jumped rather than waited to be pushed. As Walker explained later: 'None of our directors has ever wanted to be a millionaire.'

The next day, Walker went to Ford's Cheapside offices and called on Robert Adams, who, as advertising manager for the home market, was the filter through which all Ford's domestic advertisements had to pass. Adams belonged to a new breed of advertisement managers. The old school, in his own words, were 'egocentrics who used to base their decisions on hunch or histrionics'. Adams himself, an ex-archaeologist who was appointed by Ford at 33, believed that 'an effective ad-manager should steer the agency very positively – otherwise they may shoot off

[2] Although there are roughly 500 agencies altogether (250 belonging to the Institute of Practitioners in Advertising) the top five placed roughly a quarter of all the advertising which went through the agencies. The estimated billings in the UK in 1964 for five of the biggest agencies were: S. H. Benson £17 million; Colman, Prentis and Varley £19 million; the London Press Exchange £20 million; Mather and Crowther £14 million; and J. Walter Thompson £19 million. Comparison of billing figures, however, is complicated by the different criteria applied by the agencies in arriving at their totals.

at a tangent'. He regarded it as one of his ambitions in life to raise 'the low level of British automotive advertising'.

Walker, in a rare reversal of roles, told Adams he was sacked; but added that R C N were ready to handle Ford's advertising until they had found a new agency. Adams accepted the dismissal, and they parted. On September 29th, Walker duly wrote to the Ford Chairman, Sir Patrick Hennessy, who replied that it had all come as a great surprise to him.

So began the strange, involved ritual by which a major advertising account changes hands.

But the Ford affair was much more than just a large account moving agencies; it was a classic example of the advertising world at work. It typified the instability of this £500 million industry,[3] the suddenness with which the fortunes of agencies change, the continual competition for new business. It was one of the internecine struggles which create the neuroses and the unease which seem to be endemic to advertising.

In this inbred little world the agency grapevine works quickly and efficiently. Apart from gossip in the pubs and coffee-bars which agency men tend to frequent, there is a vast 'old-boy' network of people who have already worked in half a dozen firms and who are shrewd enough to cultivate their lines of communication carefully in case they should want to move again next year.

Indeed the grapevine is so good that it is difficult to launch a new product or a new advertising campaign without its details being known by rival firms months before it bursts upon the public.[4] The men who produce television commercials for several agencies may talk indiscreetly; printers setting up type for a new campaign of newspaper advertisements do not hide the fact from the casual visitor; and advertising men in newspapers and TV companies can easily tell their friends which agencies have booked space for the months ahead.

So, although the R C N decision may have come as a surprise to Sir Patrick Hennessy, it certainly was not news to many shrewd agency men. As soon as the separation became official, almost every big firm in London was in the hunt for the Ford business. Within days there were callers waiting in the cream painted lobby at R C N to ask Ernest Walker how they ought to go about landing the account.

Adams, on his side, was suddenly required to recommend another firm to the Ford management and this, from the agencies' point of view, put him in a position of considerable power. He had roughly six months in which to find a new agency, but the field was large and scattered. London has nothing to compare with the golden mile of Madison

---

[3] This represents roughly 2 per cent of the national income. In America, by comparison, the proportion is nearer 3 per cent, in France under 1 per cent.

[4] Many advertising men disagree with this: they say that security arrangements within agencies are most strict.

Avenue. If there is any Mecca to which advertising men aspire (particularly those in American-owned agencies), it is Mayfair – but there are important agencies in Knightsbridge, off the Strand, in the narrow lanes north and south of Fleet Street, dotted all over Holborn and even in the less fashionable regions to the north, off the Tottenham Court and Euston Roads.

Ford did not want another small agency. They were looking for a firm which handled at least £3 million worth of business, which had other big clients – and they needed an agency which would improve on their current advertising programmes, services which, they thought, only a big agency could provide.

Adams drew up a list of about thirty who topped the £3 million mark, and took a closer look at each of them. Half a dozen were immediately disqualified because they already did advertising for other vehicle manufacturers – for it is a convention of the agency business that the same firm cannot advertise for competing companies.

McCann-Erickson, British subsidiary of the second-largest agency in the world, were out of the running because they had the Ferguson tractor account – Ford make tractors as well as cars. So were Colman, Prentis and Varley (advertising agents to the Conservative Party) – they handled Austin Cars. So were Dorland Advertising (Morris), Crawford (Vauxhall), Pritchard, Wood (Rover) and Erwin, Wasey, Ruthrauff and Ryan (Sunbeam).

The same convention put one of London's most successful agencies, Mather and Crowther (responsible for the campaign 'Drinka Pinta Milka Day' which, apparently, came out of a harrassed executive's inspired attempt to cram his advertising message into four words for a poster), in an almost intolerable dilemma. Mather's had just been given the Standard-Triumph account which at that time had an appropriation of only £200,000. Regretfully, Adams had to strike Mathers off his list.

Another large British agency, S. H. Benson, who had been doing the Guinness[5] advertising for more than thirty years, were able to by-pass the same convention. They already handled the advertising for Austin's commercial vehicles, but Adams discovered that – with Austin's consent – they could give it up if something more lucrative came along. That pleased Adams. From the beginning, he favoured Benson; he was looking for 'creative' advertising and thought they would provide it.

Early in October, he made his first move with a cautious approach to the agencies still left on the list. Obviously, he said, Ford did not want

[5] In January 1965 Mather and Crowther merged their interests operationally with Ogilvy, Benson and Mather of New York to form the holding company of Ogilvy and Mather. David Ogilvy is Chairman, and Donald Atkins of Mather and Crowther is Vice-Chairman.

to commit themselves at such an early stage, but he would like an opportunity to have a look round.

In the world of advertising, appearances are vitally important. Though most British agencies are not so sumptuously appointed as their American counterparts, they still take their *décor* pretty seriously. Big accounts may depend on the first impression of visiting chairmen; so the agency boss may stuff the building full of modern art, to give an impression of creativity, or surround himself with antique bric-à-brac to suggest well-bred opulence.

Adams liked a modern, functional *décor*, and reacted sharply both against the reproduction Regency which some of the more affluent agencies favour, and against the cream-and-brown dowdiness which others use to create an atmosphere of austerity.

The *décor* of one of London's biggest agencies left an indelible mark on his mind. The walls were 'a monotonous cream', the lift was 'cantankerous', the corridors 'finicky'. 'I felt like the White Rabbit in *Alice in Wonderland* when I was there,' he said. This was an agency, incidentally, which was not short-listed.

In some agencies, which obviously set out to project themselves as gay and creative, Adams found 'reception rooms decked out like drawing-room comedy sets from the 'thirties. In others,' he said, 'there was an "anyone for tennis?" atmosphere, usually accompanied by large bowls of luxuriant flowers. Sometimes the hollyhocks were just too big.'

To Adams it appeared that there were broadly two kinds of receptionist. About half were 'toffee nosed debs, who always seemed to be in the middle of telephone conversations with very intimate friends' – and made their distaste for interruption only too obvious. The other half were impeccably uniformed commissionaires with clipped, military manners whom he half expected to frog-march him in front of the agency director.

In the hunt for new business, the agency boss is a crucial figure. In the rising firms, the chairman not only acts as a presiding father-figure who lends an air of tradition to the place – he also knows the right people in the high echelons of the City and the business world. In the declining agencies, he is merely a living reminder of the triumphs of the past.

At each agency, Adams was given a whistle-stop tour, followed by coffee – nothing stronger, since he usually called at ten in the morning – and the best cigarettes the agency could afford, invariably from a silver cigarette box. Most of the agency bosses were polite and courteous, but not pressing. Despite the post-war American invasion – about half London's big agencies are American-owned – the Madison Avenue huckster is still a rare bird.

At only one leading firm – American-owned – was Adams given the hard-sell treatment which is common in New York. The agency boss pinned him to the wall like a butterfly: 'We desire to have your account, we deserve to have your account, we *must* have your account.' Even then, Adams suspected the heavy huckster approach was only used because the boss thought Ford would be impressed by it.

So the list was getting shorter. Other agencies did not do the sort of business which suggested that they would be good at advertising cars. They knew a good deal about detergents, or chocolates or cosmetics, but had never handled what Adams called 'consumer durables'.

As the October days moved on, the number of candidates still in the race shrank rapidly. There were seventeen names, then ten, then seven. Adams made a final call on the seven. They were: J. Walter Thompson; S. H. Benson; Masius and Fergusson,[6] an agency which had taken over the European business of the legendary American firm of Lord and Thomas when its owner sold out; the London Press Exchange; Foote, Cone and Belding, another off-shoot of Lord and Thomas; Young and Rubicam, also American-owned; and G. S. Royds. Four were American, three British.

From these Adams, in consultation with the Ford management, prepared a final short list. For various reasons, Masius, Young and Rubicam, and Royds were eliminated, and this left four agencies, two American and two British.

But before he drew up his report for his director, Adams did a little behind the scenes investigation into the four. He discreetly approached companies who had been or were still served by one or other of them. For instance, he talked to two of Thompson's present clients – Reckitt and Colman, and Champion Plugs – and one former client, Brand's Pastes, to find out what they thought of the agency. The reply: first-class. He checked up on why the London Press Exchange had lost the Remington Razor account and why Foote, Cone and Belding no longer handled Batchelor's Peas. In both cases, he discovered the loss had been due to reorganization by the client. His inquiries also yielded a warning not to underestimate Benson, with their very English tendency to under-sell themselves.

With all this information, Adams sat down and composed a long and exhaustive report on the four. He commented on them under three main headings – 'creative ability', organization and 'executive characteristics'. Adams had already decided that advertising men tended to fall into two categories. There were the 'creative' men, often Oxbridge, always intellectual, who saw advertising as a game which could be won by sheer

[6] In July 1964 the agency changed its name to Masius, Wynne-Williams. See Chapter 11.

smartness and brilliance; and there were the 'marketing' men, usually with a background of hard selling, who believed that the 'creativeness' of an advertisement could only be measured on a sales graph of the product advertised.

But in the case of one agency, Thompson, there were underlying political issues to assess as well. In the British advertising world, American parent companies can be embarrassing. In Thompson's case, the fact that their parent already handled Ford advertising in America and round the world to the tune of $80 million a year, might have proved doubly embarrassing. They were, on the one hand, so closely associated with the Ford name that they could hardly compete for other car accounts in Britain. On the other, there may have been qualms in the minds of some people at Dagenham at the prospect of hiring the same agency as their American bosses.

From this point of view, Ford's change of agencies could hardly have come at a worse time for Thompson in that American Ford's bid to take over the British company (which became public in November 1960 and succeeded in the following January) was already anticipated at Dagenham. But in the event the Ford Chairman, Sir Patrick Hennessy, officially stated that they would look at all agencies with no prejudice whatsoever.

Thompson's top London executives had done everything they could to allay Ford's fears. Bill Hinks, their chairman, as well as Sandy Mitchell-Innes, one of the deputy chairmen, had assured Adams that there would be no interference from New York, either then or later. Thompson, for their part, adhered rigidly to that promise. Throughout the battle for the British Ford account which followed, they refused to pull their American strings and indeed, when things were going badly and New York looked like intervening, top-level action was taken to see that the Americans stayed out of the fight.

For the rest, Adams could find little to fault at Thompson. Their creative work, he said, was high-grade and though they were then going through a major administrative reshuffle, he found their organization streamlined, if elaborate.

Of the London Press Exchange, on the other hand, he wrote that their organization was something of a headache. There were no less than fourteen semi-autonomous companies in the group, each with its own particular function. For instance, the agency had created a separate company, called Intam, to handle overseas advertising. They had set up a specialist agency, St James's Advertising, to work for clients in the City. The group had its own printing firm – the Fanfare Press – its own separate research unit and even a subsidiary – Merchandising and Marketing Development Limited – which did everything from training a company's sales force to advising them on what sort of goods they should be selling in five years' time.

At first, this seemed like a 'ghastly octopus' to Adams, but he soon began to understand. The object of breaking the agency down into specialist companies was simply to attract as much business as possible. If firms did not want L P E to do their advertising, they could still hire St James's Advertising to place their company reports in the financial press, or get brochures printed at the Fanfare Press or get advice on what they should pay their salesmen from Merchandising and Marketing Development. Adams agreed with a top American executive's verdict on L P E: 'A superb machine for making money', and he found the executives he had met personable and frank.

At Foote, Cone and Belding he liked the fundamental, contemporary *décor* and was impressed by the good manners of everybody he met. He thought the agency boss, Brian MacCabe, was outstanding – and his only question-mark against the agency was whether it might not be too much of a one-man band. With Benson, he could find little wrong. He gave them a glowing testimonial and said that no agency in London did better creative work.

The report went off to John Read, then Ford's sales director. He approved it and collected together a group of executives – himself, Adams and four other senior sales and marketing men – to go round the agencies. Three of the six knew little about the agency world, and particularly for their benefit Adams drew up a check-list of twenty points which they could bear in mind and mark off during the course of the visit. He also personally sent copies to each of the four agencies, so that they knew exactly what Ford were looking for.

The check-list started off with the question: 'Do the building in which the agency is housed and the service personnel that man it suggest modernity, efficiency and progress?' and went on to cover almost every imaginable criterion. Was the agency philosophy 'sound and convincing'? What kind of accounts did it hold? Was the 'client list' impressive? Did it include advertisers of durable consumer goods? Did the executives impress in terms of 'experience . . . and sensibility'? Was the agency a team or a one-man band? What about their creative work for TV and newspapers? What marketing and research services did the agency have? What did the team think of the man who would be handling the Ford account if the agency won? And finally, the crunch question, 'to what extent is the agency felt to be American, felt to be British?'

Armed with this comprehensive yardstick, the Ford party set out on October 26th from Cheapside in two Zodiacs to visit Foote, Cone and Belding in Baker Street. They arrived at ten o'clock to see the presentation of the agency's talent and resources which had been prepared for them.

Brian MacCabe received them and impressed the entire party with a smooth run-down on the agency's philosophy and business.

Then they were taken downstairs and several account executives[7] spoke about problems they had encountered – and solved – when dealing with other clients. One young man's performance was particularly memorable. He was wearing a waistcoat which was clearly too small for him, and no braces; as the band of shirt grew wider, some of the Ford party became absorbed in speculating whether he would succeed in finishing before his trousers actually fell down. MacCabe stage-managed the entire presentation, prompting and interpolating as required.

When it was all over, the two Zodiacs arrived at the door and whisked the Ford party back to Cheapside. Read had laid down that they would not discuss individual agencies until they had seen all four, so there was very little conversation, other than the usual banter on the odd things that had caught their eye.

On the following Wednesday, November 3rd, the party set out again, this time for Benson's Kingsway offices. Adams had made his liking for the agency crystal-clear to his five colleagues, and as the party went in they were ready to be impressed. Yet two hours later Benson had virtually lost the Ford account.

Even before the presentation, nothing had gone right for them. The man who should have managed it, Donald Bain, had fallen and concussed himself and Adams asked the agency if they would like to postpone the visit until Bain had recovered. Finally, they decided to risk it, and go ahead without him.

Everything began smoothly enough. The Ford party was taken upstairs to a small presentation room with contemporary chairs, and Bain's deputy, Roger Lloyd, won their sympathy by saying he was sorry if he was – perhaps understandably – a little nervous. The Ford men were impressed by this human touch, and flattered perhaps to think they were so awe-inspiring.

Then things started to go wrong. The senior executive whose job it was to provide an account of the agency gave only the sketchiest outline, and Adams had continually to interpose questions – 'Exactly how much business do you do?' 'What accounts have you lost?' 'What representation have you in Europe?' – to dig out all the facts which the twenty-point questionnaire demanded.

By this time, several of the Ford party were becoming disenchanted and when the executive who had been detailed to talk about overseas advertising began speaking about South-east Asia instead of the Common Market countries (where Ford were making their big effort), the damage had been done. Another executive hurriedly intervened to say that they would, of course, follow the Ford flag wherever it went. The

[7] The standard title for the man who acts as the agency's link with the client. Thompson give him a different name – there he is called, with literal accuracy, a 'representative'.

correction simply compounded the original error, because Ford had, in fact, been selling in Europe for several decades.

And so, on November 9th, to Thompson in Berkeley Square. For them, this was more than a presentation to a £1 million prospective client; it put the new administration and the new managing director, Tom Sutton, who had been brought back from the agency's Frankfurt office, on trial.[8]

Sutton, therefore, had marshalled the presentation with even more than his usual thoroughness. By the time the Ford party arrived, his team were almost word-perfect. Each Ford man was escorted by a Thompson man. They sat at a line of small tables, Ford and Thompson men alternating. The room, as Adams recalled it, was 'impressive, if slightly baroque'.

Sandy Mitchell-Innes had been chosen to begin. His quiet, city banker's manner, his mild Etonian tones, were clearly intended to demonstrate that Thompson were a truly British agency. He rubbed the point in by mentioning that they shared only 17 per cent of their business with their American parent. He also pointed out that they had three new, young directors, all of them around forty.

Then Sutton spoke in some detail on the structure of the Thompson account groups and indicated the way in which the agency might work with Ford if the account were assigned to them. Next Jeremy Bullmore, with the reputation of being one of the brightest admen in London, talked in a relaxed and polished style about creative advertising. As an example, he told the story of how Thompson had evolved the concept of 'Night Starvation' in 1930 to help sell Horlicks, after they had discovered people were drinking it late at night.

John Treasure, an economics lecturer who had become Thompson's research and marketing director, gave an account of the agency's considerable research facilities. After he had finished, there was a gentle reminder that Thompson were already working very successfully for Ford elsewhere. To make this point, Sutton had chosen a man who handled Ford accounts in Paris and Antwerp – and who would manage the business in Britain if the agency won.

There was a coffee party, the Ford men were shown some of Thompson's ITV commercials – and before they went out of the door, they were presented with bound copies of the presentation to study at their leisure. They were suitably impressed – they agreed afterwards that it was the best presentation they had seen – but awed. The monumental efficiency of the show gave at least one of them 'a colossal inferiority complex'. 'Perhaps it was a bit soulless,' a Thompson executive admitted long after the battle was over.

[8] See Chapter 3.

Finally, on November 25th, the Ford party made their way to the last agency on their short-list, the London Press Exchange. The presentation which followed was totally unlike the one they had seen at Thompson. To begin with, the atmosphere was relaxed, affable, almost homely. The early speakers illustrated their talks with charts which they tried to hook into what looked like an old army blanket draped over a blackboard. The charts kept falling off in a pleasantly amateur sort of way, but the Ford men felt there was a genuine, almost boyish eagerness to win their business. 'It was a Boy Scout sort of attitude – rather attractive,' Adams recalled afterwards.

Everything was going beautifully for L P E. They split the Ford party into four, and sent them off to see various aspects of the agency's work. Then the two sides settled down for a round-table discussion, which took the form of a cross-examination between prospective clients and prospective agency. Mark Abrams, head of L P E's research subsidiary, led off ably and the Ford men were entirely happy. Quite suddenly, however, things started to go wrong. In the account of the presentation carried by *Advertising Age*, the American weekly magazine which is the nearest thing the industry has to an international journal, the L P E speakers then 'touched on the attitude of dealers to the selling of cars'.

What actually happened was that the head of L P E's subsidiary Merchandising and Marketing Development Limited, John Telford Beasley, began to hold forth about car dealers – and more particularly Ford dealers – and the way they handled their prospective customers.

Beasley had sent his men to find out what actually happened when people went out to buy a car. His conclusion was that, although Ford dealers were more efficient than those of other firms, the overall standard was still pretty appalling. And while the Ford sales executives listened, he said so in no uncertain terms. The dealers were offhand, they did not know of Ford's facilities, they were inadequately supplied with promotional material, and so on in the same vein.

Several of his colleagues were dumbfounded. At least one who had been in on the planning for the presentation, had no idea Beasley intended to speak. 'It wasn't planned in the least,' he said. 'Our idea was not to tell Ford about cars, but about the agency.'

As Beasley went on with his evidence – and he spoke for about twenty minutes – the atmosphere grew heavier and heavier. Adams himself restrained an impulse to crawl under the table. 'It was,' he said later, 'a devastating critique of our methods – inferior literature despatched late, bad advertisements and poor sales promotion.' (Even to the outsider, Beasley's verdicts seemed a little harsh – Ford, in fact, have always had a progressive sales policy.) On the L P E side, there was mounting unease as they realized things were swinging against them. 'We were all hoping he would shut up, but he didn't,' one executive recalled.

Eventually Beasley finished, and the Ford party left in a huff. When they got outside, there was complete silence and it was left to Read to break the ice. 'Well,' he said heavily, 'we said we wouldn't talk about agencies. Let's take a little time to reflect. Maybe a critical agency is an agency worth having.'

In any case, they had to go back to L P E the same afternoon for an hour long presentation at Intam, the subsidiary company which handled overseas advertising.

At L P E, there was despair. For days after the presentation, Beasley was conscious of fingers pointing at him all over the agency and voices saying: 'That's the man who lost us the Ford account,' even though the agency had recognized all along that they were up against stiff competition.

'I got the feeling that morning that Ford weren't really interested in us,' recalled Mark Abrams. 'I felt they'd included us simply because we were the biggest British agency. We used to handle Daimler and Singer, but we didn't know much about the mass car market.'

David Dutton, the agency's managing director, seeing a million pounds' worth of business slipping out of his grasp, telephoned Adams to say that he had an uneasy feeling things hadn't gone well. Adams agreed. Dutton assured him that Beasley's contribution had been an error of judgment, that he was most terribly upset, and asked whether he, Dutton, could do anything. Adams told him that he could drop a note to John Read if he wished.

The Ford party met a week later in the Cheapside offices to make their final choice. The punters were all confidently tipping Thompson, with Foote, Cone and Belding as a possible outsider. Everybody assumed that strings had been pulled in New York and that the issue was cut-and-dried.

But the Ford men thought differently. Adams, as expected, plumped for Benson, though he admitted that he had not been impressed by their presentation. After a very full discussion, there was complete agreement among the group who had investigated the four agencies that they should recommend L P E.

So the battle was apparently lost and won. Ford's top management still had to approve the choice and sign a contract, but these seemed to be mere formalities. Yet, though the struggle was all but over, the infighting went on.

Tom Sutton, afraid that Thompson was being excluded for political reasons, suggested another meeting with Adams. Over lunch Adams was non-committal and Sutton came away more convinced than ever that Thompsons were in a cul-de-sac, with nobody at Ford to help them out.

Brian MacCabe also rang Adams and said he didn't expect Foote,

Cone and Belding would get the account, but that he was just about to carry out some reorganization in the agency, and it would be useful to know if it would come their way. Adams replied that he didn't think it would.

The only interest which Ford U S A took in the selection of the new agency was to request a copy of the appraisal which had been made before the final selection. A copy was sent – but, having looked it over carefully, they replied that they thought it was a sound piece of work and they did not propose to interfere.

On January 2nd, Allen Barke, Ford's managing director, accepted the party's recommendation. The company's lawyers drew up a contract for Barke and L P E to sign: they got it all on to three pages, compared with the twenty-six which contain the agreement between Ford of Detroit and J. Walter Thompson in New York.

Adams then rang David Dutton and told him Barke was coming to see him. 'Does that mean we've got it?' Dutton asked eagerly. 'I'm not supposed to say,' Adams replied, 'but yes, it does.'

On January 12th Barke arrived at L P E and everybody took their seats in the T V theatre. Barke began to speak in his slow and deliberate Lancastrian fashion. 'Well, gentlemen, I've seen and heard a lot about your agency from my colleagues, and because of that I've come along today because I want to satisfy myself that you can do the things they claim for you.'

He stopped, and there was an awkward pause – a moment of surprise for Dutton, who had thought this was going to be merely a formal occasion. It occurred to both Dutton and Adams that Barke had not, after all, signed the three-page contract. Dutton recovered quickly and began talking about the size of the agency, of the various services they could offer. Barke listened, puffing away at his pipe, and then interrupted, speaking just as slowly and just as deliberately as before: 'Well, we've decided to appoint you as our agents as from April 1st. We'll send you the agreement in due course.' Then, the business being done, he swept off in his personal Zodiac.

So began the honeymoon between Ford and L P E. Elsewhere there was disappointment. Benson wanted to know how they had lost, and John Read saw Robert Bevan, Benson's chairman, to explain. Car preferences also changed. Sandy Mitchell-Innes drives a Humber Hawk these days. Sutton still has a Zodiac. At L P E David Dutton enjoyed the splendour of a new blue Ford Galaxie. One battle was over for L P E: another was just about to begin – how to retain the affection of their notoriously demanding new client.

2. The 100 mph Dream

So L P E had won, and the agency bosses congratulated themselves. But by winning the Ford account they had done far more than add a million pounds a year to their business; they also thereby took on the job of helping to lead Britain into the status age which had been developing throughout the 1950s as old class-barriers were being undermined by the new and widespread affluence.

The agency world in London as a whole had been slow to recognize the appearance of the new status-hunters – those whom one advertising executive, in the jargon of the business, called 'the C2 commuters who drink lager instead of beer, smoke tipped instead of plain, eat plain chocolate instead of milk, and the young AB executives who've just acquired an open-plan and garden in the suburbs'.[9] However, from the mid-1950s onwards, there were a growing number of campaigns addressed to this market. Mather and Crowther, for example, ran the Batchelor's 'Hostess' campaign for Batchelor's tinned peas quite early in the 1950s, addressing it to 'socially mobile C2 housewives' and using models and settings a degree or two higher in the social scale than the actual users of the product. Later campaigns like the Hat Council's 'If you want to get ahead get a hat' – followed the same line.

'Snob-appeal', of course, had long been an accepted advertising gimmick. Even before the war, duchesses had been recruited to recom-

---

[9] In the agency world, the English class-structure is generally broken down under letters of the alphabet:

Group 'A', Upper Middle Class, according to the definition of one big agency, have incomes of £1750 and over, employ servants and include company directors, professors, high-level local officials like town clerks, and high-ranking Army officers.

In the 'B' Grade (Middle Class £950–£1750) are placed, somewhat whimsically, junior executives, head librarians and Army officers up to the rank of Major. They are thought likely to live in a 'semi' in the suburbs.

'C' is divided into two: C1 (£950–lower middle-class) includes another curious hotch-potch – nurses, junior lecturers and shop assistants with responsibilities: C2 (£15–£20 a week) are skilled workers – 'engravers, long-distance lorry drivers and miners'. A C2's wages may on occasion rise to £30 a week, but even then he should not be counted as C1.

'D' are unskilled workers (£6 10s–£12) – 'railway porters, tailors, privates in the army and shop assistants without special responsibilities'.

'E' (under £6 10s) are simply labelled 'The Poor'.

mend Ponds' cold cream; the traditional quality fashion advertisement was seldom without its background of foxhounds and huntsmen, and those for drinks conveyed an air of upper-class ease by showing venerable gentlemen consuming their sherry in front of Goyas. Much of this was muted and implicit. But, even more important, the traditional snob advertising did not offer you a place in this true blue world; it merely informed that you might like – through a particular product – to breathe for a moment its purified air. The important thing about the *new* status advertisements was that they invited you to take a couple of steps up the social ladder, and to keep climbing.

Even the advertising for the motor car – the very seal and hallmark of the new affluence – remained stolidly conventional, however. The cars in British advertisements were just machines – the advertisements said they worked, but that was all they did say. The promises they made – 'performance', 'reliability', 'economy' – were what Robert Adams of Ford called 'the gorgeous dead words which the car industry has been using for years', and there were seldom any real people in them – 'just the car', as Adams said, 'sitting there four-square and beaming out at you like a great fat baby at a baby show.'[10]

Rarely was there any suggestion that ownership of a particular model would up-grade you socially – let alone bring you sexual success. Even Jaguar contented themselves with 'Grace . . . Space . . . Pace'. Part of the reason for this restraint was the down-to-earth nature of the motor moguls, part the fact that in the post-war years they scarcely had to advertise their cars to sell them.

But in America, where the sales war had gone on unabated, the depth psychologists had been digging away for over twenty years to uncover the deeper motives which made people buy cars. As far back as 1939, Dr Ernest Dichter,[11] whose work was described by Vance Packard in *The Hidden Persuaders*, had adumbrated his theory that the convertible was

---

[10] The research head of Thompson, Dr John Treasure, has remarked that 'status is not as important in Britain as in America because our home-life is more closed than theirs.'

Even as late as 1963, most car firms stuck to traditional slogans. The Hillman Imp was heralded simply as 'an inspiration in small-car design'; the new Jaguars as flatly as 'début of the new Jaguar 3.4 and 3.8 "S" models'; the Vauxhall Viva with the line: 'Now the Vauxhall Viva – the one-litre car with the millionaire ride'; and the Rover 2000, photographed standing alone on a beach with the wind and the waves, was headlined 'Rover engineering takes motoring years ahead'. The Ford Consul Corsair (headline: 'Flair Everywhere') was also photographed on a beach, but with it were a couple of swimsuits; and when the advertisement appeared in *The Sunday Times Colour Magazine* another couple were pictured beside the car, the girl in low-cut evening gown, the man in his tuxedo.

[11] See Chapter 12.

a man's 'mistress' while the saloon could be equated with his sedate 'wife'. And it had long been axiomatic on Madison Avenue that the automobile was one of the most powerful of status symbols.

The result was that frequently the American car advertisement set out to evoke a dream-world in which the would-be owner could see all his longings satisfied. They led him away from unpleasant reality into a land of mink and tuxedos and unattainable women.

Ford's arrival at L P E was Britain's most dramatic introduction to this Madison Avenue dreamland, and to the American-style status advertisement. Other agencies were taking the same road in a much milder way – Thompson had suggested with Player's Bachelor tipped cigarettes that tipped smoking was a criterion of social standing – and a new vocabulary was being minted for the benefit of the status-hunters; the era of the 'trend-setters', the 'pace-makers' and the 'taste-leaders' had begun.

Few agencies, however, used such a strong status line – along with a variety of other promises – as did L P E with the Ford advertising.[12] Whereas most of the car makers preferred to keep their advertising conservative, Ford – and particularly Robert Adams – wanted to blaze new trails.

Ford, of course, were engaged in a *guerre à outrance* with the British Motor Corporation. They were fighting to maintain their 30 per cent share of the home market, and 1959 had been a crucial year in the struggle. B M C (who had something like 40 per cent) had beaten them into the baby-car field with the Mini, and although Ford replied with the even more successful Anglia, B M C had clearly stolen a march.[13]

Adams had a variety of ideas about how to fight the advertising side of this war, some of which were very close to those of Dichter. This is how he expressed his philosophy on car advertising: 'A car is intrinsically a rather dull mechanical contrivance, duplicated by hundreds of

[12] L P E deny that they concentrated on a status promise in the bulk of their campaigns. 'Most Ford advertising,' they say, 'emphasizing the functional advantages of the product, said then, and says still, things like "Get a real car for your money", "Big Car Motoring at Small Car Costs", "100 mph Motoring in the Grand Manner", none of which *exclude* status – but none of which concentrate on it.'

[13] Ford did not drop the idea of going into the baby-car market until the middle of 1962. They decided, on the basis of market research, that there were going to be too many in the field (they knew the Hillman Imp and the Vauxhall Viva were on the way), and that the future lay with cars of bigger-than-Mini proportions. They abandoned their baby-car model and launched the Cortina to exploit the gap between the small and medium-car classes.

thousands of others. It only has meaning to a reader or viewer when you have tailored a particular mood, personality, aura, sex – call it what you like – for it, and you match this image you have created with the dreams of your customers. 'A car purchase, I'm sure, is Freudian,' he said. 'When a man buys a car, he's probably making the second most important acquisition in his life and – if the first was a wife – he lavishes the same affection on both.'

But to Adams, as to many other people from the birth of the automobile, a car was also a status-offering. 'Of course,' he went on, 'the British are going through a car-status wave which the Americans have already had. Notice how the English love to leave their cars in the driveway so that the neighbours notice, and when they put them into the garage at night, this again is all part of the love relationship, like putting the car to bed.'

'Motor cars,' he concluded, 'are not sold for rational reasons, they're sold for emotional reasons. Watch the care an Englishman gives to his car – he looks after it much better than his wife, she's got to fend for herself. So when you're talking to people about cars, you've got to speak to the heart as well as to the head, you've got to sell the sizzle, not just the steak.'

'Selling the sizzle' meant a complete break with convention, away from advertisements full of 'marketing propositions which try to isolate the exclusive features of your model, or what you kid yourself are its exclusive features'. What Adams wanted L P E to do was 'to wrap the car in these great emotions, and use fresh, vivid words that still mean something'.

To critics who questioned his use of 'persuasion by emotional appeal', he returned the adman's stock response. 'We live in a society which lives by selling,' he said. 'People can think for themselves, they can make up their own minds. In my view, the only offence advertising can commit is to be misleading.'

Adams, as he admits, is 'an odd bird in industry, but it's a living, and advertising offers an outlet for any creativity'. He had had a curiously uneven career. After two years at a Redbrick university after the war, and another two as a management trainee with Tube Investments, he found himself in cycle publicity (as manager of a team of professional racing cyclists among other things). He then moved into the Ford job in 1956, at the age of 33. For recreation, he escaped as often as he could to 'the silence of the desert', excavating Roman cities in North Africa with Sir Mortimer Wheeler.

At home in Surrey, he has 'an orchard of twenty-three apple trees' and drives a Capri, the nearest thing Ford of Britain have to a convertible. 'It makes me feel good to drive it, with its white body and red upholstery.'

25

Adams had already begun to put his theory of car advertising into practice before L P E took on the Ford account. On November 25th, 1959, while Rumble, Crowther and Nicholas were still handling the Ford business, there appeared in *The Times* an advertisement which a L P E executive called 'the battle hymn of the affluent society'. Its headline read 'Four Bedrooms, Three Children, Two cars' and it showed a £5000 house with two cars – Zodiac and Popular. 'This ad,' said Adams, 'put the stamp on the Affluent Society.' At about the same time came an advertisement for the Anglia with the heading 'We can't help showing off our Anglia' and a background with a house which was clearly private but at the same time near enough to be council, and two people showing off their car to their friends. The baseline of both these advertisements was 'Be First on the Road with Ford', which had obvious connotations of both status and speed.

Adams wanted to see L P E – an agency fully conversant of course with status as a weapon in advertising – develop these themes; and so, many discussions took place at L P E to decide how the proper balance should be struck between stressing these emotional reasons for buying cars and putting over the functional advantages they had to offer.

Such was the glamour of the Ford business that most of L P E's account executives jealously coveted the job. There was surprise when Adams picked Angus Shearer to supervise the account. Shearer was particularly good on consumer accounts like Corona drinks and McDougall flour, but hardly the rugged personality everybody thought Ford would want.

Shearer then set about collecting his team. Fortunately, L P E had just appointed a new young creative director, a 31-year-old Oxonian named Roger Longrigg whose ideas matched Adams's own. Then, after a few months, L P E gave Bryan Oakes, a Durham graduate from Doncaster, the job of handling the copy writing. He soon established a close rapport with Adams, and indeed Longrigg and Oakes admirably complemented each other, representing the two streams which feed the advertising pool.

Oakes came from a C2, upper working-class background, and was himself living through the status revolution he wrote about. A story from his university days showed how important status was to him personally. 'I'd been playing around,' he recalled, 'and the local council cut my grant for a term. That moved me to sit down in the garret in the condemned property we lived in and write down all the things I wanted out of life. Part was metaphysical, part was sex, but far the biggest section was on status, detached house, car in the garage – that's what I wanted.' He added that L P E had a lot of people from his kind of background.

Now he has six children – four of them at the best local private school – four bedrooms in his Victorian house in Surrey, and two cars – Victor Estate and bubble-car. He also edits the church magazine.

Oakes had graduated in 1951 in English, and although the university appointments people had consigned him to the Civil Service, he won one of four Hulton advertising scholarships and went to Alfred Pemberton, then a medium-sized agency in Park Lane. At Pemberton, he worked on Cerebos, Bisto and Saxa Salt, and toured the country for three months with the Bisto Kids. From there he went to Odhams, Dorland's, and Pritchard Wood (where he did some work on Rover cars). Then, just after being appointed a group head, he left and found a job at L P E.

Roger Longrigg, on the other hand, was distinctly AB. From Bryanston, he had gone to Oxford, where he had belonged to all the right clubs, the Carlton and the Canning among them. 'The purest chance' brought him into advertising. He failed the Foreign Office entrance examination – 'thank God, it wouldn't have done for me' – and through friends and connections found his way to McCann-Erickson as a trainee copy-writer at £500 a year in 1952. He soon went to Colman, Prentis and Varley, where he worked on the Shell account, and on to Mather and Crowther as group head. He became a director of L P E at 33.

Now he lives in Berkshire and is also a two-car man (Jaguar and small Austin). 'I fish when I can, go racing as much as I can, and bet more than I should,' he said, putting his thumbs into his yellow braces and puckering his thin, donnish face. He also writes books, six under his own name – including a novel partly about advertising called *A High-Pitched Buzz* – and others under a pseudonym.

He noted the new social mobility – England is a class-ridden society, but the new with-itness is classless' – and observed that 'a great many consumers want a product which will make them feel one-up socially'. With his background Longrigg could afford to look down on the status battle with some irony. 'Don't forget,' he said jokingly, 'a car has to satisfy big needs – social advancement, sexual success – and world peace.'

But, the irony apart, Longrigg's philosophy of advertising is to operate with almost military efficiency in formulating a campaign. 'You've got a product, Blobbo,' he said, 'and you must offer people something – anything from a hard practicality like 2d cheaper to "makes you a bit sexier". I think we should forget the idea that advertising can push products towards the housewife – we should create a magnet which will pull her to the product. The chemical change is in the housewife.'

'Then, once you've decided what your proposition is,' Longrigg went on, ' – and it must be a Unique Selling Proposition,[14] you must go about it with the most ruthless professionalism.'

The agency's first launch of a new model – the Classic – came in 1961, only a few weeks after they took over the Ford account. Not surprisingly, with time so short, Adams had difficulty in getting exactly what he wanted. Even so, the agency's basic strategy (or 'central consumer proposition' as they call it) of stressing the car's style plus performance plus up-to-date modernity was accepted and the original headline suggested was the one finally used –

> 'Take a long look at the long low look
> Set the style, make the pace
> With the all-new Consul Classic from Ford.' –

Indeed at the end of it all Adams described the agency's efforts as 'an absolute dazzler of a campaign'.

First of all, though, he recalled, 'they offered me conventional ads – they got too tangled up in the car's mechanical features.' He went round to L P E and told them what he thought. 'You've got to catch the mood of the car,' he said. 'It's flamboyant, it's striking, this is a car that will set a trend.' He advised them to go and see *La Dolce Vita* – 'that's the mood you've got to get.'

The young agency men were delighted to find such an adventurous client and immediately went out to Rome Airport to take the pictures for the advertisement. Adams was delighted with what they brought back – 'the car standing there white and somewhat sinister, with the chains and necklaces of airport lights round it.' Nor was this going to be a conventional launch; Adams suggested that the Classic should be announced to the public at midnight parties all over the country. Some of the Ford management held their hands up – and said that no one would ever turn out. But the midnight parties were a triumph; 250,000 people arrived, and at places like Reading, there were cars parked for a mile round the dealer's showrooms where the Classic was on show.[15]

Nor was the new-style advertising to be merely a matter of hunch and flair. Part of Ford's effort to hold their share of the home market was

[14] The theory of the Unique Selling Proposition (or U S P) was first drawn up by Rosser Reeves, one of America's most articulate and successful admen. As enunciated by him, the U S P must be three things – it must be a definite proposition, it must be unique – something the opposition cannot offer – and, finally, it must sell. See Chapter 9.

[15] The fact that the Classic was never a complete success had, perhaps, more to do with its shortcomings in performance and price than with the advertising.

a comprehensive research programme into what car buyers wanted. This market research programme (the appropriation now runs well into six figures) gradually gave the agency men more and more information. A continuous series of studies was mounted to reveal how well people liked the models they had – whether Ford or competition – what exactly they were looking for in their next purchase (this broken down by car-class and owner-group), and what they particularly disliked.

Long before the launch, in fact, the agency was told who was likely to buy the model, why they would buy it, how many would buy it and where they would buy it from. They were then supposed to be in a better position to draw up a copy-platform aimed accurately at the potential market.[16]

And just to make sure that the advertising message would get across loud and clear, L P E almost invariably drew up two or three different copy-lines and tested each of them against a sample of 300 or 400 people – to find out which was most effective.

Even after the launch, the barrage of tests continued. As the Ford programme got under way, there were introduction day surveys among showroom viewers; surveys on 'new model awareness' to find out how successful the launch advertisements had been; two-monthly studies to show what 'image' the car had with the public; surveys of early buyers, by class, income, size of household and so on; and the same thing again, repeated after six months and a year of ownership.[17]

And in addition to these routine tests, Ford followed standard practice by doing a piece of depth research into 'the emotional appeal of

[16] Nine months before the Cortina was put on to the market, the agency were told that it would have most appeal to under-45s and heads of families with children. They were told that its appeal was fairly spaced over the classes, that its price, fuel economy and good external appearance were its main attractions. They also knew that it was likely to cut Anglia sales by 40 per cent, and Classic sales by 32 per cent.

[17] One thing these surveys did produce, L P E say, was confirmation of the importance of product information in car advertising. 'The public want to know the details about a car – particularly a new car. Consequently, the main Ford campaigns prepared by L P E emphasised the consumer benefits in functional terms of the Ford cars. The Zodiac Mark III was introduced with 'Enjoy the new luxurious 100 mph Zodiac Mk III'; the Zephyr 6 was introduced as 'the crispest ever statement of the Zephyr formula'; the Cortina as 'Big Car Motoring at small car costs'.

A study of early Cortina buyers showed that 57 per cent came from households without children (which seemed to contradict the pre-launch research), that 40 per cent were in the £1000–£1500 bracket, that 45 per cent read the Daily Express, 26 per cent the Daily Telegraph. It also revealed that 86 per cent of buyers were 'very well satisfied' or better, compared with 62 per cent with the Zephyr 4, and 56 per cent with the Mark III Zodiac.

cars'.[18] This was a useful way of testing Adams's ideas and the result seemed to justify him. A small sample of people were interviewed and the subsequent report showed that it was social prestige which counted, however much the interviewees might try to hide the fact. 'The research made plain,' said Bryan Oakes, 'the self-deception people practise. They really want self-confidence and to be one-up on the neighbours. They expressed their desire in practical ways – such-and-such a car has got more power or room. What they mean is "I feel a bigger person in an Anglia than in a Mini".'

The team at L P E now began to turn out the sort of advertising that Adams wanted, emphasizing the functional advantages of the product, but also ushering in the dream-world of higher status, where speed and sex were a natural part of the High Life.

For instance, while the Mark III Zodiac was introduced with 'Enjoy the new luxurious 100 mph Zodiac Mk III' (and all the main Zodiac campaigns contain the ton-up promise) one of the colour advertisements was captioned 'Dream of Power' and the copy promised that the car was 'a dream come true. 100 mph. With wide-awake urgency'. Beside it stood a young man in a dinner jacket gazing into the eyes of a girl in white ermine. The Zephyr 6's appeal was simple and direct: 'Why come second when you could be first?' The new Anglia became 'Success Car for the Sixties', and by May 1963 the Classic, whose main campaigns continued on 'style-setter' or 'pace-maker' lines, became in one series of advertisements 'Beauty with Long Legs'. The copy underneath the headline read: 'The car will go fast. With impassioned acceleration and long-legged power.' Beside the car stood a woman, veiled and aloof, with a bare midriff. 'She looks unattainable,' commented John Bell, the account executive, 'even slightly far-fetched. The implication was that you might get the out-of-the-ordinary – you certainly don't get the girl next door with this car.'

'We're offering people dream-fulfilment,' said Oakes. 'You feel you've arrived in your own mind and in the world. Everything we do suggests to people that they can improve themselves, rise a class or two.'

And to encourage even small-car owners to believe that they had arrived, L P E used a time-honoured technique: they endowed some models with an enhanced status aura by showing in the advertisements people of a higher social grade than those who usually bought the model.

Oakes explained their philosophy quite simply: 'In our ads, we always

[18] Depth research simply means talking to the same person, or group of people for an hour instead of two minutes; it is usually conducted by one of the tame psychologists agencies employ or hire, and as one of them said, 'it is a fringe benefit that any good advertising research programme must contain today'.

give people the important facts about the car, the basic consumer benefits. In addition we always give a hint of the people who might use the car – but we play it up a bit.' He pointed to an Anglia advertisement. 'Here, for instance, the kids obviously go to private school and the mother is efficient, a little bit cool but marvellous in bed. There's gloss, gleam, the size, the bigness – this, we're saying, is the life you'll be living.' Yet Ford knew from their research that at least 50 per cent of Anglia owners earned less than £1500 a year. (A further 24 per cent of those asked refused to say what they earned.)

Again, the campaign for the Zephyr 4 which came out at the end of 1963 had one advertisement that read 'Join the Big-Car Set the Shrewd Way'. This, the agency say, 'got over the size and economy of the car' which was then developed in copy. They had been afraid that with their old advertisements, which showed six men in bowler hats getting into the car with the headline, 'Takes Six in Style for Less Per Mile', they were, in Oakes's words, 'guying it too much'. Some Americans who came over from Ford of Detroit thought so too, so the agency decided to make a more overt attack on status. The philosophy behind 'Join the Big-Car Set . . .' was, said Oakes, 'if people caught a glimpse of you in the Zephyr 4, it could be taken for a Rover 3-litre'.

This gimmick of the status-sellers is known in the agency business as 'trading the product up' and it is widely regarded as a perfectly legitimate sales weapon.[19]

The larger models do not need 'trading up'. In the Zephyr 6 advertising (research had shown that 50 per cent of owners earned more than £2000, 20 per cent more than £3000), the main promise of performance was accompanied by a hard and direct status implication. 'In that case,' said Oakes, 'with the slogan "why come second when you could be first?", we were quite unashamedly offering it to people who wanted to have an edge – aggressive types.' The advertising, in short, was clearly intended as bait for the front runners in the rat race.

Oakes admitted that they had occasionally gone overboard in their excursions into the dream-world, for instance with some of their advertisements for the Mark III Zodiac, 'The atmosphere got too show-businessy,' said Oakes. 'The promise was the status, but the image was wrong – it became out-of-this-world stuff. The correct image is the £5000 sales manager going up the M1, not a buccaneer chasing up the autostrada.' On this model too the agency took a heavy beating from

[19] J. Walter Thompson, for instance, used the James Bond idea to 'trade up' Angel Face lipsticks – a product aimed largely at mill-girls in the North and shop-girls in Oxford Street. 'What we wanted in the advertising,' one of their executives said, 'was the sort of cold-blooded upper-class passion, thrown away but deadly serious underneath. Danger, sex, sophistication – that was it.' Angel Face, he said, had 'no buyers towards the upper-class'.

Ford and were asked to give the advertising a much more businesslike air.

Nor was this the only problem the Mark III posed. There was also the matter of speed. Should Ford come right out and say it was a 100 mph car – and risk the charge that they were encouraging speeding? The tag was adopted in Britain without a great deal of discussion. In Ireland, on the other hand, where Ford – as John Bell said – have a 'very good image', the debate went on for weeks. 'Some people said we couldn't encourage speeding,' recalled Bell, 'but we finally said 100 mph, not so much to suggest that people should do it but that the car has a lot of power.'

Sex was implicit in the new High Life mixture and was most obvious in the advertising for the Capri. This was by no means a new weapon in the sales war. As far back as 1934, a L P E survey had noted that 'An Exploitation of Sex Interest was also normally rewarded by extra attention from men'.[20] But this certainly was the first time that sex had been used so overtly to sell cars, and it was indeed with the Capri that L P E came nearest to emulating Dichter's philosophy of convertible-as-mistress. They had a good idea who would buy the car. 'Who'd buy it? we asked ourselves,' recalled John Bell. 'A bachelor, or a married man who'd like to behave like a bachelor.'

'The man who buys the Capri,' said Bob Adams, who owns one himself, 'is 40-ish, hair probably flecked with grey, with ideas about his virility. It's also bought by the wives of expensive business men, with ideas I won't go into now.' A study of the early buyers of the model showed that 86 per cent were ordered by individuals, only 14 per cent by companies (a very high proportion indeed for Britain, where more than half the cars sold are bought in fleets by companies); that 40 per cent lived in one or two-person households; that only 30 per cent had children living with them.

So the Capri was sold as a 'personal' car. 'Let's Go with the New Capri', said the advertisements, which showed people in evening dress on the beach at dawn, or walking into the woods in evening dress. The copy read: 'Behind the wheel a man feels power – and a woman feels freedom.' 'We gave it the convertible image,' said Bell, 'fresh air and freedom to give romanticism rather than healthiness. This wasn't the Summer County kind of healthiness, jumping over stiles and picking buttercups – it wasn't that sort of fresh air.' 'The whole thing was so romantic,' recalled Adams, 'it really thrilled you.'

This, then, was advertising for the new affluence, with its promise of status and speed, and its atmosphere of verve and virility. To some

[20] A Survey of Reader Interest in the National Morning and London Evening Press, 1934. As for women, the survey said 'the most effective appeals are those concerned with Vanity and Sentiment – particularly about Children'.

critics, it looked like the exploitation of anti-social urges and, sometimes, like an excessive harping on sex. But to many advertising men, some of whom even think of their activities as one way of breaking down class barriers, it seemed a perfectly reasonable practice; and Ford and L P E themselves consider that 'this interpretation distorts Ford advertising policy by giving the impression that the company, since 1961, has placed undue emphasis on status and sex. Of course these have played a part in Ford advertising,' they add, 'because they are part of everyday life but they have not played a disproportionate part which some of this chapter would have us believe.'

The new-style status advertisement had had its supporters at L P E before Ford arrived. For instance, there are in the agency layouts dating from 1958 which presents Bournville as Cadbury's 'sophisticated' chocolate. Roger Longrigg believed that people wanted products which made them feel 'one-up socially' and the agency set out to tap this with the 'sophisticated' line.

'I'm a plain girl,' announces one of the advertisements in the campaign, underneath a picture of a girl in a crash-helmet. 'I like plain, simple things. A plain Facel Vega or two. A few simple Derby winners. And Cadbury's Bournville chocolate. . .'[21]

Similarly with petrol, L P E decided that National Benzole, another of their accounts, should become the 'petrol for with-it-people'. National Benzole had gone through a series of image-lifts which had never quite come off. At first, it was unique – 'there's nothing like National Benzole'; then it became what Bryan Oakes called 'sound, middle-of-the-road petrol, photos of Rolls-Royces and racehorses, terribly posh and respectable'.

The sales graphs did not respond, so, said Oakes, 'we decided to become more aggressive.' L P E first mounted the 'Go ahead with National Benzole' campaign in 1962 – 'just a man filling up and zooming

[21] The reasons people buy chocolate – according to the depth psychologists – are interesting. Longrigg said the attraction of nut chocolate was that 'it satisfies people's aggressive urges – they like to bite through the nut. You defeat the thing'. That was why Cadbury's Whole Nut – 'the chocolate that gives you something to bite on' – promised 'biteability'.
Roger Longrigg went on: 'Adult attitudes to confectionery are commonly tinged with a feeling of guilt that echoes early childhood appetites for luxuries in which over-indulgence was often frowned upon. Pocket money was spent on sweets and chocolates because of the immediate pleasure they gave, not because they were nourishing.
'The fact is, however, that chocolate is nourishing as well as appetising. Its food value has always been an important product attribute, and it is for this reason that it has long been the practice of Cadbury's to make advertising reference to its milk content.'

off and being admired by people – fairly pedestrian stuff,' Oakes commented. 'But for 1963 we created the Getaway People.'

'They were the people who did the good things,' he explained, 'the jet set, clean-limbed beautiful girls, the gods and goddesses who did exotic things. We used expensive cars – E-Type Jaguars and Aston Martins – and the promise was that, if you get this petrol, you're aligning yourself with those wonderful people, midnight drives on the beach and so on. Of course, it's tough luck – you don't happen to have a Jag just yet, or a girl like that, but any day now . . .'

To Longrigg, who master-minded the 1963 campaign, the petrol also promised rejuvenation of a sort. 'With this,' he said, 'you're recovering your lost youth.'

Other agencies were also getting into the status hunt in a somewhat new way. Thompson, for instance, who more than anybody else adhered to the 'Mum' philosophy of aiming to hook the housewife, were entering the field with the Player's Bachelor account. 'It's smart to smoke tipped' was the line proposed for the campaign in the South of England; in the North, where tipped smoking was still regarded as suspiciously effeminate, the line was to be different – merely suggesting that tipped cigarettes conferred social prestige.

These ideas were finally thrown out, but Bachelor was still launched as the 'trend-setter' among cigarettes. 'This is the Tip, This is the Blend, This is the Smoke, That's Setting the Trend' went the jingle. Unfortunately for the agency, Bachelor did not set the trend towards tipped smoking – the report of the Royal College of Physicians on lung cancer in the spring of 1962 did that much more effectively.[22]

So a new wave of advertising gathered momentum, and gave the acquisitive society a push in what some of the agencies thought was the right – or rather the most profitable – direction. But the agencies also took a push in the direction of Madison Avenue, a trend most of them furiously resist despite the spread of American financial control within the industry.

It also brought on yet another of the periodical attacks on advertising. The critics charged the agencies with playing yet another confidence trick on the consumer, of offering Nirvana in an £800 car or even a box of chocolates. And, though the advertising industry is more ostentatiously concerned with maintaining its standards than any other, it did not

[22] Sales of Bachelor continued to decline after the 'trend-setting' campaign. Tom Sutton of Thompson felt that they might have gone too far by showing very young people in the advertisements, 'very outward-looking people with whom few of the existing smokers could identify themselves'. Thompson then did a piece of depth research with 200 or 300 men and women – and found Bachelor smokers were much more conservative than had been thought. Now Bachelor simply offers 'the full reward of tipped smoking'.

seem to find anything particularly dangerous about the status revolution.

As for Adams himself, he resigned his job at Ford in October 1963. His reason was simple – as the servant of a huge corporation, he had felt more and more pressure to conform as the years went on, and he felt that he had to move or go under. So when a disagreement with the Ford management arose which meant conforming on a major issue, he walked out.

3. Face-lift in Berkeley Square

At 5.30 on the evening of June 16th, 1959, the telephone rang in the Frankfurt office of Tom Sutton, then managing director of J. Walter Thompson's highly successful German office (one of forty-one in twenty-five countries). His secretary answered it and told him: 'Mr Meek is on the line.' There was nothing unusual about this. Sam Meek was the vice-chairman of the New York parent company in charge of international operations, and Sutton spoke to him frequently, sometimes several times a week.

Sutton picked up the telephone. Without preamble, Meek asked him to fly to London immediately for a meeting on the 18th, 'to discuss general problems'. Again, nothing unusual; the agency were hard at work laying their plans for 1960, and the meeting might have been almost routine.

But the call set problems for Sutton. June 17th was a public holiday in West Germany, and since he wanted to go to London with the plans for 1960 neatly packaged, he had to ask his secretary and accountant to work throughout the holiday. This he did and having spent the 17th hard at it, he flew to London that same evening.

The next morning, after a night's sleep undisturbed by any premonition of what was about to happen, he had breakfast with Meek at the Connaught Hotel. Sutton immediately began to talk about his problems in Frankfurt, but Meek stopped him short. 'We won't discuss them for the time being, Tom,' he said. 'We've another problem to talk about, and I'd like Doug Saunders and Bill Hinks to be there.' Colonel Douglas Saunders was the Thompson chairman in London, a father-figure of the advertising industry, and Bill Hinks, a North-countryman had joined the agency in the 1920s and was at this time managing director.

Sutton assumed that an important meeting about Thompson's European operation was in the offing. Later that morning Meek and he went to Hinks's room, where Saunders and the managing director were waiting.

Saunders then dropped the bombshell. 'As you know, I shall be retiring at the end of this year,' he said, 'and the agency has decided to appoint Bill Hinks as chairman. We feel it would be a very good team if you came in as managing director.' He explained the new management set-up and the meeting finished shortly afterwards.

Sutton, 'delighted and terrified', astonished at the turn of events, hurried back to Frankfurt the next day to tell his wife and family that they were going back to Britain. When he arrived, he found a heap of packing boxes in the hall. Surprised, he asked his wife what they were. They contained some of the ornaments from their English home which they had sold three weeks previously after holding on to it since 1952, when Sutton had first gone to Frankfurt.

Sutton had reason to be both delighted and terrified. He had succeeded to what was then the largest advertising empire in London – handling £13½ million worth of business in 1959 – but it was an empire whose absolute supremacy over its competitors was declining. Thompson needed a Beeching – and Sutton was the man chosen to wield the axe.

The truth was that, in the lush advertising years after the war, the agency had run to fat and earned a reputation for hiring Etonians with carnations rather than people with brains. Sandy Mitchell-Innes (himself an Etonian and one of Thompson's two deputy chairman) retorted that the only Thompson man he could remember wearing a carnation was an Harrovian, but the reputation none the less stuck.

In a sense, the image of well-bred smoothness was a quite deliberate one. Douglas Saunders, the retiring chairman, suffered from the feeling that advertising was a low-level activity and rather below the salt. He compensated for this sense of inferiority by recruiting as many of his executives as he could from the right stables – the more notable public schools, preferably followed by the Guards or the Green Jackets.

Saunders himself had gone into advertising at a time when it was dominated by brilliant individualists – and it was by such men that Thompson had been built. 'Before the war, there was no management here,' as Mitchell-Innes recalled. The first Thompson office in London had been opened in the 1890s merely as a business for the buying and selling of space in the Press. For a time it had closed down, and not until after the 1914–18 war did it become an advertising agency. By then the business had been acquired by Stanley Resor who, having bought out the original founder, Commodore Thompson, in 1916, was to run the agency for over forty years.

But even by the 1920s, Thompson's London office was still an obscure little affair, with a staff of eighteen and premises in Bush House, in the Strand. Their biggest account was Sun-maid raisins, for whom they spent £40,000 a year – 'we thought that was pretty big then,' said Hinks.

Thompson made their name with a series of brilliant campaigns in the 1930s. They invented the concept of Night Starvation to sell Horlicks as a bed-time drink. They also persuaded Rowntree to change the nature of its business – from over a hundred different products to a handful of branded lines – and then induced the firm to package their chocolates under the name Black Magic, instead of selling them anonymously and loose.

The most notorious Thompson campaign was the affair of the duchesses. In America they had had the idea of selling Pond's cold cream by persuading prominent socialites to give it a testimonial. This had been so successful that they brought the idea to Britain and set about recruiting duchesses. Hinks was given the job of finding the first duchess, and the campaign became so well-known that the aristocracy were soon writing in, asking to be included. On the strength of these successes, Thompson moved from Bush House to Berkeley Square – the first of the big agencies to go into the West End – and by the time war came their billings had grown to £2 million.

After the war, Thompson flourished even more successfully. When Sutton came to power, they had perhaps the most catholic selection of accounts in London. Among other things they advertised toilet-paper for Bowater-Scott and Eno's Fruit Salts for Beecham, lipstick for Chesebrough-Pond, hearing aids for S. C. Ingram, Smarties and Black Magic for Rowntree, South-West African Persian Lamb for the Karakul Industry Advisory Board, Rose's Lime Juice, Airwick, and Corn Flakes for Kellogg. At one and the same time, they served the Butter Information Council and sold Spry cooking fat for van den Bergh. Under Stanley Resor, they used to refuse what the Americans call hard-liquor accounts, but did publicity both for the French National Committee for Wine and the South African Wine Farmers' Association.

They also gave their services free to – among other organizations – the British Horse Society and St Andrews University.

In those early post-war years, Thompson had made their name with an honest-to-goodness, 'value for money' style of advertising, in which the copy was sober, rational and down-to-earth. One of their cheese campaigns was typical. The research had shown that most of the cheese consumed in Britain was taken by workers for midday snacks, so the headline was 'Cheese is a man's meal'. The opening proposition was invariably supported by a very solid body of words. 'Don't forget, we're a copy agency,' as one executive said. 'We believe in saying a thing in 500 words because if they are well written and put forward real and interesting consumer benefits, they will be more effective than 5 or 50.'

The trouble was, as the years went on, that other agencies caught on to the 'value for money' style and rising competitors like Mather and Crowther took it a stage further by injecting life and wit into the Thompson formula (vide 'Drinka Pinta Milka Day'). The agency began to lose out by reason of a general dullness and predictability – and even some of the agency's best creative men began to feel discontent at the rut in which they seemed to be stuck.

The entire agency needed a complete face-lift. Even the Berkeley Square premises, lacking the panache for which the New York offices were famous, exhibited merely a rather dowdy Britishness. In the reception-room you sat in cream-coloured, plastic-covered chairs while a receptionist with a deb voice directed visitors to their destinations. Smart young men wandered in and out, the names Jeremy and Christopher were for ever in the air, and there were peonies in the telephone alcove.

Upstairs were floor upon floor of dull corridors, white-painted or else tiled in brown cork squares. Many of the offices were just cream-coloured boxes, obviously furnished in bulk. Such colour as there was in the *décor* was of the traditional sort. Hinks's room was furnished with an air of cosy antiquity, with Corinthian column lamps and a large Victorian oil-painting of people taking the air along the front at Eastbourne. Mitchell-Innes, too, favoured discreet period furniture.

This was the advertising factory Tom Sutton was recalled from Frankfurt to manage. It was still highly successful, but flabby, self-satisfied and more than a trifle dull.

Sutton did not seem to fit very well into the Thompson poshocracy. Of Austrian descent, half Jewish, Sutton, (whose father had earned his money from the feather business), had read Modern Greats at St Peter's College, Oxford. As a statistician, he decided market research offered the best opportunities and in 1949 joined the British Market Research Bureau, a Thompson subsidiary, unaware that it was in any way directly connected with an advertising agency.

However, he soon moved into advertising – and in 1951 left Thompson to be advertising manager at Pasold. The following year, the agency recalled him. They had tried three times to start a subsidiary in West Germany and three times they had failed. In 1952 they sent Sutton, 'one man with a typewriter', as he said later. When he left in 1959, there were 310 people working in the Frankfurt office.

Sutton succeeded in Frankfurt for a number of reasons. He worked with imagination and frenetic energy; he was an organization king, capable of fashioning a highly efficient machine; and he was very persuasive with prospective clients. He was an efficiency expert with a talent for bringing in business.

But the question remained whether these techniques would work in Berkeley Square, where individual freedom (even to the extent of an afternoon off during the Wimbledon fortnight) was almost an article of faith. Certainly Sutton was a novelty in the agency. As Mitchell-Innes remarked: 'We'd never had anybody like that before – Tom's a very good businessman.' Sutton, in fact, represented a new wave of advertising men, wholly different from the nabobs of the first generation.

So, when he first arrived in Berkeley Square, he trod carefully. He began to cast a critical eye on the way the Thompson organization was working, but when he was offered Douglas Saunders's old office, he turned it down. Too many people, he thought, would resent the step. Instead he moved into an unpretentious office on the third floor and quietly broke the Thompson tradition by putting in modern, functional furniture – with green leather chairs and a Picasso and a Dufy on the walls. His only concession to antiquity was outside the door, in the alcove where his secretary sat, where he hung two Venetian prints, one of them of the Doge's Palace. 'Tom's office,' a colleague said, 'is really an operating theatre.'

The operation Sutton performed on Thompson's well-upholstered body was urgently needed. The agency's turnover of staff – they had lost only three account executives by normal departure during the 1950s – was so low as to seem like 'constipation' to Sutton. But in less than two years, much of the unnecessary fat had disappeared. At the end of 1961, Thompson had 918 people on their books; by April 1963 and with the same business, they had only 815.

Sutton preferred not to over-emphasize the changes he had made. 'We sacked some Old Etonians,' he said, 'but we also hired some and promoted others.' Sandy Mitchell-Innes, on the other hand, admitted that they had been 'slimming like mad. First of all, we haven't replaced any who've elected to move on. Then we've got rid of a certain number of people. Parkinson has had a good innings, but he's had his day here.'

One of the agency's junior executives put the change even more sharply. 'Sutton's arrival,' he said, 'was like changing from a monarchy to a republic. All the flunkeys went and he set out to make Thompson into a money-making business geared to profit.'

But the Sutton revolution meant much more than a reduction in numbers: it involved a major reorganization within the agency and the application of numerous new concepts. When Sutton took over, Thompson was divided into creative departments – copy, art, T V and so on. The idea was to draw men from each to deal with particular accounts, but the departments had grown apart and communication between them was poor. The problem was to bring about a better understanding without sacrificing the flexibility which enabled the agency to have as many different account groups (between 150 and 200) as there were account problems. As one Thompson representative said – 'The system put too much responsibility in too many hands. To run it properly, you needed scores of people capable of taking ultimate responsibility – and there aren't that many in London.'

Sutton regarded it as one of his most important jobs to rationalize this structure with the aim of getting more cohesion, but at the same time keeping the flexibility to choose the right combinations of people for each account.

It took him two and a half years, though he maintains that changes are bound to continue as in as dynamic an organization as an agency no system or arrangement can ever meet all the needs of the time. What emerged in the first phase were a small number of creative groups, twenty to twenty-five strong, with writers, art directors and T v producers permanently attached to them, and a group head who had real responsibility and power to plan the advertising strategy and content of millions of pounds' worth of advertising. The groups were still not completely self-contained, and movement between them continued, but the change suited the brighter creative men, who had been complaining that they were not being promoted to jobs of real responsibility. 'In the old days,' said Jeremy Bullmore, 'the copy group head only had the copywriters under his control, and yet he was responsible for the whole of the advertising. This was obviously wrong.'

The same sort of process swept through the media department, whose job it was to draw up schedules for the buying of space and then to buy it. In the autumn of 1962, Sutton brought in a young, grey-haired Oxford economist called Christopher Higham, to inaugurate the new régime. As Higham said, the Thompson practice had been to split the department down the middle – with the planners, who worked out which were the best buys, on the one side and the buyers, who picked up the telephone and did the hard negotiation, on the other.

As it stood, the buyers had considerable power and responsibility although they did not do any of the planning and were performing what was really a clerical job. They were the agency's front men when it came to contact with the media executives. Sutton thought this was out of step with the changed circumstances in the media world and feared that, in a buyers' market, the arbitrary decision would result in inflexibility and slow service. He enthroned the planners – the slide-rule boffins of the media department – as the heads of groups which contained both buyers and planners. And Thompson took on more university graduates to head the groups.

Sutton pushed this programme through with the same intense energy as he had shown in Frankfurt. He probably works harder than any other advertising man in London. Always in his office by eight o'clock, when the pressure is on he occasionally gets there as early as six. Between eight and nine, he clears up the previous day's unfinished business and at nine, coffee for six arrives automatically. At that time on every day except Mondays, the small management group which effectively runs the agency meets. Sutton – who in committee has the reputation of being extremely brisk, with no time for diversions – heads the group of six men though he avoids the word 'chairman' which has obvious political connotations in the agency.

The average age of the group, when they were appointed in 1964, was 38, and though Hinks and Mitchell-Innes still come in every day, they only join the group now once a week.[23]

At 9.30, the agency officially starts work, and at 9.45, when the management group has broken up, Sutton opens the day's mail, and dictates replies. Almost every Tuesday morning he joins a Review Board on the problems of one particular account. Every second Friday, Sutton meets the agency's senior creative men from 9.45 to 10.30. He works on five accounts personally – two of them, Persil and Bachelor cigarettes, from the Unilever and Player's stables, but the other three are not large clients – so that 'I understand how the agency works'.

His lunch diary is generally booked for a fortnight ahead. If he is taking clients out, he either uses Thompsons' own excellent dining-room or else books a table at the Bon Viveur, the Guinea, the Berkeley or the Connaught. At all these places, the squat, bustling figure commands quick service. One nearby restaurant he avoids – 'the service is so appallingly slow and I like to get on with it.'

In the afternoon, there is the same tight schedule of meetings and Sutton seldom leaves the agency before six though not often later than this. Monday to Thursday the evenings are usually taken up with functions of one kind or another – and he stays at a house in South Eaton Place. On Friday nights, he drives his Zodiac down to his small country cottage at Warninglid in Sussex and carries on working. One day – either Saturday or Sunday – he leaves completely free from the agency's affairs and devours anything political he can lay his hands on.

Once a good athlete, he now chooses to ignore an expanding waistline by proving his fitness as often as he can. He did the London to Brighton walk in under fourteen hours, and when he went to Moscow with the

[23] The idea of the new group came from Hinks, who said that he would be retiring in a couple of years' time and that they ought to start thinking about the future. Sutton and two new directors, John Treasure and Christopher Thomas, picked three of the agency's brightest young men to join them. The six went away for a weekend together to get to know each other better – and now they meet much more regularly than in the old days, when the management committee only got together once a week.

Roy Thomson cavalcade he swam in an air temperature of zero Fahrenheit. (The water was 83 degrees.)

As far as his way of working is concerned, he seems to have modelled himself partly on Stanley Resor (though Sutton would deny this) with whom he spent three or four hectic days in March 1959.

Resor was then in his eighties, but as energetic as ever, and Sutton well remembered their last day in Berlin together. 'In the morning Mr Resor went to East Berlin, then did a tour of the new buildings in the West, and went to catch the 5 p.m. plane to Frankfurt. It was late, so we didn't get to Frankfurt till eight or nine. When we arrived, he insisted on having a dinner party for us – and then took the 11.30 sleeper to Paris.'

But although he has close friendships with the top men in the New York parent company, Sutton seldom goes to America. In 1962 and 1963 he did not cross the Atlantic once, and in his first four years of office, he only spent nine days there. This is strong evidence to prove that Thompson function as an independent British agency, though New York (with a 50 per cent share-holding) has final control. Furthermore, there are only four Americans in the London office, none of them on the board, and in all the seven European offices the total is only nineteen.

The Sutton New Deal took time to work and there were disasters – the failure to land the Ford account was one of them. The graph of business went gently upwards – £15.5 million in 1960, £17.2 million in 1961 – but then fell back to £15.7 million in 1962. There was the impact of television tax. Further, some accounts were lost – Gomme Furniture, Courtelle, Vaseline Hair Products, Tetley's Teabags and Mackeson among them – and the gains – Oxo, Campbell's Soups, Kodak, Findus, United Breweries – had not had time to take effect. 'Nor,' said Sutton, 'had our measures to increase operational efficiency become fully effective.' But 1963 was a slightly better year, and the 1964 billings of £18.8 million were much healthier.

The surgery had been performed. Sutton did not seem to feel any more at ease than he had when he first arrived, but he had done the job he was hired for. He had successfully brought the carnation era to an end.

Sutton wielded the axe, but he was strongly backed by men who had risen with him to fill the vacuum of power which the retirement of Douglas Saunders created. One of them, Dr John Treasure, was disposed to be even more ruthless than Sutton. 'Inefficiency,' he said, 'is more immoral than anything else. When I see it, I lick my lips. It's almost an aesthetic pleasure cleaning it up.'

Treasure's room is spare, almost academic – as befits a man who was once a University lecturer in Economics – with an easel in one corner, prints of Welsh scenes round the walls and a view of the London Hilton from the window.

Treasure rose rapidly. He came – like Sutton – to the British Market Research Bureau to do some research, and stayed. Four years later in 1956, he was B M R B's managing director; by 1960 he was deputy chairman and also research and marketing director of Thompson itself. Now he is a member of the management committee and is frequently one of its most incisive voices.

He has got to the top because of a sharp mind and a total commitment. 'I'm a whole-hogger,' he said, 'and I have a very strong competitive instinct. I like doing things better than anyone else.' However, he still finds it hard to look upon himself as a career advertising man.

He certainly believes that the future – both at Thompson and in the agency world as a whole – may lie with high-powered research men like himself. 'Look at the fabulous post-war growth of McCann-Erickson in America,' he said. 'It all happened when Marion Harper – who came up through the research department – was made president over a lot of others at the age of 35.'

Research men, he thinks, make good agency heads because they represent 'the highest level of intellect in the business', because 'if they're any good, they are always rooting out new ways of solving problems', and finally because they are continually involved in marketing problems at the highest level.

The fact is that, in agencies like Thompson, the research boss now holds a crucial position. Big clients have become more and more concerned with the logistics of advertising – is the product going to hit 70 or 75 per cent of C housewives? – and they are gradually moving towards the attitude of American companies, who want at least three levels of research before they embark on a major campaign. In this sort of situation, the man with the facts and figures is all-powerful. His findings increasingly form the foundation of the big campaigns; if his figures suggest that the advertising has been wrong in the past, the account group and client concerned may very well change it. Thompson's top creative men are only too well aware that sheer instinct and hunch count for rather less now than they did. 'Slowly,' as one creative group head remarked sadly 'market research is becoming everything.'

As research boss, Treasure exercises an effective kind of birth control over the sort of advertising Thompson produces. The cumulative research of the agency has produced a body of ultimate truth about the nature and buying habits of the British public – and Treasure is its guardian.

The basis of Thompson's version of this truth is quite simple: '80 per cent of sales in consumer items goes to women over 25 in the C2,

D and E brackets,' explained Treasure, 'and they are interested in kids and the home – sex is just a nuisance to most of them. They're interested in sex between the ages of 15 and 25. After 25, it is the children/Mum axis which matters – the feeling that the family really appreciates them. We know that because we've done studies on it.'

This is the heart of the Thompson philosophy, more fundamental even than the 'value for money' concept. Although Treasure says that they are only interested in the mother-child relationship 'when it is relevant – and we believe it is highly relevant for many household goods' – Thompson are often thought of as a 'Mum agency'. The first of the agency's 'Mum' campaigns was the one they mounted after the war for Persil. 'We were the first Mum people, and we've hung on to her ever since,' said Christopher Cross, who handles the Persil account. 'Mum likes to be told about herself by somebody who understands her lot. If she feels the manufacturers understand her, then she's much more likely to go for the product.' In this case, the philosophy seems to have worked; Persil still holds well over 30 per cent of the washing powder market despite the fiercest competition. And, almost as though to proclaim his allegiance, Treasure has a Picasso mother and child hanging behind his desk.

All of which lends an added air of respectability to the Thompson image. Treasure, like Sutton, was at pains to emphasize how discreetly the agency conducted itself by comparison with some others. 'There is a very high standard of behaviour here,' he said. 'We never entertain clients excessively and we don't lay on girls and night-clubs.'

Talking about the advertising industry as a whole, Treasure conceded that a 'certain amount of sex' was used in advertisements by copywriters 'who've read a child's guide to Freud'. In nine out of ten cases, one of two people were responsible, 'a young woman who produced the campaign in all innocence or a young fellow with a second from Oxford'.

But 'are you brave enough to wear Angel Face Double-O colours?' asked one of the best-known television commercials in the 1963 Pond's campaign. 'They're sheer murder. Shameless, passionate colours, that stay soft, smooth all day.' They had used the James Bond idea, he said, not only because of its suggestion of high living and excitement, but also for its sexual overtones. These, Treasure added, were good associations for cosmetics.

Treasure also thought that market research in the 'hidden persuader' sense had had its day. Out of the £10 million spent on market research each year, he doubted if more than £2 million was spent on motivational research.

It is true that most studies simply unearth the facts of the market – like, for instance, Thompson's work on Rose's Lime Juice. When the account came to the agency, the advertising had centred on Hawkins the butler – a figure from the 1930s – who strongly recommended Rose's for hangovers. Thompson immediately did a consumer survey on who actually drank it, and found that the vast majority were middle-class folk who liked it because they thought it refreshing. This apparently came as a thunderbolt, so the advertisements were changed to scenes of summer, with Rose's shown as a refreshing drink. The sales went up considerably as a result.

Thompson have also done research to find out what the Lux advertisement 'Nine out of every ten film stars use Lux' meant to women. The results made it plain that few literally believed the claim but it was, even so, anyone's judgment whether it was accepted at some subterranean level.

Treasure said he could certainly see no harm in ordinary persuasion. 'Everybody,' he said, 'is a persuader, and if you're trying to persuade people about things, you have to dramatize and overstate a point of view.' There were a good many 'white lies' in advertising, and Thompson had occasionally become involved in this kind of thing – 'it's created partly by an instinct of workmanship, a desire to do a really thorough job' – or possibly under pressure from the client.

Their advertising for Nimble bread can serve as an example. The loaf was slightly starch-reduced and smaller, so that if a slice of it were compared with a slice of ordinary bread, there were less calories, though the difference was very, very small. If you ate two slices, then you were back where you started. The early advertisements for Nimble used the claim 'Be Gay, Be Young, Slim with Nimble', but in course of time this claim disappeared and in the later advertisements a loaf was shown which melted into a picture of a slim girl – with the strong visual implication that Nimble helps you to slim. This kind of compromise must occur daily, not only at Thompson but in every big agency.[24] Treasure himself is involved in it more than most, since he advises both the I P A and the Advertising Association about public relations for advertising.

For himself, he wholly approves of the changes that the Sutton régime has brought in the agency, though one wonders if he thinks they have gone far enough. 'The average age here has gone down,' he said, 'and the agency has also become much less certain of its own superiority, much less dogmatic, much less insular, much more open to outside influence. The Establishment has weakened although there

[24] In 1955, the C. J. Lytle agency was fined £10 for an advertisement which said 'Jaffa grapefruit is rich in protective Vitamin A and wards off colds and winter ills'. Analysis showed that the Vitamin A content was so small that you needed to eat 120 a day to get the normal human requirement. In 1965, Libbys were fined £100 for claiming that some of their products contained Vitamin A, when in fact they contained none.

has certainly been no weakening of authority. And,' he added, 'the creative men will listen more to the research people.'

Another power behind the throne at Thompson is a much more traditional figure, Sandy Mitchell-Innes. He is, in fact, probably the most influential member of the Old Guard left, though he, like the chairman, Bill Hinks, is due to retire very shortly.

Mitchell-Innes is a small, shrewd man with a military bearing who came to Thompson in 1934. He had tried accountancy in the city, but 'couldn't add or subtract' and then had gone out to India for seven years with a firm of bill and exchange brokers. When he came back, the slump was at its worst and he spent some time selling roofing tiles – 'frightful fun, though they weren't frightfully good tiles'. From tiles he moved into tea, which he did well, and which decided him that he was 'a salesman by nature'.

Selling tea took Mitchell-Innes – again by sheer accident – to New York and into advertising. He was taken to the Harvard Club by a friend, who assured him that advertising was the highest form of selling and that, if Mitchell-Innes was interested, he knew somebody at J. Walter Thompson. Eventually Douglas Saunders took him on in the agency's London office.

Now he is regarded within the agency as a shrewd client contact man, who has the right connections and who can be relied on to bring in the business. Mitchell-Innes deprecates this view. On the one hand he denies, with a characteristic tightening of the lower jaw and squeezing the words out of the corner of his mouth, that friends can be decisive these days – 'that age has long gone' – and on the other admits that he did play a part in getting the giant Oxo account.[25]

He lives in a much more relaxed style than either Sutton or Treasure. He comes in at half-past nine and breaks off when he feels like it – 'I never stay longer than I have to, especially in the summer.' He lives in Hertfordshire or at a town flat in Mount Street, drives a Humber Hawk and a Victor Estate wagon, his clubs are the Bath, the Savile and the Arts – 'two too many' – and he is reputed to be comfortably off, though he himself says he will not retire with very much.

Mitchell-Innes's influence in the agency is hard to define, but none the less real. Certainly he does far more than give Thompson an air of venerability and tradition. He still takes ultimate executive responsibility for several of the agency's largest accounts – among them Rowntree, Oxo, Campbell's soups and Beecham, and for twenty-five years he handled the Horlicks advertising, before handing it over to John Treasure. He also – and this is perhaps the crucial point – has the sort of

[25] See next chapter.

46

social contacts at the top of British business which nobody else in the agency has.

It has always been one of Thompson's proudest boasts that they attract the best creative talent in London. Sutton showed how important he thought the top creators were by centralizing power in the hands of a few exceptionally able men.

One of them, Anthony Pugh,[26] has an office on the eighth floor. On the wall outside is a Spanish tag: 'A dios rogundo y con el mazo dando' which Pugh translates as 'Pray to God and keep hammering away'. On the desk inside are scattered toilet-rolls, Smarties, packets of Corn Flakes and huge cardboard Oxo cubes. From this untidy office Pugh controls the fate of several million pounds' worth of advertising – including the Kellogg, Kodak and Bowater-Scott accounts.

In his team he has five copywriters, ten art directors and two T v producers – and they live in the warren of tiny offices which surrounds Pugh's.

Pugh himself is forty with thinning blond hair and a pale, sensitive, mobile face. He chain-smokes and always seems to have at least four boxes of matches somewhere about his person. He read English at Cambridge and emerged with 'a very poor degree' and the distinction of having edited several magazines. He went to the B B C, became a producer and turned out programmes on the history of art which had, he says, 'an audience of three, all of them in East London'.

After a time he felt he could stand 'Reithian didacticism' no longer, so he left. The Cambridge appointments people kept him fed with vacancies, one of which said that there was an advertising agency which was considering taking on a graduate. 'So I came along here,' said Pugh, 'and I asked for Sir Walter Thompson. I thought a place like this must have at least a knight at the helm.'

Pugh had to go through the standard Thompson battery of tests and interviews, perhaps the most thorough and exhausting of any agency in London. One young executive said he had had sixteen hours of interviews before being offered a job. The round of interviews is followed by an intelligence test and then half-an-hour or so with a psychologist – 'not free association stuff rolling round on a couch,' as one young recruit explained, 'just this chap making sure I wouldn't go bonkers in the first six months.' All this in quest of what Thompson call 'inquisitive minds which do not think in ecstatic terms'.

Pugh passed the visual intelligence test, but failed the writing side of it, largely because he spent all his time doing a parody of Dickens. Despite the lapse, he was hired as a copywriter.

As a race, copywriters are unfortunate animals. They start life at

[26] Pugh moved to Masius, Wynne-Williams at the end of 1964.

about £700, live in untidy little cubicles stuffed with paper and are continually harried for their copy. They also operate under a curious contradiction; they are the main source of ideas and inventiveness in the agency, yet they often have their words hacked about until they are quite unrecognizable. 'The everlasting sorrow of the copywriter is the utter anonymity and meaninglessness of what he writes,' as one Thompson group head explained.

To survive successfully, they have to be both emotionally involved with what they are trying to advertise – 'I've found you have to think about your product as though you were actually making love to it,' said one 23-year-old – and yet utterly detached when their copy is mutilated.

This often induces a mild schizophrenia, particularly in women copywriters. Some group heads at Thompson think women are totally unsuited for the advertising life (not Pugh, who met his wife there) – one called them 'inflexible, with the general inventiveness of the potato, and they become so emotionally involved that they often crack up completely.' Not everybody is so sweeping, but it seems to be widely felt that women get too involved with their own brain-children and that they are too subjective in their approach to products. Even so, Thompson has two group heads who are women.

'Unless their subjectivity is normal,' said Pugh, 'that's to say coming from the great broad belly of England, it's dangerous.' Bernard Gutteridge, who has been copywriting since before the war and now acts as a sort of father confessor to the Thompson creative department, told a story to illustrate the point. ' "The trouble with you women," I said to one of them, "is that you always argue from the general to the particular." "*I* don't," she piped back.'

As newcomers to the advertising game, sometimes from highly intellectual backgrounds, copywriters also suffer most fiercely the doubts which occasionally afflict even the most dedicated admen. Pugh, for instance, never likes doing copy for toothpastes or soaps. Another group head disliked writing patent medicine advertisements.

These twinges grow less sharp with the years, and a senior copywriter in the agency said he liked doing patent medicines 'because you have a target'.

Copywriters in a big agency like Thompson usually console themselves with the dual compensation of rapidly rising salaries (the able survivors comfortably top £2000) and a somewhat second-hand sense of power – 'at best you even get the feeling that you are moving goods off the shelves', as the 23-year-old put it.

Pugh, as one of the people who has survived successfully, has developed his own technique and principles. 'I'm not at all worried about the truth about a product,' he said with a faint smile. 'I'm more concerned with the truth about people. The writer has got to involve himself with their hates, loves and resistances – and then he must colour their lives a little and try to make them happier and more exciting. That's the millenium.'

To Pugh this does not mean creating dream-worlds – 'I get annoyed if I have to imply that buying plastic bath-mats will change everything,' though it may mean falling back into the ordinariness which, he believes, often characterizes Thompson commercials. 'I don't like copy to be thought of as a separate language, full of bright epithets. I do like to think of words being spoken – I like to think of what people would say in life and then write it rather better. For instance, if you think of Corn Flakes, you can dream up words like "double-crunchy, deep-brown flavour" and so on, but if I said "Corn Flakes are very good, aren't they?" you'd probably answer mentally "Yes, they are".'

With a market which for most products is 80 per cent female and a team that is 70 per cent male, Pugh thought one of his main strengths was 'a very queer – no, it can't be that, I have four children – a very feminine approach and feel for things. For instance, I hate strong noise and I think the female ear is tied to a different frequency level: strident things give them a pain physically. I like to be quiet and confidential – though that's an awful word. The Americans will tell you, if you've got nothing to say, then sing it – but I prefer to have something to say.'

He also tries to avoid sheer cleverness because in his experience women do not respond to it. He talked about the advertising they had done for Smarties. 'For a long time,' he said, 'we did dotty advertising which said that everybody liked Smarties. This was palpably untrue, because only the kids did. The sales stuck at 100 tons a week, so I thought we must find out why kids liked them – in psycho-analytic terms.'

'What we discovered was that children like collecting lots of little things – so we thought of the phrase "what a lot". Then I taped my own children's voices playing with lots of Smarties, and they said "WOTA-LOTIGOT" and "WOTALOTUGOT". We thought we'd put this on TV in clever cartoons. You'd think it would be fine, with policemen taking their helmets off and Smarties falling out, but the sales didn't shift. Then I thought, why don't we show them the people who're supposed to be eating them, let's just get ordinary kids, not television children. Then sales roared, because the women in the audience could identify themselves with the thing.' This is why Pugh prefers to think of Thompson as a 'domestic situation' agency rather than just a 'Mum' agency, even though it is the Mum who does the buying.

He works mainly at home – 'I've never done anything constructive in the office' – and has what he calls 'a ten-day creative cycle'. 'I produce perhaps three days of good stuff,' he said, 'then I relapse into total inertia and lassitude.' He tries all his ideas out on his wife Caroline –

'she's got a totally instinctual reaction, so there's always a running stream of consciousness to dive into.'

The creation of a new advertising campaign may start in any one of a number of ways. A new client may arrive at the agency, an existing client may have a disastrous slump in sales, or simply be bored with the advertising he is getting. In any case, the first sign of trouble is likely to be the account representative rushing into Pugh's office and complaining that all is not well. Only too often, the demand comes in the period between July and September, when the agency is already desperately trying to complete a heavy schedule of winter campaigns, with a skeleton staff working fifteen hours a day. Whenever it comes, the new campaign is likely to take six months, perhaps eight, to mount.

If it is a new product, Pugh gathers all the information he can from the client. If it is already established on the market, he calls for information about the past advertising, all the marketing recommendations that have ever been made, all the market research that has ever been done. There are huge volumes at Thompson which contain all the past advertising they have done on products – and the market research is collated in a series of thick blue books. There are also charts – 'on Corn Flakes, for instance,' said Pugh, 'there might be 100 charts going back to 1934, and from them you can easily see what disasters you unleashed in the past.'

From this mass of information, Pugh and his team on the account have to try to formulate answers to five questions, known within the agency as the Thompson T-Square. The questions are: what exactly are we selling? who is most likely to buy it?; when are we selling it?; where are we selling it?; how are we going to sell it?

At this early stage, a crucial figure in the agency network – the controller – comes into the picture. In other agencies he is known as the traffic man and it is his job to try to keep track of the progress of the campaign as it moves forward. He is responsible for seeing that all the target dates are met from the moment the first requisition is made to the time when the advertising is launched upon the public.

At this stage he only issues Pugh with a general planning requisition, with the account name and a job number – say P123. Copies go to the typographical and art buying departments, so that they are ready to receive specific orders at a later date.

The controller is a man who lives by the calendar. Bruce Youngman, one of Thompson's seven controllers, is surrounded by them. They are scattered all over the walls, and he even has one inside his cigarette case. On the wall facing him is a vast progress chart covered with pink, blue and yellow tags showing how many jobs are under way and where they are in the agency. At the end of August 1963, there were thirty behind schedule. (The controllers, says Sutton, always arrange for a built-in time reserve.)

Youngman, a dapper, smooth-haired man with spectacles and the suggestion of a moustache, seeks to preserve an impression of calm, but finds it difficult. It is practically impossible to conduct an intelligent conversation with him in his office. The phone rings constantly, and men with a variety of mysterious errands rush in and out.

'Bloomsbury Advertising say it's not in the book,' said one of Youngman's clerks plaintively. 'Well, try the old number,' he suggested. The phone rang. Youngman consulted the calendar in his diary: 'The sixth deadline will be on Thursday night,' he said and put the phone down again. Then a man with a Cockney accent came in brandishing a toilet roll with the word Bravo printed on it. 'I want to bring this business to a head,' he said obscurely, and disappeared into a jungle of technical jargon. Youngman sat, listened resignedly, hedged and finally the man retired with the toilet roll, still shouting.

Once the requisition has been placed with the controller, Pugh calls a full meeting with his team. There might be twelve or fourteen people there – copywriters, art directors, a T V producer and representatives from the media and marketing departments, with the account representative putting the client's point of view. With all the sales figures and any available market research before them, they set out to decide what sort of broad approach they ought to take to the advertising.

These gatherings can go on for at least a fortnight, and the group might meet four or five times. On a new account like Kodak, there could easily be a dozen original planning sessions, each of them letting loose a flood of correspondence among the members of the team. Memoranda fly about the group, suggesting bright ideas, trying desperately to define the aims of the campaign, whether they should plump for Press or TV, what display material they should create.

These occasions are apt to have a ponderous solemnity which is sometimes not borne out in the end-product. 'One of the patent absurdities of it all,' said another Thompson creative group head, 'is that you often find twelve people with combined salaries of £25,000-£30,000 discussing how to do a show-card. All that time and effort from so many highly-paid people pontificating away and finally producing on a platter something such as "People like Pongo".'

The meetings often last two or three hours and, in Pugh's experience, they are usually dominated by the writers. 'They're really actors as well,' said Pugh, 'and they're always throwing up their hands and shrieking "Oh, Christ!" They've got strong views on everything. But the statistics men quieten it all down. Mind you, we don't have any pyrotechnics here, we're a pretty sober, intellectual crew.'

'Slowly the Jeremiahs and Cassandras water down people's enthusiasm. The art director usually pipes up with: "But you must get glamour into it." rather plaintively. Slowly we get nearer to our objective.'

If Pugh thinks it necessary, he asks for a fresh piece of market research, but this inevitably delays the campaign's progress and is only resorted to in extreme need – which is in less than 10 per cent of cases. An outside survey – with a sample of several hundred – might take a month to set up and a month to formulate the results. With the client breathing hard somewhere in the background, a much more likely solution – if research is needed – is a quick survey of a sample of Thompson's own staff.[27] If it happens to be a food account – and Thompson currently have almost a score of them – a good deal can be done in the experimental kitchen of the agency's own Home Economics Department. 'Home Ec' tests products and the recipes which use them, makes up most of the specimens used in TV commercials and even helps clients develop new products. Twice a month, the agency top brass lunch there, sitting on drug-store stools at the plastic-topped bench.

When the series of planning sessions have agreed a broad approach to the advertising, smaller, more parochial meetings within Pugh's group begin, and continue almost daily. 'We ask ourselves,' said Pugh, 'how, specifically, are we going to communicate this what to that who'. First of all, the copywriter has to isolate the 'promise' the product offers and reduce it to one, or at most two, short sentences.

Then the art director has to decide how the promise can best be illustrated. He may want to use photographs in preference to drawn art work, and, particularly at Thompson, he may have a mass of copy to contend with. The art men – 'perpetual adolescents' one Thompson group head scathingly called them – continue their passionate search for 'glamour' and are very likely to suggest that the pictures ought to be taken in Egypt.

Dozens of possibilities are tossed about, dozens of layouts prepared. The art buying department is consulted on the best artist or photographer for the job. It is their job to keep in touch with the visual side of the world in advertising – and they keep the work of nearly 1000 artists and photographers on file. ,

If the campaign is proposing to use television, the TV producer in the team begins to work out draft scripts. Sometimes he also uses a storyboard – between six and nine miniature TV screens drawn down the

[27] Thompson, like other agencies, are very conscious of losing touch with the mass-market by virtue of being a somewhat closed community. As a measure of their concern, they send two or three people to Butlin's each week, where they keep a chalet – and people like Christopher Higham, the media director, go ten-pin bowling in Streatham because it 'intrigues me to be surrounded by working-class people. It's dangerous to become isolated from the 75 per cent who leave school at 15'.

length of a piece of paper – to indicate the way in which the pictures will fit in with the words.

Thompson have perhaps a dozen film-producers – small companies like Augusta Productions in Bruton Street or Francis-Montague in Paddington Street – whom they use regularly. The director may be called in very early in the campaign planning to discuss casting (Thompson has its own casting department). TV commercials are an expensive business. Performers are highly-paid – a celebrity might earn £1000 for a series of three commercials, starlets generally pick up perhaps £300 – and the cost of studio equipment is very high. In the autumn of 1963, three thirty-second commercials for Campbell's Soups took two days of studio time to make. The total cost: £6,500.

At some stage, Pugh has to decide where the focus of the campaign is going to be – will it be half-pages in the women's magazines, full-pages in the national dailies, fifteen-second or thirty-second commercials? Again, the debate goes on, and the bright ideas flow. 'Someone is sure to say "We must show this dramatically on TV",' said Pugh, 'and then I have to say, yes, but we've only £75,000 to play with and that would last us precisely a month and a half on TV.'

When he has decided roughly what he wants, Pugh again calls in the media man. '"Jeremy," I say – he's always called Jeremy somehow – "what'll give us the best buy?"' The media man goes away and produces a White Paper which shows the circulations and audiences of the media Pugh is proposing to use, how many housewives will be covered – by age and class – and what the discounts are. The placing of the advertisements is a major factor in the timing of the whole operation, because peak-time TV spots have to be booked at least four months in advance, and the premier positions in the national newspapers require at least three months notice.

As the campaign begins to take shape – a month or five weeks after the original demand – the complaints begin. '"I can't write it," the copywriters always tell me,' said Pugh, '"I'm attending an I P A conference in Torquay." Or maybe the excuse is that he hasn't got enough information to go on. Then the media men want you to do it on half-pages instead of full pages, and the marketing men start bleating that they can only sell what they believe in – which is just humbug.'

When the scheme of things has been roughly drafted out – and there may be twenty or thirty different pieces in it – it goes to the agency's lawyers. It has to satisfy them on three basic points. Can the claims be proved – or at least not disproved? Could it offend public taste? Does it attack or denigrate a competitive product – is it 'knocking copy' in fact? If there is any doubt, counsel's advice is taken and, in the case of pharmaceutical products, one of a panel of consultant doctors is called in.

Now, at last, comes the presentation. This is the moment of truth, when the agency puts its proposals before the client. (The client has, in any case, been kept in touch with the campaign's progress.) A big presentation at Thompson, with perhaps £1 million worth of advertising on the chopping-block is a dramatic occasion.

Very often they are held in the large upstairs sitting-room of the eighteenth-century house which the agency is using in Hill Street, just off Berkeley Square until the lease runs out in a few years time.[28] The room has a brass chandelier and a large and exceedingly ugly oil painting of the Crystal Palace obscuring one wall. For the presentation, small period tables and chairs are set out and boards hide the painting of the Crystal Palace.

The account director – the board member who carries ultimate responsibility – emerges for the presentation and generally slumbers gently over a cigar, giving off an air of confidence. Then there are the account representative, the creative group head and the media man. On the client side, the team is usually headed by the marketing director who is going to carry the burden of the presentation. With him is the advertising manager – 'said to be bright, but showing no signs of it' thinks the creative group head – and the manager of the brands being shown.

The agency usually opens with an analysis of the marketing picture – the product and its competition. Then the creative group head talks about what he thinks they are offering consumers ('the consumer proposition') and how the advertising might do the job. He answers questions as he goes. 'You can almost see them coming,' said Pugh, 'it's like badminton, you watch the shuttlecock of a question out of the corner of your eye. You've got to fend them off and keep the initiative, otherwise you're sunk.' Finally comes the media presentation – how and where the agency proposes to spend the client's money.

If the marketing director is American, he is likely to be appreciative but doubtful. 'I see exactly what you're driving at,' he might say, 'but it doesn't look like hard-sell to me. I think we've got to have more consumer-benefit.' The advertising manager, perhaps slightly too young for his job, adopts a nagging attitude – 'most interesting, though I can't say we've agreed to spend so much more'. With the marketing director present, he sets out to give an impression of being tough with the agency.

When the presentation is over, and all the objections have been met, the agency team usually take the client men to lunch. It has been superbly laid on in another room in the Hill Street house, a room which

[28] At the time of writing, Thompson are building a new presentation theatre in one of the wells of the Berkeley Square building, while in the other there will be a television workshop. This is part of a complete redecoration (cost, about £200,000) which will replace the agency's depressing cream-and-brown with a much brighter and more modern colour scheme.

has a pair of firedogs and two paintings – a portrait of Stanley Resor by Augustus John and a study of dead birds by an unknown artist.

Before lunch, any Americans in the party may opt for whisky on the rocks, the English stick to gin and tonic. Lunch is lightish: smoked salmon, steak (au naturel, for the benefit of the Americans), beans and potatoes with probably a nice plain rosé; and lemon soufflé. The conversation is about holidays and children and the cost of living.

With this stamp of approval, the campaign can now go rapidly ahead. The controller issues new numbers for each piece of work – four figures for Press work, five for non-Press – and each is given a record-card which stays with it until the advertisement appears. Youngman runs through 10,000 of these jobs in eighteen months.

Through requisitions issued by him, the finished art work is put in hand; the copy goes first to the typographical department, where the best type-face is selected, and then through the printing department to one of the six block-makers employed by Thompson. If different sizes of blocks are needed – the advertisement might be appearing in the *Daily Express* and the *Daily Mirror* as well as in the women's magazines – a Lucie camera is used to scale down each layout to the correct size. Contracts are put out for the television commercials – and they are shot, edited and a music track added.

Meanwhile the media men are hard at work. They may have to wheedle and negotiate for the TV spots and newspaper positions they want. Speaking for a big agency, which spends £10 million a year on air time and £6 million or £7 million in the Press they are entitled to a little extra consideration, and they usually get it.

And then, at last, the campaign appears – and all that is left is to sit back and hopefully watch the sales graphs.

4. Katie and the Cube

Giving the image of a product a face-lift is one of the services which advertising claims to be able to perform. The product is not changed; it is merely that the public is persuaded to think of it in a different way. The classic case of this technique is what J. Walter Thompson did for the Oxo cube.

By the winter of 1957, the directors of Oxo Limited were uneasy about their Company's progress. The sales of their main product – which over the course of half a century (the Oxo cube first appeared here in 1910) had almost become a part of Britain's folk heritage – were still very high, but they were below the record level achieved during the post-war rationing period and for some years had been completely static.

In an effort to get things moving Oxo's managing director, Tommy Sycamore, who had joined the Company in 1954, had already completed a reorganization of the whole business – production, administration and sales. It was now time to re-examine the Company's advertising policy and approach.

At that time, the advertising budget was not particularly large for a company of Oxo's size: the advertising policy had been essentially one of reminder, using every type of advertising medium available. Oxo advertisements appeared on vans, railway stations, buses, bus tickets, television, newspapers – everywhere in fact where an advertisement could be fitted. Most of them sported a bull as a symbol of Oxo's strength-giving properties, and they recommended the penny cube – rather as if it were a patent medicine for cooks – for drinks and sandwiches and stews.

Sycamore went to Thompson to see an old friend of his, Sandy Mitchell-Innes. Mitchell-Innes agreed with him that they did seem to be having 'rather a dull time'. He already knew about Oxo's sales position because the product had been on Thompson's Retail Audit panel for some time. The Retail Audit then covered a sample of 350 shops all over Britain and involved a close and detailed check on sales every four weeks.

Sycamore was impressed that Thompson seemed to know their predicament so well, and he kept in touch with Mitchell-Innes. Mitchell-Innes, meanwhile, continued to watch the way Oxo was moving, and shortly he ventured some conclusions. He told Sycamore he thought there was nothing wrong with Oxo as a product. It was simply that the public had begun to think of it in the wrong kind of way: in other words, its image was blurred.

'Oxo has got two images,' he told Sycamore. 'One for drinks and one for cooking, and the advertising is spread about all over the place. I think you should put your money into one medium – television – and into one use, cooking. That will clear up your image.' Sycamore had been thinking along similar lines himself – and so in the spring of 1958, he decided that it was time to make a change of agency and put the account into the hands of Thompson.

The agency appointed a group to handle the account; Bernard Gutteridge was to do the initial creative planning and, a little later, Anthony Pugh was given creative control. Christopher Thomas, now a member of the agency's board, became the account representative.

The agency did not feel any need to undertake a large new research project at this stage, and in any case they had only six months in which to mount their first campaign – by the autumn of 1958. So they did a quick survey, lasting only a week and consisting of only a small number of interviews, to find out what people felt about Oxo.

The survey, small as it was, completely confirmed Mitchell-Innes' and the agency's suspicions. Oxo had come to be regarded as a synthetic product, a substitute for the real thing. Its biggest sales had been during and after the two wars when meat was short, and in the Depression when it became a cheap substitute for beef. Because of this it was connected in people's minds with the hungry 'thirties – and therefore associated with poor people and poor cooks. As meat had become more plentiful after the second war, Oxo had slipped lower and lower in the public mind.

Pugh drew the same sort of conclusion from the early research. 'Here,' he said, 'was a product that had been chewed in the trenches, a very cheap little thing with the context of Jarrow.'

At the early planning meetings there was little disagreement as to what the agency needed to do. As one of the young marketing executives put it: 'We clearly had to up-grade the product socially – to clear away the prejudices which had built up about it and show that it was being used by young, with-it people. Then we had to concentrate our effort into one medium, and finally we had to show what in fact was true, that Oxo was made of nine perfectly good ingredients.'[29]

The first job was to find the right vehicle to dispel these 'social prejudices'. To Pugh, this meant showing Oxo being used in a domestic setting; to Gordon Thomson, the media man in the group, it meant 'taking it off the streets, lifting it out of the public arena and putting it in the home'. Posters with bulls were out; television with people was in.

It was Bernard Gutteridge who gave the campaign its first theme. He had driven up to St Helens by car with Sandy Mitchell-Innes to see another of the agency's clients, Beecham. 'It was a thick, muggy day,' he recalled, 'and on the way back we started talking about Oxo. Suddenly we came behind a bus and there was one of those ads in orange and brown saying that Oxo was a very fine drink. I remember saying, "That's the kind of thing we must do away with, Sandy".'

When Gutteridge got back to London, he sent for his copywriter – a girl named Joan Drummond – and began to visualize for her the kind of domestic, husband-and-wife situation which he wanted to see Oxo in, the kind of situation which would dramatize the new youthful image the agency were trying to project.

---

[29] Oxo is made up of hydrolized protein, beef stock, beef extract, desiccated beef, flour, yeast extract, caramel, salt, spices and onion powder.

'Basically,' he told her, 'we want the idea that the chap is after the girl for her sexiness as well as her good cooking, and we need a slogan to keep us on that line.' Joan Drummond went away and came up with 'Oxo gives a meal man-appeal', which was to be the campaign's base-line.

As Christopher Thomas admitted later: 'Rationally examined, we're still not quite sure what it meant.' Others in the agency criticized it for being vulgar, but it provided the right focus for the planners.

Television was clearly the natural medium. Apart from the fact that a domestic situation could not be adequately portrayed in flat print, this was the golden age of the TV ratings, with relatively low costs and colossal audiences for the commercial channel. As Gordon Thomson said: 'If it had been now, the story might be different, because the cost is a lot higher.'

But it did not prove easy to evolve a series of commercials which won general approval among the planning team. In fact, the debate soon became a row. Pugh supervised the making of two commercials – one, as he said, 'the usual idiot thing of a girl in a fantasy kitchen throwing up a large cube and singing – the other a documentary deal with a straight-forward woman presenter.' The second commercial was ultimately to produce 'Katie', the Oxo housewife.

Several of the planning group favoured the fantasy advertisement – 'a song and dance in a wire kitchen', as Pugh scathingly put it – and the argument was so sharp that the agency decided to submit to arbitration. A small sample of the public was asked which they preferred, and fantasy (even in wire kitchens) proved more acceptable than realism.

Pugh was now in a very difficult position. Either he had to submit to the majority, with the backing of research – and no advertising man likes flying in the face of figures – or else risk going ahead on his own hunch.

Pugh thought it over and then made his mind up. 'I decided,' he said, 'that the wire kitchens stank. I said to myself – "Where do we go from there?" – the thing had no growth potential and I thought, if only I could find somebody like my wife, with that same age and class, as the presentor, that would be it.' He stuck his neck out, rejected the results of the research and went for the documentary treatment.

Now Pugh began to search for the sort of person who could embody the image of the new Oxo-user the agency wanted to create. 'I went back home and talked to my wife,' said Pugh, 'and we began to look for a name. We wanted an expressive name, not something like Lois. Mary would have done, but Mary Smith is the archetypal advertising pattern. The thing kept going through my mind – K-K-K-Katie come into the Kitchen. Katie, I thought, was an OK name, it had a sort of bravado, a devil-may-care quality about it. What Katie Did, you know. It was also, I felt, a floury-handed name.'

And Katie it was, though the group meeting considered between twenty and thirty names altogether. Now the problem was, what sort of woman should Katie be. This was crucial, since it was to be Katie's job to dispel all the prejudice which had suggested that Oxo was an old-fashioned, cheap product. Thomas thought of her as 'a fairly pleasant version of a modern young housewife, who lived in a nice, not very ritzy house. As for her class, we thought we should make her fairly indeterminate – as classless as possible. We thought of her husband (Philip) as being someone in a fairly good clerical job, at the beginning of the executive ladder if you like.'

'We also had to make Katie the sort of woman who watched her pennies,' he said, 'because we wanted to work along with the butchers, who couldn't sell their cheaper cuts of meat. This was right for Oxo, since we wanted Katie to use it for casseroles and stews.'

Pugh imagined Philip and Katie 'living in Ealing, with Philip playing rugger on Saturdays. I did wonder at first if it wasn't going to be too smart for Lancashire'. But a much greater problem in his mind was to get a girl of the right age and appearance. 'We didn't want anybody so young that she would be flibbertygibbet and put older women's backs up.'

Thompson, in fact, were struggling desperately to create a multi-class woman – someone who would keep the old Oxo buyers as well as capturing new purchasers whose position and status were not at all clear – apart from the fact that they were up the social ladder. Isolated from the world to which they are selling, agencies often reach hopefully for an image which they think will capture the class they are aiming for. It is, at best, inspired guess-work.

But Thompson realized that Oxo would still be selling most of their cubes to older, more conservative women – and they knew from a study they had done of the eating and cooking habits of housewives that the younger, more adventurous cooks were still in a minority. They therefore decided to attack this smaller group through a second medium – the women's magazines.

The Katie they picked was a complete unknown. She was a repertory actress who had never appeared on a television screen. She was twenty-seven and she had no particular accent, and she did not have what Pugh called 'the actress manner. So many of these girls declaim – they can't just say things, it's always like Shakespeare at the Old Vic.'

It seemed that they had picked a central character as unexceptionable as it was possible to be. But three of the senior creative women in the agency made it known that they thought the team's choice 'absolutely wrong'. Other women, they said, would hate Katie because she was too attractive and would arouse latent hostility from older women.

To answer this criticism, Thompson hired Jonathan Routh to make a 'Candid Camera' type film, in which he asked twenty women, many of them elderly, what they thought about Katie. The result was surprising. Eighty per cent said they actually liked her, whereas in tests of this type a large percentage is usually totally indifferent. 'We feel she's one of us', was a typical reaction.

There were other objections which Pugh recalled. ' "Of course we should be in a mess if this Katie was knocked down by a bus, shouldn't we? The trouble is, she's the star and not the product." People were so afraid of putting all our eggs in one basket.'

It was Pugh's idea that they should not only concentrate on television, but pack all their spots into one night – Sunday. He wanted the thing done in three episodes, the first one showing Katie preparing the meal, the second showing Philip eating it ('my God, this is good') and the third showing the couple going off to bed. 'After all,' he observed, 'this episodic treatment of things is traditional in British Life – think of Dickens, the Archers and the Dales.'

So Thompson hired a TV company, Augusta Productions, to make their commercials for them. They had to shoot between twenty-five and thirty for the first season, and though there is some economy in numbers, the cost was still perhaps £1000 each. The job was big enough to build a complete set of a kitchen, which itself cost over £1000. Particular care had to be taken with the furniture in the kitchen because every piece helped to establish the status of Katie and Philip. But the shooting went ahead quickly and the commercials were ready for launch date in October 1958.

The other point of attack was the women's magazines, on which Thompson spent one-third of their allocation. There were several reasons for having this second string. 'First of all,' said Gordon Thomson, 'we wanted to use the magazines as a way of up-grading the cooking level by offering slightly unusual recipes. This was image-building, but it was also providing a service to the housewife. Moreover, the magazine offered us a complementary coverage – we again hit some of the people we caught via TV and still had an overlap of 40 per cent.'

'Gourmet goulash' and 'boeuf strogonoff' were two of the recipes offered in the first campaign. 'We tended to include rice,' said Christopher Thomas, 'though, mind you, in those days we didn't expect anyone to use the recipes.'

But there were other problems associated with the magazine advertisements. What, for instance, was going to happen to the famous Oxo bull? This seemed to be an instance where it ought to be kept, so the agency tried to find out whether people liked their Oxo made from castrated animals or whole ones. 'They said they liked whole ones,' recalled Gutteridge, 'so we put a picture of an obviously masculine black bull in the first Press ads.'

Then there was the question of suitable illustration. Here the agency decided that they would not use Katie, but show young couples instead. Again it was Gutteridge who provided the impetus. At one of the planning meetings, he said to the art director: 'You've got to think up some new visual look for these colour pages in the women's mags. What you want is a nice romantic picture of a chap and girl – and it might be a painting instead of a picture.'

George Butler, the art director, said he knew just the man for the job, an Italian artist called Tempesti. One of his staff immediately flew out to Italy to hire him.

Katie was duly launched in October, with Oxo's full approval and backing, together with the full pages in the women's magazines. One showed a man being pursued by a woman with a dish; another had the line 'Men fall in love with girls, but they marry good cooks'. The campaign duly ran from October to March, the normal span of most winter food campaigns.

But, unfortunately, very little happened to the sales graphs and the agency team began to get anxious. 'There wasn't any shift at all,' said Thomas, 'and we were desperately worried.' There was even talk of mounting a campaign on the old style, advertising Oxo as a drink. Oxo themselves, meanwhile, were not unduly concerned. As Thomas said: 'They never turned a hair, they were far less worried than we were.'

There was only one ray of hope on the horizon. This was the result of research Thompson had done into people's attitudes to Oxo in January and February 1959, three months after the campaign had been launched. This showed a marked improvement, clear indication that the image was changing in exactly the direction Thompson wanted. The agency clung to this faint hope even though it was not mirrored in sales figures.

By the spring of 1959, of course, they had to begin thinking of the campaign for the following winter and there was fierce discussion as to whether they had taken the right line or not. The men who had favoured the fantasy ad were inclined to feel rather superior, but in the end Pugh's views prevailed – and Katie was booked for a second season.

There were changes, of course. As Thomas said: 'In the commercials, we felt we had tried to cram too much in. Katie had too many words to say, so the message was not absolutely clear and simple. Katie was too brittle, slightly nervy, gabbling a bit and with cooking this is not the right impression to create. So we cut out a number of words and incidental details.' Nor did Katie any longer do any straight selling at the end of the commercial: this, the agency felt, was superfluous and destroyed the reality of the mood.

By this time, the agency felt Philip and Katie were well enough established to launch them in the magazines as well. So along with lines like 'Men always seem to go for gravy and for girls who know how to make gravy taste rich and meaty' went pictures of Philip with Katie in his arms and the caption 'Suddenly it's spring'. They also changed the timing of the TV commercials to fit the pattern of buying better – most housewives bought their Oxo on Thursday, Friday and Saturday. So the commercials no longer appeared only on Sunday.

In January and February of 1960, Thompson duplicated the piece of attitude research they had done the previous year: again the results were encouraging. But, even more important, the sales figures had begun to move. Mitchell-Innes was very relieved. 'I shall never forget the meeting when the figures showed a slight shift upwards,' he said.

The advertising, and Oxo's own efforts, were beginning to bear fruit. The company themselves, apart from a powerful sales drive, had also begun to do further research into the packaging of the cube. For a long time, it could not be displayed on the counter because it needed to be kept in tins – a severe handicap for what was often an impulse purchase. Oxo devised a new form of protective wrapping which meant that the cube could safely be taken out of the tin, and this also helped boost sales.

Now that the figures were going in the right direction, the agency set themselves to consolidate the position. As time went on, the sexual content of the Katie commercials faded and 'Oxo gives a meal man-appeal' was replaced by a simply flat injunction 'Don't forget the Oxo'.[30] As Thomas said: 'At first one of the important things was to make people sit up and take notice, to show them that something had happened to Oxo and this was our way of doing it.'

There were also difficult exercises to cope with, like the introduction of Katie's dining-room. All the furniture and decorations were indications of her class and status. The agency chose a very neat *décor*, and even occasionally permitted Katie some candles on the dining-table. (Again the agency's idea of life in the middle class seemed a trifle bizarre). Philip was clearly climbing the executive ladder, and by 1963, when they were attending the ballet together, progress was visibly being maintained. Katie herself grew older – a sound thing in the agency's view. 'It's good to have as your image an older married woman who's a more experienced housewife,' said Thomas. (In 1964, for that matter, Katie suddenly had a baby.)

Then, as Katie became more established, the people next door were brought into the commercials, with a scatter-brained wife called Muriel to act as a foil for Katie's well-planned housewifery. 'They were all,' as Thomas said, 'semi-detached people.' This fact in itself raised problems, because it tended to imply that Oxo had a restricted class appeal. So

[30] The latest (1964–5) campaign has gone back to 'man-appeal'.

Thompson introduced a C2[31] Dad for Katie – 'bald, retired, rather blunt, he could have been an old-fashioned retailer,' said Thomas. 'Her mother was useful too, because she brought in old-fashioned recipes like steak-and-kidney pie. It all served to keep the class appeal varied.'

Gutteridge was angry at this decision, however. 'It was very off-putting,' he said later, 'to have anything interfere when you'd got them slotted nicely into classlessness.'

1960 had seen another departure. A new Philip had to be introduced because the old one felt that he was getting dangerously type-cast. The agency went to tremendous lengths to produce three or four commercials in which Philip did not actually appear. 'His hand would pick up the telephone in the clubhouse,' said Thomas, 'and he'd say he would be late for lunch, but you never actually saw him.' The new Philip did not appear until November. When he did, he became very popular – particularly with husbands – partly because he was somewhat stouter than the first Philip and partly because at this time the agency decided that previously Katie had been a little too dominating and therefore now allowed Philip to get the better of her occasionally.

1960 produced a further problem. Oxo were always reluctant to raise their prices, partly for historical reasons. Baron Liebig, the firm's founder, had made it a principle of his business that they sold their product for the lowest currency of the country concerned. In the 1950s, however, the 1d cube became $1\frac{1}{4}$d and then $1\frac{1}{2}$d and finally, in 1960, Oxo decided to increase it to 2d (which was, after all, only double the 1910 price).

Thompson used unusual tactics to cope with the increase. As Gordon Thomson explained: 'We decided we'd have to keep widest possible coverage to take in all users – and to keep Oxo before the public in a favourable light.' The agency took full pages in the national dailies, in which butchers standing among their sides of beef recommended Oxo cubes to the housewife. In the event, the rise in price seemed to stimulate sales rather than deflate them.

From Oxo's point of view this had been a most successful operation. True that by 1963 they were spending substantially more on advertising in absolute terms, but with sales nearly 50 per cent up there was more than enough to pay for it. The number of users had only increased marginally, but the people who did use Oxo bought it on a much larger scale. And yet no real change had been made to the product itself.

Katie had done her job of image-building and prejudice-dispelling. The agency's claims for their own achievement were modest. The marketing men, in particular, acknowledged the overriding importance of the changes Oxo themselves had made in their own sales approach and the

[31] See page 22, footnote 9.

innovations in packaging they had introduced. But one thing at least they could claim. 'Nobody,' said Christopher Thomas, 'would think of Oxo as old-fashioned now.'

5. Guinness *is* Good for You

Advertising, by its very nature, is a serious business and nobody, least of all the British business man, pays the outrageously heavy costs of advertising his products for the fun of it. But in the past this element of heavy seriousness has not always shown in the advertising itself. Advertising may have been serious, but it was not always entirely humourless and this vein of humour provides one of the few discernible trade marks of British advertising from the mid nineteenth century to the present day. It may not have been always very good humour but it was there. Now it looks as if its days could be numbered.

For one of the old ideas which the *nouvelle vague* of Anglo-American admen are doing their best to hit over the head is the idea that people will buy your products because your advertising amuses them or charms them or simply cheers them up. 'Buying,' says David Ogilvy, 'is a serious business. Nobody buys from clowns.'

And for better or for worse this particular criticism seems to be echoed by the people who control the budgets and direct the policies of the leading agencies in Britain. One of the most interesting examples of this new trend at work is the story of one of the minor mysteries of contemporary British advertising—the sad and revealing tale of where the Guinness animals went.

The Guinness Company started advertising their stout as far back as 1928 when they ran a pilot campaign in Scotland, following it up with a full-scale national campaign which has continued with only occasional interruptions ever since.

The reason behind this was that the company was in rather an unusual position. At Dublin they owned what was then the biggest brewery in the world (and is still one of the biggest in Europe) but unlike most other big breweries in this country they had been resisting the tendency to buy large chains of tied public houses and off-licences through which their beer could be sold.

They were manufacturers, pure and simple, and the Guinness board realized that if they were to remain so against the growing competition of the other brewers (through whose pubs they were already having to sell their beer) they would somehow have to create a national awareness of the name of Guinness. It would have to be a unique name. Ideally every potential stout-drinking man and woman in the country should believe that there really was something about Guinness which set it apart from the common-or-garden stout which other brewers produced and were only too anxious to sell in their own houses.

This was the start of a campaign which, during the thirty-seven years it has run, has become possibly the last of the British advertising classics.

That it did so was partly due to the Guinness Company themselves, who realized from the start how closely the advertising was tied up with their own future and so were willing to pay far larger sums over far longer periods than most British companies of their day. It was also due to the agency they employed and which still holds the £1¼ million Guinness advertising account. (Because the Guinness Company makes its poster bookings and certain other expenditure direct, the agency is eligible for its fifteen per cent commission on roughly half this figure. Guinness is still, however, easily the largest single brewery account in Britain.)

S. H. Benson is now one of the largest advertising agencies in this country, with a total billing for 1964 of about £17 million. It advertises Johnnie Walker whisky, and is proud of having had Bovril as one of its clients since 1893. It has the more dubious credit of having coined the phrase 'adds brightness to whiteness' for Omo. It established 'Pink Paraffin' as a brand name by advertising, although paraffin had been so coloured and so called for many years. It joined forces with Mather and Crowther in backing David Ogilvy to set up the one and only British advertising agency to compete successfully on Madison Avenue. And it must take some responsibility for the growing bosom consciousness of Britain. For it was Benson's who triggered off the first shot in the American-inspired female foundation garment war in this country with a highly successful campaign in 1955 for the International Laytex Corporation. The advertising for the Playtex roll-on was specially written for the British market, but John Mellors, who was copy chief at Benson's at the time, says that the Playtex bra was sold largely on its American origins. 'There was a definite feeling in those days that the bosom was one area where the Americans really had a significant lead over Britain.'

But despite this, Benson's remains the most purposefully non-American of the British agencies at the top of the league. If a British tradition of advertising does survive, Benson's is its undoubted repository.

It is not the oldest surviving agency. (R. F. White and Son were in fact active before 1800.) But, perhaps because it has developed the habit of hanging on to its clients for so much longer than most advertising agencies, it seems more conscious of its history than any of its big rivals.

Benson's was founded in 1893 by the retired naval officer whose name is now enshrined in the business and whose distinctly frosty portrait still takes stock of visitors as they cross the reception area of the present offices just opposite Holborn Underground station. And today something more than just the name and the portrait of the agency's founder seem to survive. The firm has kept the reputation he gave it for its copy and its creative work and many of the executives seem to adopt a certain breeziness of approach as if they had just stepped off the quarter-deck themselves.

It is easy to over-emphasize the nautical element in the agency and the management are insistent that the brass bell hanging in Reception with 'S. H. Benson' engraved on it is not a ship's bell but only a very ordinary bell which happens to *look* like a ship's bell. But the fact remains that down to the present day ex-naval officers have continued to hold important positions in the agency and that the atmosphere of the place is identifiably different from any other agency in London.

One way this distinctness shows is that Benson's seems anxious to appear more patently culture-conscious than the run of leading agencies. At a time when the fashion is for close carpeting and a certain blandness of *décor*, Benson's continues to decorate its miles of corridors with reproductions of type faces and photographs of its classier advertisements, and the agency owns a collection of paintings by some very respectable British painters.

They are also proud at Benson's to have had several well-known writers working in the agency in the past. (For some reason admen have a curious inferiority complex over 'real' writers and seem to draw a certain comfort from the knowledge that a few men and women of letters actually began their careers in the agency business.) Before you have been long inside Benson's you are likely to be reminded that Cecil Woodham-Smith once worked there and that Dorothy Sayers, 'another old Bensonian', was there as a copy writer before the war and based her advertising agency in *Murder Must Advertise* on Benson's. There is even a small brass plaque on the wall outside the chairman's office commemorating the fact. It was unveiled by 'Dorothy L. Sayers, M.A.' in 1950.

But until recently much of the success as well of the character of Benson's stemmed from one man – Robert Bevan, who retired from the chairmanship of the company in March, 1964. A large, kindly, cantankerous man with a splendid voice and a habit of peering at newcomers over the top of his spectacles, he always managed to look like the sort of elderly housemaster legends are formed around.

'I don't,' he would say, 'like shrieking advertising. I don't like to be bored. I can't stand people who talk about advertising philosophies. And,' he added, allowing a faint, Alistair Sim-like chuckle to creep into his voice, 'I never forget that there was once a Provost of Oriel who said, "show me a researcher and I will show you a fool". A little hard. A little unnecessary, but I think I know what the man meant.'

It was Bevan, more than any other single individual, who will always be associated with the great days of Guinness. This association dates back to 1928. He had just joined Benson's as a junior copy writer when the men from Guinness arrived. He describes the early days of the Guinness campaign with relish, and he describes it well, for it is something he is proud of. He tells how that great old-timer, Oswald Greene, maestro of 'reason why' copy, originator of the Mustard Club and famed advocate of Hennessy's Brandy and the *Encyclopaedia Britannica*, was put in charge of the campaign. He tells how he and Greene started off on some of the advertising business's earliest consumer research on the people who were drinking Guinness – 'We spent an awful lot of time in an awful lot of pubs.' And he tells how all the time Greene was searching for something the advertising could say about Guinness which the people who drank it actually believed.

'Wherever we went, whoever we spoke to, we kept coming back to the idea people had that Guinness did them good. It was the genius of Greene that turned this general idea into a copy line that was a masterpiece of the obvious – "Guinness is good for you". It may sound very easy and very obvious now, but in those days a slogan like that was really revolutionary.'

The slogan was placed below a picture of a large glass full of a dark brown liquid, and the long, long haul of Guinness advertising had begun.

'From the very beginning,' said Bevan, 'we knew that we would have to hammer away at the main theme of Guinness doing you good,' and for many reasons the hammer was wielded ceaselessly. 'Seven Good Reasons Why Guinness is Good for You' declaimed an early piece of copy with a generosity that would be impossible today.[32]

'1. Builds strong muscles for sports.
2. It is good for the nerves.
3. It is good for the blood (also the complexion).
4. It is a splendid digestive.
5. It gives a permanent sense of greater health and strength.
6. It is beneficial to the aged.
7. It helps you to sleep.'

[32] Because nowadays the tighter rules of the IPA forbid the making of any claims involving health whether they be true or otherwise.

At the same time someone at Benson's got the bright idea of circularizing doctors asking for medical support for the idea that Guinness actually did people good. This was taken very seriously, and the Guinness company has always taken great pains to foster the goodwill of the medical profession.

To this day every doctor in the medical directory is sent a richly produced *Guinness Book* in the interests of seasonal good-will each Christmas, and on occasions a letter has been sent to every doctor in the country asking if he would care to report from his own experience on the benefit Guinness has been to his patients. Guinness are reluctant to reveal just how many favourable reports came in last time. (They have always promised the profession that they are *not* trying to collect material for some sort of 'Ten Thousand Doctors Can't be Wrong' story). But from the way they talk it seems as if at least 10,000 doctors did send some sort of favourable reply.

Guinness sometimes do quote from doctor's letters in their advertising, but this is done only after permission has been obtained from the doctor concerned and almost every precaution in the book has been taken. When we asked Tommy Marks, a former Guinness advertising manager about this, he made it clear that he regarded the thousands of doctors' testimonials, all safely filed away at the Guinness headquarters at Park Royal, as an asset of the most satisfactory sort.

'All the same,' we asked him, 'do you really believe that Guinness demonstrably is good for you?' He said he was convinced it was, but wouldn't know where to start if he had to prove it by chemical analysis. 'It would be rather like trying to prove the benefits of a day at the sea. It's good for you but you can't analyse that either.'

As the Guinness advertising got into its stride and this homely message began to do its job of suggesting to people that Guinness really was something special, certain rules began to establish themselves about the advertising. The first of these was that the ads should never show an actual Guinness drinker. As Bevan said, one of the first aims of the advertising was to correct the idea that Guinness was the staple drink of dockers and charladies, and it was felt that to show a single representative Guinness drinker would be to destroy the chance of establishing it as the 'entirely classless' drink that maximum sales demanded it should be.

And at the same time the advertising gradually became a softer and softer sell. Of the first twenty-four Guinness advertisements Benson's prepared, fourteen had the 'Good for You' message hard and clear, and in the early 'thirties the copy was still inviting stout-drinkers of all classes to try Guinness for strength. But then, gradually, a little more of the character of the people behind the advertising began to seep through. By 1933 the Guinness glass had a smile on its face, and two years later it was felt that the time had come to make a joke out of something that might otherwise have become too tedious for civilized men to inflict on the long-suffering British public.

After a visit to the circus at Olympia, Benson's art director, Dicky Richards, got the idea of a keeper chasing a sea-lion who had stolen his glass of Guinness, and the first animal in the Guinness menagerie appeared on the hoardings with the slogan 'My Goodness, My Guinness'. In 1936 there was an ostrich. In 1937 a lion, and as the joke caught on and the sales of Guinness continued to rise, the old hard selling slogan of 'Guinness is Good For You' remained only in this punning form. From 1938 Good For You posters disappeared entirely from the hoardings for nearly a quarter of a century.[33]

Instead the aim of the advertising seemed to be to associate the idea of Guinness with cheerfulness and good nature by allowing everyone to join in a sort of nation-wide family joke with an element of thoroughly clean, slightly smug sea-side postcard humour about it. For here at last was that supreme rarity – advertising which the client enjoys paying for, the agency enjoys preparing, and the public enjoys looking at. And the humour was not confined to the seaside postcard variety. Rex Whistler was hired to illustrate a beautifully printed *Guinness Book*. A pelican joined the other Guinness animals, and copywriters were busy composing rhymes like

> 'My mother said
> I never should
> Miss my Guinness
> – As if I would.'

It was all very cosy. The advertising was considered a great success, and the goodwill for this cheerful, friendly Guinness company was intense. But there was one tiny, bad-natured question which no one seemed particularly concerned about because the answer was thought to be self-evident. Did goodwill sell Guinness?

Well, did it? In 1936 production was 750,000 barrels, and in 1951 it was 2,000,000 barrels. Figures like these were good enough for anyone, and when the advertising picked up again after the war, the humour was still there. A Guinness clock was put up in Piccadilly Circus, the Guinness animals returned, and the happy copy line ran, 'What's the time? It's Guinness time.' There was always time for a Guinness.

But despite the production figures, and despite the air of general euphoria at Park Royal, the question of the real effectiveness of the

[33] Guinness add: 'In a sense it is not strictly true that serious "Good for You" posters disappeared entirely from the hoardings for nearly a quarter of a century, since a serious design appeared in November 1956, bearing the words "Guinness Goodness – At home too".'

advertising remained unanswered. In 1951 the Guinness company made the first serious attempt to answer it.

It was not a particularly sophisticated attempt, and it had no immediate effect on the advertising which went on much as before. At the time only the most perceptive would have realized which way the wind was blowing, but in the light of what was to happen it was probably as important as the occasion when Oswald Greene and Robert Bevan set off on their tour of Guinness-drinking pubs in 1928. They started a national survey to find out who actually drank Guinness.

For one of the remarkable things about the whole business of marketing Guinness was that although by now it had been nationally advertised for twenty-three years, nobody knew who *did* drink it. At Benson's and Guinness it seems that there were two schools of thought on the subject. One was the 'everybody' school, who thought that the advertising had done its job so well that Guinness had really become a classless drink which was being sold to cheerful, good-natured people right across the market. The other was the exact opposite. This school felt that, despite the advertising, Guinness was still being drunk predominantly by women, and could never forget that every Punch cartoon that showed a charlady still had her drawn with her attendant glass of stout.

In fact, as the consumer survey showed, neither was right. It was largely a male market, and the typical Guinness drinker was much older than most people had thought.

Clearly both facts were important, but on their own they were not enough, and the real value of the survey was to reveal to the Guinness company how much they had to learn. For vaguely it was felt that there was something slightly absurd in spending nearly £1 million a year on advertising when you really did not know to whom you were appealing. So Guinness began trying to find out.

The first thing they had to discover was really the key to the whole future of Guinness as a popular drink. One thing that worried them was the age element in Guinness drinking. Did it mean that the market for Guinness was a dying market like the market for spats and moustache cups and Gold Flake cigarettes? Or was there a chance that Guinness was one of those mysterious products like deaf aids and rupture appliances which certain members of each generation turn to as age catches up with them?

At Benson's some people thought that Guinness should make more of an effort to capture the younger drinker in the face of possible competition. Others, including Peter Hadley, until recently the director in charge of the account, firmly believed that Guinness was a drink to which people 'graduated' when they were a little older and that, as Hadley put it, 'no amount of advertising could hope to persuade a substantial number of younger drinkers to drink it'.

It was important to know which was true, and one of the men who was brought in to find out was George Wigglesworth, an economist who had studied before the war under Hugh Gaitskell at University College, London, and worked for the last five years with the British Export Trade Research Organization. Wigglesworth is a dry, profoundly sceptical man. As a person he is about as different as can be imagined from the gentle humourists who were responsible for Guinness advertising in its heyday. And as he is now at the head of Public Attitude Surveys, the organization through whom Guinness carry out their market research, this is a fact to be borne in mind.

One of the first things he helped to establish after his arrival was that the Guinness market was in fact a 'replacement market' and that the taste for Guinness genuinely was something that came with age and maturity, so that no one at Park Royal need worry too much if young men in their early twenties could not be persuaded to drink it. But once they had established this, Wigglesworth and the rest of the Guinness researchers went on digging in an attempt to unearth, once and for all, that elusive but invaluable individual, the four-square Guinness drinker. What sort of a man (or woman) was he? What was it about the drink that appealed to him? What was his class and his income? And why did he change over to Guinness in his late twenties and early thirties?

To help find the answer to some of these questions, Dr. F. E. Emery, an Australian psychiatrist at the Tavistock Institute and the author of a paper on 'Differences between the Communication function of the Mass Media', was asked to help with some of the more abstruse psychological implications of Guinness drinking. From now on not a motive was to be left unturned.

In the meantime, things had been changing in the world outside. From the middle 'fifties on, the beer war had been hotting up, and before long some of the fighting had spread to the previously peaceful territories of the stout market. Whitbread had acquired the Mackeson company, and in a brave attempt to recruit a new and more youthful individual to the ranks of British stout drinkers, were advertising it on the zippy but slightly nebulous copy line 'There's a promise in a glass of Mackeson'.

But before this Guinness had been trying to attract the same market and no one at Guinness seems particularly proud of their efforts. Gay young people were shown enjoying themselves with Guinness in punts. Others were seen picnicking with crates of the stuff at Stonehenge. All that Tommy Marks will say about this is that the campaign was well under way before he joined the company.

The start of television advertising gave another jolt to the air of self-confidence the advertising had inherited from before the war. For Benson's tried to translate the sort of humour that had worked so well on the hoardings into the commercials. It was not always very sucessful.

Looking back, what is surprising is not that the Guinness advertising changed, but that it continued as it was for so long. And when change came, it was to arrive from an unexpected quarter. For it was at about that time that the careful men who had been digging away for so long in research began to feel that they had unearthed something significant at last. It had taken so long because, as George Wigglesworth says, 'It took us nearly ten years to start asking the right questions.'

Even today Guinness are remarkably coy about disclosing exactly what Wigglesworth did discover. 'There's so much beer advertising about that still seems to miss all the points that matter that we're not anxious to give away secrets that cost us a lot of time and a lot of money to find out,' says Alan Wood, the former advertising manager for Hovis who had succeeded Marks as Guinness advertising manager in 1962. (Marks had just been promoted to take charge of the new Harp lager Guinness launched in that year.) But what seems to have been the essence of the Wigglesworth line was to start by regarding drinking as a normal, rather than an abnormal activity.

In 1962 Wigglesworth was in America, and in an interview he gave to the *Chicago Times* he was quoted as follows. 'We know that the drinker to excess is abnormal, but to me the person who doesn't drink at all is abnormal as well.' The people he was interested in and whom he considered 'normal', were those who 'drink and smoke in moderation to relieve the stress and strain of modern life'.

But who, in Wigglesworth's terms, were these 'normal' drinkers? Presumably they were not the indulgent drinkers – the heavy topers and solitary boozers who drank to get drunk. Nor were they really the social drinkers – the people who drank at parties and in pubs primarily because it was the expected thing to do and because it offered an excuse for the company.

From the way the Guinness advertising has developed it is clear now that the man Wigglesworth was after was really in neither of these categories. His drinking would be an expression of his very normality. He would lack the instability and irresponsibility of the indulgent drinker. He would also lack the self-conscious motives of the social drinker. He would be steady and responsible. He would drink because he enjoyed what he drank, because he felt he had earned it, and because he thought in some obscure way that after a good day's work he needed to put back some of the energy he had expended on his job.

This seems to have provided the brief on which Dr Emery and the Tavistock Institute were to labour during the months to come. And it was from Dr Emery that Wigglesworth's 'normal' drinker was to receive definitive classification. He was, said Emery, taking over a term first used by Freud's disciple, Melanie Klein, in her work on children, a 'reparative' drinker. More important still the market researchers seem to have discovered that it was among the ranks of the reparative drinkers that the true Guinness men were thickest.

Once this idea had been seriously accepted it tended to undermine the foundations upon which the whole of Guinness advertising had been carried on for the previous quarter of a century.

For if you knew the character of the Guinness drinker as clearly as the researchers claimed they did, it should not be difficult to get advertising with far more specific claims on his loyalties than sea-lions, keepers and kangaroos. More serious still, it was a moot point whether he was the sort of person who would be influenced by humour at all. And worst of all, there were actually people at Benson's and at Guinness's who were openly confessing that there must be an end to the sort of humour that went into the advertising.

Wigglesworth was among them. 'Who ever heard of an economist with a sense of humour anyhow?' he said. But so was Alan Wood, 'I felt we were in danger of becoming altogether too self-conscious about Guinness advertising. Everything had to have the Guinness touch and it was this constant need to be witty or funny that was absorbing us rather than what should have been at the heart of what we were doing – getting out and selling Guinness.

'We were like one of those witty fellows,' he added, 'who have been known for years as the life and soul of the party. To start with you're glad to have someone like that around, but there usually comes a time when he is so invariably breezy that whenever you see him you say "Oh God!". I think we were getting dangerously near the time when people would say "Oh God!" when they saw another Guinness poster.'

Some of the Benson people had long been feeling the same way themselves. Among them was Peter Hadley, who had been growing increasingly disturbed at the number of people who, as he put it, were saying 'Of course I love the Guinness advertising but I never actually drink Guinness myself'. Even before Wood, he had formed the opinion that humour would have to go, at least for the time being.

As Wood himself put it, 'In its greatest days, Guinness advertising was not funny all the time. If you say something you honestly believe in you don't always have to say it with an apologetic giggle.'

So it was agreed between Guinness and Benson's that, for the time being at any rate, the humour should be played down and the advertising should get back to its urgent if antediluvian message about doing you good. In due course Benson's produced some admirable advertisements to that effect, with the message in good white lettering and a picture of a glass of Guinness looking as sober as it is possible to make a glass of stout look.

At the time, if you spoke to people at Benson's and asked them

c*

whether the old days of Guinness advertising were dead at last, they would talk about getting back to the original, orthodox message of the great days of Guinness, and say something about the pendulum having to swing between hard selling and soft selling, between harsh realism and gentle humour.

But when they said this, the last thing their words meant was that the Guinness animals would make their comeback one fine day. For now that the legendary Guinness drinker had apparently been unearthed at last and now that the energetic Mr Wigglesworth was finding out more and more about him every day, no one was going to have him ousted by a menagerie of funny animals that should have been buried with Christopher Robin.

Instead, in the autumn of 1963, the new Guinness posters were finally depicting what was, presumably, the world's first official portrait of the Guinness drinker himself, produced in the flesh after thirty-five years of anonymity.

To the casual passer-by this new face on the hoardings might have appeared remarkable only by nature of its outstanding ordinariness – an everyday sort of chap in a raincoat about to take the top off a glass of beer. But that, the researchers might have replied, was the object of their entire exercise. For the Guinness drinker, like the 'normal' drinker Wigglesworth mentioned in his interview with the *Chicago Times*, is an ordinary sort of chap. A nice chap. A decent chap. Not a neurotic but not necessarily a hearty, conventional beer-drinking man either. He could be a solid, mature man who drinks because he has earned his drink.

One gathers that there was considerable heart-searching both at Benson's and at Park Royal before the new Guinness drinker was actually let loose on the public. Several of the attempts to photograph him for the campaign were rejected as unsuitable for one reason or another. Conferences were held to decide how long his hair should be and whether the nails of his left hand should have just a tinge of dirt behind them. (Ultimately it was decided they should not.) The pros and cons of his raincoat were discussed. Misgivings were expressed about his age. Altogether Cecil B. de Mille can hardly have taken more trouble over one of the apostles or John the Baptist.

'Guinness drinking,' says Wood, 'is primarily an attitude of mind rather than a matter of class or income, and we settled on a poster that would show a certain type of man – a responsible, down-to-earth fellow who savours his drink. By showing him in our advertisements we were trying to establish a bond of sympathy among similar men everywhere who drink after work as a reward for work done.'

The new copy line, 'Reward! You've earned that Guinness' developed straight from the research and looks as if it might rival, not only the animals, but the Guinness is Good For You claim as well. Indeed, Wigglesworth tends to regard 'doing good' claims for Guinness as irrelevant. 'After all,' he says, 'we're selling beer, not tonic or cough mixture.'

From the latest Guinness advertisements there are signs that the work of the researchers could become the basis for a new, cautious style of humour in its turn.

But whether it does or it does not, it is clear that the old Guinness humour is over. The toucan, the sea-lion and the kangaroo have had it for good. The most popular campaign in Britain is put in the attic because they say it no longer works.

In its place Mr Wigglesworth has given us the mature, serious face of the Guinness drinker to remind us of the reward that is ours for one-and-tenpence a bottle – a responsible, solid face. And the nails of the left hand are quite clean.

6. Patrick Dolan

In the spring of 1946 Emerson Foote, one of the principals of Foote, Cone and Belding, the agency which had succeeded the American arm of the old Lord and Thomas empire, walked into the Marguery Bar on Park Avenue in Manhattan. Standing at the bar was the man he was looking for. Patrick Dolan was then earning $25,000 a year as manager of one of the largest New York printing companies after five years in Europe with the Office of Strategic Services, the Americans' secret intelligence outfit.

Emerson Foote had a better proposition for Dolan. He asked him if he would go back to Europe to start up a new business for the agency. The terms were attractive. Foote, Cone and Belding would put up $100,000 in capital for three years and if by the end of that time the business was grossing $1 million in billings, Dolan would be given a 25 per cent share in it. The salary was $25,000 a year with a $15,000 expense account in addition. Dolan accepted.

The decision had more than personal significance, for Dolan was to spearhead the post-war American invasion into the gentlemanly corridors of the British advertising world. Thompson, of course, were in Britain long before the war, but a good many others moved in during the 1950s so that today eight of the top eighteen agencies are controlled from America.

In time, many of these agencies blended easily and successfully into the London scene as Thompson had done before them, but Dolan was different. To this day he does not fit. He does not belong to the advertising men's clubs, he does not attend advertising conferences, he never makes speeches – 'I'm too busy to waste my time,' he said. Instead he has become one of the most successful and richest men in the agency game by bringing his own brand of hard salesmanship to bear on a world where real salesmen are curiously rare. To this day Dolan still despises the traditional type of agency boss – 'old dodderers who want to keep the status quo' – and he still goes back to New York every two months because he needs to.

'It's like a horse-doctor's syringe of adrenalin,' he said. 'In New York I get real stimulation, that's where I really recharge my batteries.'

So there were no spiritual connotations in Dolan's decision to return to Europe. Although he was the son of Irish emigrants who had left home for Chicago when he was twelve, his roots were in New York. But the war had left him broke and with no chance of setting up a business on his own account. On the other hand, he knew Europe and liked it.

That was why he accepted Emerson Foote's offer; he might not have been so enthusiastic had he known the opposition his arrival would arouse.

Dolan arrived in London in March 1946. He took a suite in the Savoy Hotel – 'the only place I knew besides Claridge's' – and began operations. His arrival was the signal for attacks in the advertising press and there was a good deal of talk about 'the American invasion'. Dolan still believes that the attacks were inspired by the late Mike Masius. Masius had bought the London link of the Lord and Thomas empire, and thought Foote, Cone and Belding should stick to America and keep out of his territory. That was one thing Emerson Foote had not told Dolan.

In a curious way, the attacks brought Dolan one benefit at least – his secretary. She was working with the *Advertiser's Weekly* at the time, saw the advance proof of the article about Dolan, was intrigued by the attack and decided that he was probably looking for help. She walked round to the Savoy and asked for a job. Dolan hired her then and there, told her to go out and get a typewriter, a desk and some paper. She and Dolan are still together.

He built up the rest of his staff in an equally *ad hoc* way. Sydney Whitcombe, who is still Creative Director of Dolan's agency, was interviewed by him sitting in his bath.

Jack Swaab, now a top executive with Colman, Prentis & Varley, was another recruit. Swaab was a young army officer who wanted to break into advertising. He made the rounds of the agencies, but got nowhere. They all wanted to know what experience he had and the only qualification that Swaab could offer was a Military Cross and an eagerness to learn the business. He told Dolan his story. Dolan laughed and said 'How would you like to go out and get me some coffee?' Swaab hesitated, then said he would go. 'Right,' said Dolan, 'throw away your umbrella and bowler hat. You can stay, you're hired.'

Soon Dolan was out hunting for business. He did not, to put it mildly, approve of the conventions which governed the advertising business in London. He could not see why chasing accounts held by other agencies should be regarded as poaching. He recognized that in Britain lip-service was paid to the *status quo* but that, in fact, there were many ways of manoeuvring round the approach to new business. 'In the States,' he explained, 'every account is free grabs for anybody. Keen competition results in better work and there is no nonsense about poaching. Anyway, I didn't give a damn.'

His first visits were to companies which were serviced by Foote, Cone and Belding in America. 'If it was a client of F C B in the States, it was as much our client as anybody else's. In any case,' he added, 'being from F C B only got you through the door. Then it got real tough because most of the ad-managers thought you'd tell tales on them back in the States, which is stupid, but they are human.'

Once Dolan was through the door he was hard to get out. Nor did he, as he said, take anyone to lunch at Lord's or to the American Bar in the Savoy.

Within nine months of arriving in London he had reached the target billing of $1 million and had taken over big accounts like Frigidaire, Lockheed, Kleenex and Kotex. He had spent $80,000 of F C B's first $100,000 and for that he had capitalized a company for £20,000. The agency's first offices were in a flat above Sir Bernard Docker in Claridge House.

Dolan hadn't succeeded without making a certain number of enemies. 'Almost every piece of business we got,' said Dolan afterwards 'had to come from someone else, so I'm afraid I left behind a long line of un-requited lovers.'

Within three years Foote, Cone and Belding were billing $5 million in Europe.[34] But things were not altogether happy. Dolan was complaining of interference from Harry Berk, at that time the agency's Vice-President in charge of International Relations and Dolan's immediate boss. Dolan had just won from Gillette the big Toni Home Permanent Wave account and had brought the Toni Twins to Europe to start the campaign. When Dolan was away on holiday in Spain, Berk came to London and, according to Dolan, changed a lot of the planning. Dolan

[34] This figure includes billings in London and in New York for European accounts.

flew back to London from Spain, threw Berk out of the agency's Hill Street offices and set out for New York without a bag.

According to Dolan, Foote had privately been promising him for the previous two years that he would remove Berk. Dolan now insisted that it had to be done, and done then and there. Foote vacillated and eventually told Dolan he could not do it. So Dolan promptly walked out himself.

He was now out of a job and an office. He was offered jobs in New York, but he had been away from New York for nine years, and in any case the capital requirements were too stiff for him to start his own business there. At the same time, he knew that a chilly reception awaited him if he went back to London.

Mike Masius was still hostile and the new régime at Foote, Cone and Belding was anything but friendly. Dolan therefore decided to move out of advertising (for the time being) and into public relations.

He had had his first taste of PR in the years before the war when, to add to his meagre salary as a reporter on the *Chicago Times*, he had done odd PR jobs for various charities.

Before he moved into newspaper reporting, Dolan had worked as a relief fireman on the Chicago Northwestern Railway and then as a soda-jerk in an all-night restaurant. His first PR job was promoting a Jewish charity called the Daughters of Zion. His fee, $300: and he also collected a $300 bonus from a satisfied client. Then he got a telephone call from the President of Quaker Oats, Robert Black. Black was running the St. Andrews Society and wanted to raise funds for an old people's home. Dolan brought Will Fyffe and a haggis from Scotland. The fee: $600.

He wrote his first advertising copy while working for the *Chicago Times* (his salary there: $50 a week). One night, the Promotion Manager walked into the City Room and asked if someone would write a house advertisement for the paper. Dolan volunteered, finished it in twenty minutes, and to his astonishment was paid $100.

One of his great successes while on the paper was promoting a book called *The Home Medical Adviser*. The promotion had not begun very well but Dolan discovered a chapter on the sex education of children and promptly wrote an ad headlined 'An Open Letter to the Mothers and Fathers of Chicago on Sex'. The book became a best seller and Dolan moved into the Promotion Department at $100 a week.

From there he went to the Columbia Broadcasting System, and soon became Advertising and PR boss of the new CBS Records. He also made a small fortune out of a series of 25 cent books on the great composers – they sold five million copies.

Out of the proceeds he bought the oldest book publishing company in New England for $50,000. When the war came, he gave shares in the company to a literary agent who promised to look after it while Dolan was away. When the war was over, Dolan returned to find that the man had sold out and fled to Mexico.

So the end of the affair with Foote, Cone and Belding was not the first time that Dolan had been, as he puts it, 'back to square one'.

The problem now was to raise money. He called on his Bank Manager at the Corn Exchange Bank in New York and told him he wanted to start a public relations firm. At first they offered him $25,000 but when they found that the business was to be in Europe with headquarters in London, they promptly cut the offer to $5,000. Unfortunately for Dolan, most American bankers did not think Europe a particularly good investment in 1950.

Dolan also tried to interest one of the biggest American advertising agencies (which he was later to join) Batten, Barton, Durstine & Osborn, in his enterprise. He saw the President, another Irishman called Ben Duffy; he offered him 51 per cent control of the European business if he would match his $5,000 with a similar amount. Duffy turned him down.

So Dolan registered Patrick Dolan & Associates as a New York Company with a capital of $5,000 and his father and two wartime friends as Directors. Then he bought boat tickets and a new Chevrolet and set out again for London. He took a mews flat behind Park Lane and began to build what he called 'the first serious, major P R enterprise in Europe'.

There was enough truth in his claim to influence a young English banker named Jocelyn Hambro in putting up money to back him. Hambro had been introduced to Dolan by a mutual friend, invited him to lunch at Bishopsgate, listened to his story and astonished Dolan by telling him that the bank was prepared to give him a £10,000 'line of credit'. 'Furthermore,' said Hambro, 'I am prepared to invest £500 of my own money in your English company.'

Within six months, P D A had billings of £100,000. Dolan worked eighteen hours a day picking up new business. Bata Shoes (Tom Bata, the head of the business, was an old friend) was his first big client. Then came the Dutch Bulb Growers; and Roderick Peat, the senior partner of Dolan's accountants (Peat, Marwick and Mitchell) put him in touch with Sir Frank Spriggs, boss of Hawker Siddeley. Spriggs said to Dolan: 'I am sick and tired of going to dinners and having people ask me what is Hawker-Siddeley? I want Hawker-Siddeley to become a national name.' Dolan drew up a P R brief – and got the business.

P D A grew quickly enough for Dolan to be ready to move back into advertising within three years. By 1953 he had gathered together £30,000 in accumulated profits. Again he went to Jocelyn Hambro for backing for a new enterprise – an advertising agency to be called D D W S, Dolan, Davis, Whitcombe & Stewart.

He drew up a budget for the first year – billings £100,000, income

£15,000, costs £14,000, profit £1000. Then he ran into trouble again. Dolan was told privately that he would not be given recognition by the Newspaper Proprietors Association, the body which alone has competence to grant recognition to new advertising agencies. (In America, more logically, the Advertising Association of American Agencies does the job.) The N P A's Recognition Committee examines the financial and professional competence of would-be newcomers into the agency game.

So Dolan did not ask for recognition: he just went ahead and announced his agency. Several of the advertising directors at newspapers, when Dolan wanted to buy space, retorted by asking for cash down: they were not prepared to give credit. Usually agencies work on sixty to ninety days' credit with the media and the demand for cash payment was tricky.

But Hambros put up the money and the Dutch Bulb Growers sent £40,000 as an advance payment for advertising that was not to be placed for six months.

Within six months George Pope of *The Times*, a friend of Dolan, and Stuart Mander of George Newnes, feeling that Dolan's agency ought to be given recognition, advised him to apply – and the N P A gave Dolan its seal of approval.

By the end of its first year D D W S was billing £350,000 but its early days were very tough indeed. Most of the early art work was done by Sydney Whitcombe on his kitchen table at home, but by 1956 the agency had a staff of 100 and four floors in a new office block in Bruton Street.

But Dolan was still not satisfied.

In 1960 he merged his business with Batten, Barton, Durstine & Osborn (B B D O) who ten years earlier had turned him down.

By the deal B B D O acquired 60 per cent of D D W S and P D A, Dolan kept 40 per cent, became President of B B D O International and a Director of the New York agency – and acquired valuable shares in the parent company. (B B D O has 3000 employees and 300 shareholders, of which Dolan is now one.) The move seemed logical enough. As Dolan said, 'B B D O had no business abroad. I had none in America, so it was a natural proposition.'

For B B D O, however, it was a considerable departure. Previously they had maintained a deliberate, almost isolationist seclusion within the frontiers of the United States – and they had been formally associated with the Republican Party for fifty years. Now they had bought a man who was a lifelong Democrat and a supporter of the New Deal.

How strong the ideological clash was can be seen from a story Dolan likes to tell about the day the deal was signed in New York. 'There were piles of paper all over the floor,' he recalled, 'and in came one Bruce Barton, one of the founder-members and once a well-known Isolationist

Congressman. He put his hand around my shoulders and said: "This is a big presentation?" "It is," I said. "What is it?" he asked. "It's one of those international things," I replied, to keep it simple. "Young man," he said, "the day they put that cable under the ocean, that was the blackest day this country ever had".'

The accession of Dolan to the B B D O Board created enough of a stir to carry it to the ears of John F. Kennedy who promptly invited him to dinner at the White House – the first 'B B D oer' ever to go to the White House under a Democratic President.

The merger with B B D O was followed by an invasion of the Continent with new offices being set up in Milan, Frankfurt, Dusseldorf, Vienna and Paris. (In Frankfurt, one of the agency's biggest jobs is helping recruit for the new German army.) Dolan is now spending half his time shuttling to and fro to his growing Continental network. The European business of B B D O is now running at £7 million annually, with £4 million coming from the U K, even though in 1964 either B B D O or P D A lost Hawker-Siddeley and other useful accounts like Coty, Nestlé, Morphy-Richards and Betty Crocker Cake Mixes.

Nevertheless, Dolan is still one of the moguls of the London agency game, one of the few who bears comparison with the megalomaniac giants of the early days. His office on the sixth floor of the Bruton Street building has easily the most staggering *décor* of any of London's top ad-men. As you enter the executive suite, one of the secretaries says 'hi' from behind a screen of greenery. At one end of the entrance hall is a marble bust of Marie Antoinette, at the other a tortured sculpture of a political prisoner. In some odd way this juxtaposition seems to sum up B B D O as an agency.

Dolan himself favours bold striped shirts with a small initial P D on the left breast. When you go in, he is almost invariably in the middle of a 'yah-huh-huh' telephone conversation. To emphasize a point, he flourishes a gold-plated two-foot ruler. His cuff links are gold Indian's head dollars. Above his sixteen-foot desk is a giant weathercock – 'it's a proud bird and its crows, which is important in advertising'. Most of the paintings are modern, but tucked away discreetly in an alcove is a picture of General Cornwallis surrendering to George Washington, a present from a client.

Dolan is a wealthy man by any standards. He owns a sixteenth century farmhouse in Hertfordshire with 200 acres, has a town house in South Street and an apartment in Manhattan on the top floor of a block on 66th Street and 3rd Avenue. He runs a Bentley – his sixth – and owns a power cruiser which he keeps at Villefranche. Though he works round the clock when he needs to, he always takes two long holidays – a month in the Mediterranean in the summer and two weeks in Arizona or the West Indies in the winter.

He is still, to a large extent, an independent operator. 'There's no New York interference at all,' he says. 'I legislated against it in our agreement.' But B B D O – at Dolan's request – have sent over Carroll Newton, a director of the agency, as Managing Director. Newton handled United States Steel, Lever Brothers and the Republican Party among other things. He directed the advertising behind the two successful Eisenhower campaigns and the unsuccessful Nixon campaign.

The agency's London staff includes only four Americans – Dolan, Newton, John McCormick (a recent recruit from Procter & Gamble as Marketing Director) and Fred Doerflinger in the public relations company.

Nonetheless, B B D O still retains a more unmistakably transatlantic flavour than any other agency in London. This is largely the outcome of Dolan's own militant attitudes, which he likes to contrast with the more amateur methods of some competitors. 'For us,' he explained, 'this is not a game. People hire us for our brains not for our old school tie.' He is aggressively democratic. 'We are not influenced by family or breeding' and frequently boasts that 'as an agency we are not easy to live with. We like to stimulate our clients and we do not reckon that our business is a one-way street.'

Dolan's world is a world of constant clash – 'there's nothing grey, it's all either black or white and people are for me or against me.' He believes in the *angst* of advertising. 'To do this job well you have got to be wholly committed, no 'nine to five' stuff. You have got to live with the business day and night. You have got to suffer the agonies of the damned and the ecstasies of heaven – unless you do that day by day, you're not totally committed.'

Dolan admits to being an extremely political animal – his ambition is the time-honoured goal of wealthy American businessmen, international politics – and revels in any campaign which involves the wielding of political influence. He particularly relished the joint P R-advertising battle which the agency fought on behalf of the British trawler owners in the early 1950s.

One of B B D O's big success stories is the campaign they launched for Skol lager in 1958 which turned out to be an important stage in the creation of a new, young market for beer. Ind Coope, the brewers, had been carefully watching the imports of Continental lagers from 1953 onwards. Consumer checks indicated a swing towards lighter, drier beers. In 1956 they decided to enter this growing lager market.

B B D O were hired to launch the new product. Their research indicated that the best chances for this new light dry beer were in the 20/35 age group. Dolan's men sifted through 300–400 possible names (Saxon was one of them) before finally settling for Skol. Skol was chosen because it had the right Continental connotation. They were given £30,000 to spend on the initial launch. The agency believed they were selling mainly to young people and their best hope of creating the market lay in persuading the 20–35s to try Skol. From an advertising standpoint the most remarkable thing about the campaign was that this was the first time women were used in beer advertising. Always before beer ads had been beery, with the emphasis on men and strength.

'From the start,' said Dolan, 'our ads were aimed at the young market.' And most of their customers were not likely to be heavy drinkers – later research showed 'many people drink it because they think it is not so alcoholic as it is' as one of B B D o's research men said – the advertising was given almost a soft drink feel about it. It set out to create what the agency called 'believably happy situations'. There were young girls with pony-tails and young couples kissing in swingboats, but no suggestion at all of pubs or drinking. Later on the emphasis changed to solitary young couples, some of whom looked so young that B B D O worried that they were too young to be drinkers and replaced them with older models. The dual promise was sexual enjoyment and good health.

B B D O resolved to splash the entire £30,000 in the first two months, and they were so successful that Ind Coope decided to continue the campaign. By 1959 they were selling 83,000 barrels of Skol, and although they have never overtaken Carlsberg, they can now claim 20.4 per cent of the British lager market.[35]

Not all B B D o's campaigns have been so successful. They launched an instant tea for Nestlé (Nestea) which proved to be a disappointment. They knew the tea market in Britain was worth some £150 million and hoped that an instant tea might corner a small part of it. But, B B D O say now, the product was not right and too expensive.

The campaign did at least provide some enlightening statistics on English women and their tea-drinking habits. One study revealed that there are two quite separate occasions on which tea is drunk in Britain. One is the social occasion, when the woman is the hostess and the tea-pot is an absolutely indispensable social symbol: the second is for personal refreshment, when the woman is alone. It was this second market for which B B D O aimed Nestea.

In the summer of 1963, they did a second study measuring the acceptance of Nestea among a sample of 1100 tea-drinking housewives. This showed that 1 in 5, the majority young women with families, were favourably disposed towards the idea of an instant tea. It also provided a fascinating list of tea-drinking statistics.

For instance: the British housewife consumes an average of 5.4 cups

[35] A research study on lager drinkers done for B B D O by Mass Observation Limited in 1960 showed that 1 in 3 drink lager in the 18–24 age group, only 1 in 7 of the 45–64s.

of tea a day; 65 per cent put one spoonful of tea into the pot for each person; only 33 per cent add one for the pot; 87 per cent warm their teapots before use; 91 per cent put milk into their cups before their tea, 8 after and 1 per cent don't use milk at all; 78 per cent drink their tea with sugar, 22 without; and 41 per cent strain it, while 59 per cent don't.

As an agency, B B D O has not yet broken through into the front rank in Britain and remains somewhat apart from the rest of the advertising world. This is partly because Dolan himself remains apart, a small, self-conscious American island which refuses to conform. His closest colleagues pass revealing verdicts on him. Sydney Whitcombe, the agency's art director: 'Pat has a real regard for the creator, but he is pre-eminently a salesman. He works twenty-four hours a day, I've never seen anyone who can push himself harder. His hobby is his job.' Baron Henry de Westenholz, now boss of P D A: 'He's got the biggest P R flair of anyone in London, but people either love him or they hate him – there are no neutrals.'

Part of Dolan's success with English clients has undoubtedly been his toughness and his unrepentantly transatlantic approach. Perhaps, without him, nobody would have paid so much attention to the American invasion.

7. The Breeze of Change

'If you're ill, Varley sends you a crate of champagne. If you're off somewhere on a job, he rings you the night before to wish you luck. You say to yourself, "God bless the old boy, he's human after all." And then the next time you meet him, he could quite easily treat you like the office boy.'

This, according to one executive who worked several years for Colman, Prentis and Varley is one of the hazards facing anyone who has much to do with Colonel Arthur Noel Claude Varley. And since Varley (everyone who works for him calls him Varley, never Arthur or the Colonel) really *is* the agency and has been for many years, it helps explain why this highly successful organization (it is one of the largest in Britain and has more overseas business than any other agency in the country) has its own nervous, slightly unpredictable reputation and why, among admen themselves, it still manages to appear the most exciting large agency in London.

Everyone who has worked for Varley has a different opinion about him. 'He's got the sharpest mind in London,' says one. 'He's a megalomaniac.' 'He's the one top agency man who really understands women,' says a third. 'He's so jolly clever that he just gets bored if things start running smoothly, and feels that he has to stir them up. That's when trouble starts,' says someone else.

And yet, to meet, Varley appears as an amiable, slightly portly, good-looking Old Wykehamist with a pipe and a tweed suit – rather a comfortable man these days, who has recently taken to silver-rimmed pince-nez for reading and who often prefers talking about his garden rather than his business.

During the thirty years he has had his name on a brass plate outside an advertising agency of his own, the secret of his success has been the instinctive attraction he has always had for creative people. In this his personality has more in common with a really successful press magnate or a show business impresario than with most of the people who are running large advertising agencies.

Most agency heads these days are primarily business men. Varley is this, but he is something else as well. He is a *shaman*, a person who can arouse belief, and for those who do believe in him, working for him has an excitement of its own. For a copy-writer or an art man, a spell at C P V is not an exercise in the techniques of applied merchandising. It is not the learning of a philosophy of selling or persuasion. It is a chance, quite simply, of working for Varley and being part of the unique, high-powered, nerve-wracking organization he has created around him.

The agency seems to have had something of this from the moment that R. H. Colman, Terence Prentis and Varley himself formed it in 1934. All three of them had worked at Crawford's and they had come together to enjoy the sort of freedom that only a small, brand-new agency can give. Varley was the oldest man in the agency. He was thirty-one.

When he talks about the pre-war agency it is impossible not to notice the touch of nostalgia in his words, and it is possible that a lot of what he does now is ruled by an anxiety to preserve the sparkle and the hectic individualism of the early years of C P V.

'When we began,' he says, 'we weren't concerned with doing cut-rate advertising or with telling industrialists how to run their businesses. Nor, quite honestly, did we want to make a fortune. We were interested solely in the creation of extremely good advertisements. In those days you could make a living on a rather small turnover, and really enjoy your work. And we'd take on anything. It didn't matter to us whether it was soap or a raincoat.

In fact, right from the start, Varley the businessman was as much in evidence as Varley the creator of advertisements, and there is no sign that he ever attempted to keep down the size of his agency to the point where a handful of creative people could sit back and enjoy themselves doing high-class art-work for high-minded clients.

Norvic Shoes were one of the agency's founder accounts. Varley himself brought in Horrockses cotton as another, and although the agency tended to make its name before the war as a pre-eminent fashion agency from the work it did for Jaeger, it also had a solid ballasting of beer and motor-car advertising along with Elizabeth Arden cosmetics.

But all the time the business was growing, it managed to preserve its fashionable, slightly off-beat reputation. Its parties were famous. Paul Jennings was working there. Peter Quennell, the biographer of Byron, was also one of its copywriters, and Jerrard Tickell, another of the writers on the pay-roll, occasionally brought a pair of lion cubs into the office. Until the war broke out, the champagne flowed.

And even the war failed to change C P V as much as it might have done. It made Varley himself into a colonel, and the agency was reduced to a skeleton staff, but when the British consumer market revived in the late 'forties and the heavy hand of American-styled advertising made it clear that from now on the agency world was to be a bigger, solider, soberer business than it had ever been in the past, there was a revived C P V with an office in Grosvenor Street as elegant as any fashion house, to remind everyone that advertising still had something to do with style, fashion and the less prosaic part of living.

By now the image of C P V as a purely fashion agency was more misleading than ever, and Varley himself, an indefatigable gainer of new business, had been hard at work adding to the number of its large industrial clients including Unilever, Austin, Shell and British European Airways. But even in its most down-to-earth advertising for a petrol or a soap powder, C P V was at its best when it could give the sparkle, the touch of something different that is the mark of good fashion advertising. And if one looks for evidence of how well the atmosphere of the pre-war agency had survived the war, one turns inevitably to the campaign the agency started in 1960 for a Unilever soap called 'Breeze'.

This is an interesting campaign in several ways. It has a minor place in contemporary social history as the first large campaign to show photographs of an unambiguously naked female model. It was also the first to introduce the British public to something else quite new in advertising – the idea of the self-regarding woman. And it is doubtful whether any other agency in London would have had the nerve, let alone the skill, to produce this particular campaign.

C P V had been advertising this new deodorant soap for several years before they started the campaign. The actual idea of it, like most new ideas in advertising, came as a result of something of a crisis. For although deodorant soap was new at the time in Britain, the manufacturers and the agency were at first decidedly conservative in their approach to it.

In America the campaign for a similar deodorant soap called 'Dial' had been proceeding with great success by showing smooth young women in showers talking with woman-to-woman frankness about perspiration and its associated problems. This was enshrined in the copy line 'People who like people like Dial'.

But in England the men behind Breeze felt that the time had not yet come when a soap maker could approach the English-woman with the same frank brutality. Soap advertising here had always been remarkable for its coyness and Breeze joined a long tradition of leaving the unspeakable unspoken when its first advertisement showed a fresh-faced maiden in the country, her chiffon scarf blown by the wind, and an invitation in the copy to 'get that country-fresh feeling' with Breeze.

As advertising it was unexceptional. There was only one thing wrong with it. It did not sell the soap.

In most agencies, this would have been where the motivation men came in; and endless research and bogus discussion would have followed on female attitudes to washing, to beauty and to body odour. But at c p v things were different. Instead, the campaign was handed over to Ronald Kirkwood, the agency's television director at the time. Kirkwood, a bachelor of 34, has the looks and enthusiasm of someone half his age. Since leaving c p v he has become deputy art director at Benson, where he has concentrated on building up the television department from scratch. As an individual he personifies the immediate, the visual, the instinctive approach of the art man in advertising. This was particularly so in the work he did for Breeze.

From the start he was very much on the side of the approach of the Dial campaign. 'Almost all British soap advertising was pretty wishy-washy with all that romantic stuff about being a duchess or a movie star or a beautiful lady. And I thought that our early Breeze advertisements were failing because the girls they were appealing to had changed. The post-war girl wasn't the wilting romantic young thing of the pre-war soap ads, and she was much too sophisticated for the overtones of haystacks and apple cheeks we were trying to get across now. So I thought that we should start again at the beginning and try to get across in the advertising the actual sensual pleasure a woman gets in using soap.

'This had to be done properly if it was to work. It couldn't be half-hearted or coy. That would just have made it vulgar and terrible. From the start I was aiming at using television to show women, as realistically as possible, the actual feel of soaping themselves with this soap – the luxury of it, the self-indulgence.'

And inevitably, since this was how he approached his advertising, Kirkwood began worrying about getting the right girl and how to film her. From the start he had made up his mind that, since Breeze was being sold on its all-over deodorant qualities, the advertising would have to show a woman actually in a bath. And from the start, he had taken it for granted that the only way to show a woman in a bath was with nothing on. 'She had,' as he said, 'actually to wear soap.' Questions of taste, of exactly what could and could not be shown could come later. What mattered at the moment was to find the right model and the right photographer.

'I made several attempts,' said Kirkwood, 'to audition English girls for the job. Absolutely hopeless. It's an odd thing, but English girls just don't know how to undress without making it look indecent, and the whole essence of this advertising was that we wanted to make it look sensual but not sexy.

'Finally, we decided on the photographer first. We thought a top fashion photographer like Henry Clarke was the only sort of man able to do a job like this, and as luck would have it, he produced his own model.'

Clarke worked in Paris. So did the model. The two of them came across to London, a studio was hired, and since fashion photographers are used to working at speed, the pictures on which the entire subsequent campaign was to be based were taken in one day.

'We worked away like mad,' said Kirkwood. 'We had a glass-sided bath full of detergent and warm water which we kept whipping up to make as much lather as possible, and Clarke had one assistant to keep his cameras loaded. He worked away with them in relays taking every possible pose we could need. Every now and then I would have to give the poor girl a glass of gin to prevent her freezing up. While Clarke was shooting I gave him only two rules. As far as the girl was concerned, I said that anything could show except the pubic hair. I also said that the girl should never look directly at the camera lens. You see, as far as the advertising went, she had to be on her own entirely. Once she looked at the lens, it would have meant that she was conscious of being overlooked and the whole effect would have been ruined.'

Although at first it was the nakedness of the model that was to get the new Breeze campaign talked about, this was not really its most important innovation. Previously, one of the unwritten rules of English advertising was that you must never use a really beautiful woman to appeal to women. Perhaps this was one more example of the sort of male thinking that used to dominate advertising, but it was always claimed that an excessively beautiful woman in an advertisement always ends up by alienating other women by building up resentment and envy, which hard-working housewives then work off in the one way they can – by not buying the product the woman advertises.

'We proved,' said Kirkwood, 'that the exact opposite is the case – that women of any class will identify themselves with a model *provided* she is beautiful enough. What we were giving women here, after all, was a dream, just a dream, and a dream doesn't have to be tangible. God's not tangible, but people believe in him.'

At first Kirkwood was worried by the social implications of his campaign, 'for we had been told that the lower you go down the social scale the more upset people become by nudity,' but once again, this proved less of a problem than had been feared. It may even have been an advantage for, as one copywriter explained, 'once an Englishwoman takes her clothes off she can belong to any class you like'.

But now, the Breeze campaign was appealing directly to something quite new in female advertising – to women's narcissism and their feelings about their own bodies.

'When I started writing for Breeze,' said Sue Perry, who with Kirkwood himself wrote most of the early copy, 'I suppose I worked from the attitude I had to my own naked body. I asked myself what I thought about myself when I was in a bath. The answer was that my body was something that I enjoyed pampering, so in the copy I tried to mix frankness with femininity. Previously B.O. had been a negative thing for women. Perhaps they used Lifebuoy. Perhaps they didn't. At any rate they never talked about it.

'I was trying to turn it from this into something positive. I was trying to say that however loved and gorgeous you are, B.O. is something you share with all women, but that if you accept this, accept your body for what it is by using this soap, you can feel as fresh and cool as this model.'

And so copy was produced like, 'Darling, it's no use being coy about perspiration problems. The fact is (any doctor will tell you) you're perspiring all the time: and it's perfectly natural.' Or, even more frankly, as the campaign progressed, 'Darling, why turn your back on perspiration odour. It happens all over your body. All day. Underarm deodorants are fine, but for overall protection you need Breeze soap. . . . So darling, please bath with Breeze – '

'The one thing I used to object to,' Mrs Perry went on, 'was that word "Darling". For me it immediately intruded a voyeur into the situation.'

But voyeur or no voyeur, the advertising was accepted and surprisingly successful. And the only newspaper which made any objections to carrying the advertising was the *Daily Mirror*. To satisfy the susceptibilities of *Mirror* readers, c p v finally prepared a special set of blocks of one of the advertisements with the nipples painted out.

Whether advertising of this sort did any good to the reputation of

C P V itself is another matter. However, long before, Varley had taken on another account which was to make C P V the most talked-about advertising agency in London.

The significance of C P V's work for the Conservative Party before the 1959 election lies not so much in the advertising itself, as in the fact that advertising was used at all. If the same advertisements had been used, as at first sight they might have been, to sell margarine or a health drink, they would have passed without comment. If there was anything sinister about them, it lay in the decision of the politicians to spend something like £500,000 on bringing their party down to the level of mere product advertising. Certainly, from an advertising point of view, no one can object to Colonel Varley's own remark 'that this was purely an advertising operation. Nothing more. And there was nothing at all exceptional about it, except that it happened to succeed.'

But there seems little doubt that this entanglement with politics did the agency a certain amount of harm. How much is problematical. As Varley himself put it, 'Some people think that because we are supposed to have had the effect some people think we did on the 1959 election we must be pretty good. Others think that because they may have to do business with Labour one day, they had better keep away from our influence.'

Certainly one fact is incontestable. The period after C P V took on the Conservative account coincided with the lowest ebb ever in the agency's morale. Business began to trickle away from the agency, including B E A and part of Shell. John Pearce and Geoffrey Tucker, two senior C P V executives, repeated the operation of Messrs Hobson and Metcalf four years earlier,[36] and left to form their own new agency of Collett, Dickenson, Pearce and Partners Ltd. and the Harvey wine account followed them. Fortunes rise and fall in advertising faster than in any other business, and almost overnight it seemed as if people were talking about C P V in the past tense.

It is this that makes the revival of C P V during the last few years seem all the more dramatic. For there has been nothing quite like the way the agency has suddenly taken on a batch of new clients and increased its total billings to the highest point in its history. As far as one can see, there are several reasons for this, but the most important of them reflect the uncanny way the agency has of catching on to the most important trends in the advertising business, and making the most of them.

The first of these was the international market. This is something in which Varley has always been ahead of his time, and during the discontents of 1960 one of the complaints people within the agency were making about Varley himself was that he was 'bleeding the home busi-

[36] See below, Chapter 9.

ness' to finance a network of agencies abroad. At the time many people saw C P V's elaborate overseas investments as Colonel Varley's *folie de grandeur*, and he himself made no bones about what he was doing. 'This is an immensely costly business,' he said in 1961, 'and of course your home advertising suffers. But then, at the moment, anyone can make money advertising a bull market at home. What is much more difficult and supremely worth doing is to try making a success of something really big abroad.' It has certainly been worth it so far as C P V is concerned.

In fact the building up of C P V internationally had started in earnest in 1951 when Varley hired Leslie Cort, a former director of Reckitt & Colman, to take charge of C P V's foreign advertising. 'Frankly,' he says, our whole foreign operation was a pretty good dog's breakfast. We had associates everywhere, and associates alone are not really what you want in this business. And in London there really wasn't much central direction of foreign business at all.'

Varley complains that British industry in general is unlike the major American corporations in that they have never backed individual British agencies in their efforts to set up abroad. 'There's J. Walter Thompson which was virtually started by General Motors; Erwin, Wasey was backed by General Foods and Lord and Thomas by American Tobacco. . . .'

But in fact the foundations of C P V's foreign advertising were really laid on the work the agency was doing for Shell in Venezuela. Before Cort arrived this advertising had been managed with little real success by an English executive from London. Cort, with the backing of Varley, believed that advertising of this sort could only be handled effectively through a local agency, staffed mainly with nationals from the country itself, but partly owned and directed from London.

Today C O R P A, the small agency in Caracas that C P V merged with, is the second largest advertising agency in South America, 'and beating,' as Cort says with sombre North-country satisfaction, 'the big North American agencies at their own game'. At the same time he has been able to use the same formula in various countries around the world, so that at the moment, C P V has direct subsidiaries in fifteen countries, including Italy where C P V Italiana actually directs the largest agency in the country.

It has been during the last two years that this major investment abroad has already been paying off. In 1962 C P V International reported nearly £10 million worth of foreign billing.

But the most interesting feature of all in the C P V revival is the way it appears to have come from a conscious decision several years ago that the agency was going to make a determined bid to concentrate more and more on what one director calls 'the big spending fields', the top twenty or so of the country's largest advertisers – like Imperial Tobacco, Nestlé, and B M C – a considerable slice of whose business is vital for any agency with top league aspirations.

According to Cyrus Ducker (formerly with Patrick Dolan in their own agency, now director in charge of plans and development at C P V), there is a law of increasing returns at the top of the agency business, and C P V has taken advantage of it.

'Once you're above a certain size,' he said, 'and have the right people working for you, the correct marketing set-up and are seen to be in the international field as well, you really can't go wrong. This is because the really big spenders through the nature of their own advertising and marketing set-up, require an agency of a certain size, and the number of them around in Britain is strictly limited. Now, owing to the rule against taking double accounts, the advertiser often has no choice but to take the one agency that presents itself.'

C P V hardly seem to have been backward in grasping the slightly daunting logic of all this. They had been founded because, as Varley himself put it, 'we were interested in producing the best possible advertising we were capable of.' But now they were in the position where, as Ducker said, 'the real struggle was not to produce better and better advertising, but to be big enough and have the right sort of services and personnel to match the marketing set-up of the big companies.

'To get into the big spending field we had to get ourselves a marketing set-up which was based on the sort of young men who had broken through in the selling organizations of these big firms themselves. We knew it was the roughest and toughest of worlds, but we also knew that it would give us an assured return, whereas if you base your future on handling fashion accounts or the Conservative Central Office, there is no security of tenure over the account, not even all that much certainty that it will pay off in hard cash.

'So, we adjusted our recruiting policy accordingly. Instead of taking on the glamorous young chaps we had specialized in in the past we started taking chaps straight from the big manufacturing organizations we were trying to do business with. We hired a man like Brian Adams from Nestlé, not because we thought we would get any more Nestlé business by doing it, but because the more that you recruit people like that, the more word gets round in this tight gossipy world that you have people talking the language of the chaps in the middle and upper echelons of the big corporations.'

As a result of all this, C P V has been changing, becoming bigger, more predictable and, almost inevitably, more like any other very large agency concerned with giving the very largest clients the services they want. Recently this process has even involved the inevitable link-up with the sort of large American agency against which it had held out for so long.

This agency is the American firm of Kenyon and Eckhardt. As usual in such deals, precise details of the merger are shrouded in discretion, but C P V admit that there was an exchange of minority shareholdings, in the region of 25 per cent each way. 'There was a sort of compromise, and we are in no way controlled from America. Gradually we are building a genuine partnership,' says a C P V spokesman. 'The truth is that these days any big agency without an American link-up is really vulnerable. Already we've started feeding business to each other, and I suppose that now, since the marriage, we jointly form about the third largest agency in the world. With resources like these we're already planning how best to expand into Japan, Scandinavia and Australia.'

An organization like this is a long way from the sort of agency where copywriters would bring lion cubs into the office and a new account was celebrated with champagne. And for the peace of mind of the advertising managers of the big-spending advertisers this is possibly reassuring, for it is hard to imagine C P V originating anything quite like the Breeze campaign today. Yet C P V themselves like to think that their advertising for the Gas Council, since they sacked Mr Therm in 1962, is as daring and radical as ever it might have been.

Mr Therm, in fact, was a dead man from the moment C P V took over the account in the January of that year. His cheerful face had been used to sell gas ever since the days of the Gas, Light and Coke Company in the 1930s, but although he'd kept his smile into the later 1950s the new gas bosses were very definitely to lose theirs.

Indeed, their research had showed them what they might very easily have guessed, that the British public looked upon gas as dirty, smelly, dangerous – and old-fashioned.

C P V surveyed this unpromising scene and noted that the Gas Industry spent practically all their money advertising gas *appliances* and almost none of it advertising the product itself. The thinking behind this tactic was that, if you sell people appliances, they are bound to use the gas.

The agency, scrambling hard to get out a major campaign (billing – £1 million a year) very rapidly, decided that the emphasis had to change. The Area Boards would still sell the appliances – roughly 75 per cent of their total appropriation still sells gas fires, cookers and so on – but C P V would set out to establish the merits of the fuel itself.

And because they were trying to get people to take a second look at gas, Mr Therm had to go. 'We had to imply modernity,' said Cyrus Ducker, the director in charge of the account, 'and you can't do that with a symbol which has lasted thirty or forty years. Nobody here has ever felt that Mr Therm was going to be a serious possibility for the future.'

But what was going to take the old man's place? The 'High-Speed

Gas' theme rapidly became clear once the agency had decided that what they wanted to do was to establish gas as a superior form of heat, initially in terms of its speed.

At first, however, they could not launch the new idea on television, because there existed amongst the nationalized fuel industries a self-denying ordinance against the use of commercial TV. This, the agency thought, was madness because, as they claimed 'the manufacturers of electrical appliances were spending £4 million over two years on the box, while the makers of gas appliances were only spending £140,000'.

To CPV, a television outlet appeared essential. They regarded their job as being to create for gas the 'indispensable benefit' which a virtual monopoly of lighting gave to electricity. So, the gas industry opted out of the self-denying ordinance and in the summer of 1963 CPV went onto TV with a series of mood ads which were meant to be the utmost in with-itness and modernity.

And, sure enough, the sales of domestic gas went up – 11 per cent in the first year. CPV are not disposed to make a fuss about it. They just, they said, had a better product and their job was simply to mediate this fact to the public at large. 'Gas is a superior form of heat,' said Cyrus Ducker, 'but nobody had ever been told.' Mr Therm has been buried a long time, apparently.

8. 'Ideas, Ideas, Ideas'

Although it is an essential part of the *amour propre* of an advertising agency to imagine that it has something unique to offer, there can be no other agency in London which has made quite such a bid for unique-ness as Robert Sharp and Partners of 45 Albemarle Street. It is there in the stainless-steel lift with the faint smell of *eau de cologne* that hauls the visitors up to the fifth floor. It is there in the manifestos the agency has been circulating among its hardier clients. 'We look for intelligent creative people with no respect for authority,' runs the section headed 'Recruiting' in one of them, 'who will shake us out of any dogmas we may be forming. We attract them by presenting ourselves as irreverent to the point of exaggeration.'

And it is there, most strongly of all, in the two old Eton and King's men who virtually run the agency and who established it with the express intention of making it a home-from-home for young men as bright, as heretical, and as on-the-make as they must once have been themselves.

Even today, both of them seem to make a point of appearing the last two men in the world you would expect to find inside a successful agency. Mark Ramage, the managing director, resigned from the civil service (where for a time he was secretary to Herbert Morrison) to join the agency. His conversation is a curious blend of worldliness and fantasy; he talks about advertising as if it were some esoteric game which for obscure reasons of his own he has become involved in but which, since he *is* involved, he is determined to master consummately. 'Even at school,' he explained, 'I was fascinated by advertising – as an art form,' he added hurriedly. 'For it seemed to me that much of the best modern painting is to be seen only in the modern advertisement. Some cosmetic firms – they treat their advertising as nothing but a pure art form and patent medicine advertisements always used to fascinate me as well. You see, some patent medicines virtually *were* their advertising. Without the advertisements what had you? A handful of not very effective and commonplace chemicals.'

Oliver Knox, the agency's other major shareholder, was a friend of Ramage at Cambridge (where he was a classics scholar), and included a spell in a Greek monastery in the Aegean before joining Colman, Prentis and Varley as a copywriter in 1947. He has four children and a large house in Bayswater. Despite the monastery, he is a worldlier, jollier figure than Ramage, but he seems to share with him the air of mild surprise that in advertising there is a world where it is actually possible to make money and enjoy yourself in the process.

'Anarchy and irreverence,' he said cheerfully. 'Those are the two qualities we want in this agency, otherwise, before you know where you are, you end up with people who call you "Sir" and are as dull as everybody else.'

Not unnaturally, talk like this has not endeared the agency to the solider side of the persuasion industry, which has always been anxious to stress the sense of responsibility and social purpose, the total respectability of what they like to call 'the advertising profession', and Sharp's made matters worse by broadcasting their ideas in a series of advertisements in papers like *The Economist* in the autumn of 1962. (It is interesting incidentally that while there is nothing explicitly forbidding an agency to advertise its services, most agencies have a strange reluctance to do so).

A Mr Stag had written in to *The Economist* complaining, as several critics before him had done, about the way the cream of the country's brains was allegedly beginning to be sucked into its advertising agencies. With tongue-in-cheek effrontery, Sharp's used this letter as the occasion for a double-paged advertisement in reply, with the headline, 'We're sorry, Mr Stag, the cream of the country's brains is *already* being sucked into Robert Sharp's.'

'Recently, at 45 Albemarle Street,' it continued, 'the Master of a Cambridge College[37] complained "Sharp's are robbing me of future Fellows." Firsts are dotted all over the building, together with many whose genius lies in more eccentric directions.'

'Ideas, ideas, ideas', read another advertisement the agency produced for itself about the same time, with a picture of three young men sitting, somewhat inexplicably, in bath tubs and wearing bowler hats. 'This is what you want and this is what you get from Robert Sharp's. Ideas to get more of your goods into the shops. . . . Ideas that make your product more desirable than ever. Ideas that stick in your mind like burrs.'

Most British advertising men – perhaps it is a side-effect of the guilt many of them still exhibit about being in advertising at all – are unexpectedly coy when it comes to self-advertisement, and there was a strong feeling that there was an element of bad taste about the campaign. 'A really good agency,' as one top agency man put it, 'should really be above this sort of thing.'

But behind all the brashness and the talk of anarchy and irreverence, Ramage and Knox between them were stating something of considerable importance about the way most agencies tend to operate. It was a theory which many people on the creative side of large agencies had muttered before them. The only real originality of Sharp's was that here was an agency trying to do something about it.

Put briefly, the theory has two parts. One is that, as Knox himself put it, 'obsequiousness to the client is a major curse of the normal large agency, and because of it the creative people become side-tracked from doing the most effective advertising into doing advertising which will merely please the client. As a result, largely because of this, successful agencies become great places for the operation of Parkinson's first law, as unnecessary bureaucracies of sound, reliable, second-rate men are built up, men who have been trained in the set ways of the agency world and whose tendency is to become immersed in a round of all-absorbing but entirely unproductive paper-work and conferences.'

These tendencies of big agencies provide much of the dynamic for change within the agency business by the mere reaction they usually provoke from the abler, more impatient people on their staff. This is one of the reasons for the extremely high turnover of personnel within the agencies, and it is interesting that whenever an adman manages to break away from a large agency and set up on his own, one of the

[37] Mr Noel Annan, Provost of King's.

explanations he always gives is that he wanted to get down to the simple, straightforward business of producing good advertising.

But the founders of new agencies are all too often like the founders of reformist religious sects. If they are successful they usually end up by becoming enshrined in the very abuses they set out to cure. Robert Sharp's, on the other hand, by endlessly reiterating words like 'anarchy' and 'irreverence' and by making it almost a matter of policy to recruit young men from outside advertising who seemed to show a high degree of unorthodoxy and nonconformity, were making a serious attempt to offset the very dangers that success brings with it.

For from the start one of the attractive things about Ramage and Knox was that, with that implicit self-confidence which is perhaps the most valuable gift of Eton and King's, they took it for granted that they would be successful. The one thing they never doubted was their cleverness and the ability of such cleverness to get what it wanted. 'When we started,' said Knox, 'we didn't believe that there was much in the advertising business that couldn't be done by clever people who could reduce the problem to its simplest form and then solve it by their natural intelligence. The people we needed had to have good taste, not too much faith in others and a good dose of intellectual arrogance.'

So it was that in 1955, after Knox had left C P V, they bought out the name, the goodwill (and incidentally, but most important of all, the N P A recognition) of a small technical agency owned by a gentleman named Robert Sharp who had been in the advertising business for many years and who thought that the time had come to capitalize on his assets. Sharp remained on the pay roll. The words 'and Partners' were added to his name, and Knox and Ramage, together with a photographer called Neil Nimmo and Arthur Wilson, a former C P V art director, moved into a house in Bryanston Square to put their ideas into practice. The experiment of applying irreverence and intelligence to advertising had begun.

Bright young men, mostly from Cambridge, were hired at salaries considerably above anything they would have got in other agencies at the time and set to work with a minimum of fuss and delay. (At one time Knox put a series of advertisements in the personal column of *The Times* asking for young men with Firsts. At another time they advertised on a large scale in undergraduate newspapers like *Varsity*. One advertisement under the heading, 'Sharp's go hunting for talent', included the typical line, 'Robert Sharp's can only hope to improve their service to their clients if they find more people as tireless and spectacularly brilliant as the partners themselves.' Later they held a weekend house-party, organized on the lines of the Civil Service Selection Board, to pick likely young graduates.)

And because, as Knox and Ramage intended it should, the news of this talent-spotting campaign soon got back to the people it was really meant to impress – the advertisers themselves – the 'tireless and spectacularly brilliant' young men of 45 Albemarle Street soon found themselves being credited with the sort of reputation they wanted. More to the point they began to be approached by advertising managers on the look-out for exactly the qualities they claimed to possess – ideas and originality. The new accounts began to arrive.

They were not enormous accounts by big agency standards. 'When you start an agency like ours,' said Ramage, 'your first clients tend to include a proportion of people in despair, stranded whales and notorious movers around.' But out of the despairing, the stranded, the movers around, and others Robert Sharp's were soon managing to build up some fairly solid business to back up their reputation. At C P V Knox had written copy for Viyella stockings, and when Viyella changed agencies they chose Sharp's. Douglas Collins, the remarkable tycoon who had recently built up the Goya perfume business, was impressed by the agency and entrusted them with some of his advertising as well. A little later, Spratt's decided that a new approach was needed to the pet food war and chose the partners to launch a new brand of cat food. The agency, believing that 'your cat deserves the best', christened it Top Cat. Later still came the sign that Sharp's really were getting somewhere. A slice of Unilever business is one of the most hankered-after forms of advertising in the trade and Gibbs, a Unilever subsidiary, finally chose Sharp's to take on a toilet soap called Astral.

In 1955 the agency had been placing around £100,000 of advertising a year. Five years later the billings of Robert Sharp and Partners were well past the £1 million mark. Ramage had a flat off Park Lane. Knox's sons were down for Eton and the directors were driving Lotus cars. Irreverence plus intelligence had paid off. Or had it?

The question arises only when you turn from the wild young man image the agency has taken so much trouble to build up about itself, and examine some of the actual advertising they produced. The contrast is striking. Where is the heresy, the anarchy, the irreverence? Where, one might even ask in a small voice, is the brilliance and originality? True, there was the campaign the agency launched for Truman's beers in which Miller Watt, who draws the Pop cartoons in the *Daily Sketch*, designed a jaunty old seadog with one leg cavorting above the heading, 'more hops in Ben Truman'. True, the Top Cat commercials had some very nice cat photography. And true, the idea of photographing a model against the Moroccan desert with the copy-line 'your skin gets dried up too', got the point across that Astral soap refreshed the skin.

It is unnecessary as well as unkind to labour the point, but the fact is that perhaps the strangest thing of all about Robert Sharp and Partners is the contrast between the individuality of its personnel and the ordinariness of the work they have tended to produce.

One cynical explanation is that all the talk about spectacular brilliance and first-rate intelligence was little more than a gimmick, designed in the first place to get the agency off the ground.

But this misses the point. For the young men the agency has been hiring during the last nine years really have been extremely bright. There is Ben Nash, for instance, Sharp's television director, still in his mid-twenties, who was hired straight from Cambridge where he edited *Granta* and made films. There is Michael Kaye (Marylebone Grammar and Trinity, Cambridge) who arrived at Sharp's with a first in classics and within a few months had taken over all the agency's media buying. And with the staff purposely kept down to the 50–60 mark, what Knox jokingly refers to as 'the staff academic-honours ratio' is higher than any other agency in the country.

What the Robert Sharp experiment really does prove is something about the nature of advertising itself and the effect it often has on very intelligent people who try to make money out of it.

To understand this, it is necessary to look a little more closely into several Sharp campaigns. The first is one already referred to – the happy but highly unoriginal advertisements for Truman's beers. This was an account the agency secured – 'frankly on the old boy net' – early in its career. It was a time when anarchy and irreverence could have been expected to be in full spate and yet the agency produced this resoundingly square series of advertisements around Miller Watt's cartoons of old Ben Truman. Why?

'This was a terribly difficult campaign,' said Knox, 'and we argued over it like mad. But you see, in those days most brewery advertising in this country was hopeless, for the simple reason that the brewers had always been cosseted by the tied-house system. Because of this there was no genuine competition and virtually no ways of telling how effectively your advertising was selling your beer.

'Now this account was worth £30,000 a year, and it was being awarded, quite simply, to the agency whose poster designs appealed most to the brewery directors. They were splendidly upper-class with typical nineteenth-century brewery offices tucked away in the City and we worked on the principle that we had to get at their sense of humour. The reason we went to a *Daily Sketch* cartoonist to do this for us was that we had discovered long ago that there is not much difference in Britain between English upper-class humour and English lower-class humour and I had an idea that the sort of modern, Festival-of-Britainish advertising which was all the rage for beer was the last thing in the world to appeal to a brewery director.

'And we were right. When they drove into London and saw this jolly old fellow hopping all over the hoardings advertising their beer, they were absolutely delighted. Unfortunately it was absolutely uncheckable whether we had sold more beer or not.'

But the chief point about Sharp's is that, for all the early cynicism and talk of off-beat irreverence, they soon made it plain that what they were after was effectiveness and success. They had no particular doctrine about advertising to hamper them. 'Advertising doctrines,' said Ramage, 'are always the kiss of death.' Instead Knox and Ramage were pragmatic to a degree. They might employ – indeed they *did* employ – young men who wore purple velvet ties, but when it came to the hard graft of producing advertisements to sell, they were as research and marketing conscious as Hobson, Bates or the London Press Exchange. Flair was something for their private lives. When it came to advertising, 'we would always scrap a bright advertisement,' said Ramage, 'for one which was duller but sold better.' 'The truth is,' said Knox, 'that we proceed with elaborate caution. We test every campaign we can before going ahead with it and compare a bright campaign in Reading with a duller campaign for the same product in York. If the York one works better we never hesitate to adopt it. Advertising is a pragmatic business and one can be interested only in what works.'

Pragmatism and caution paid off. The agency's campaign for Top Cat, its earliest and most considerable success, was essentially a meticulously planned marketing operation; and their advertising for the Save and Prosper Group of Unit Trusts is based on what seems an extraordinarily complex mathematical analysis of results. Indeed at times these wild young men seem to have been almost excessively cautious as appears most impressively in the campaign they launched for a slimming food called Limmits.

Ever since the end of the war it had been realized within the persuasion industry that fat people were one of the great potential targets for the advertiser in Britain. According to the figures of optimum weight agreed by the Life Extension Examiners of New York, seven out of ten British males and six out of ten British females are at present overweight. But according to a survey of slimming preparations and weight carried out by National Opinion Polls, only 32 per cent of the adult population, less than half of those who were overweight, realized that they weighed too much.

In the United States, where the situation had been roughly the same, advertisers and manufacturing chemists had been hard at work since the late 'forties making people weight conscious and offering them various preparations which would do something about it. Metrecal, one of the most successful of these, produced nearly a hundred imitators and slimming became a multi-million dollar industry almost overnight.

But this was one of those areas which seem to bring out the subtle difference between the American market and the English. Here there is a feeling that an Englishman's girth is his castle. A few agencies – most notably S. H. Benson – made it plain that they were not interested in handling slimming accounts, and although Metrecal and several similar products were marketed here (Metrecal with its name inexplicably changed to Metercal) they had nothing like the success they had all enjoyed in the States.

This was the background to the decision of Pfizer Ltd to manufacture a totally new type of slimming food and to employ Robert Sharp and Partners to advertise it in the United Kingdom.

Ramage said that although 'there was a certain amount of feeling against slimming aids which was left over from the days when unscrupulous gentlemen used to sell fat ladies tape-worm eggs as slimming pills by mail-order advertisements', he saw no reason at all why his agency should not accept the account provided it really did what it said.

The actual slimming food was a type of biscuit made of protein, flour and a form of cellulose which had the effect of expanding once it was inside the stomach and so providing a sense of satisfaction; it also contained the vitamins one needs, and it would be possible to live on nothing else. And as far as the agency was concerned at this stage, this was virtually all that there was. Before it was launched on the overweight English a pack, a price, a name and a campaign had to be decided.

Before he finally accepted the account, Ramage spent some time reading up all the available literature on weight reduction, 'just to satisfy myself'. Pfizer were still conducting clinical trials to settle questions of the flavouring the biscuits were to have and to discover the long-term effect of taking the biscuits, whether it should be eaten with milk or other low calorie food, and whether it had any unexpected side-effects. 'Well – constipation for example.'

Apparently it did not. The clinical trials were a total success and the campaign could go forward.

Working with 'very sophisticated clients', Ramage was determined to leave as little as possible to chance. The Neilsen organization was asked to prepare a complete survey of sales, advertising costs and similar information of all other slimming preparations already on sale in Britain. National Opinion Polls were hired to prepare a detailed consumer survey on the size of the potential market and on attitudes to slimming by class, area and income. It was felt that there were four possible ways of selling the product to choose from: through the chemists on medical-type advertising, through grocers' shops as a sort of crispbread, as a shock-tactic diet to be used for rapid slimming, and as something to eat almost as a matter of routine enabling you to cut out a single meal a day and becoming almost a matter of habit.

'There was,' Ramage said, 'no clear lead which of these we should follow, so we staged distinctly different trial campaigns in four different towns.' The towns chosen were Ipswich, York, Huddersfield and Northampton. This was because each of them had a population of around 100,000 and were roughly comparable in social make-up. The advertising for the new product was confined to local newspapers, and the tests were equivalent to spending £100,000 nationally in two months. As Ramage said, 'research on this scale is rare and calls for extremely rational clients'. But he insists that logically it was the only way of reaching a decision.

During the tests different names, different prices and different advertising themes were chosen and the chemists and grocers were visited regularly every two weeks to check on exactly how many packets had been sold. But long before the test-time was up, it had appeared quite clear that by far the most profitable method of selling the biscuits was as a food for gradual slimming to be sold at the cheaper price range through grocers' shops and supermarkets as well as chemists. Unlike American women, the potential slimmers of the four towns showed that they regarded rapid slimming preparations as something 'a bit extreme and exotic'. The tests also made it clear that of all the possible names the agency had tried out, 'Limmits' was by far the most memorable.

And so Pfizer had a name, a price and a potential market for their product. But anyone attempting to persuade a nation to slim is venturing into a social and psychological minefield where the most apparently harmless claim can suddenly explode in his face, as a further piece of research revealed, which was also commissioned by the agency.

Its first finding was fairly obvious. This was that whereas women can usually be persuaded to worry about their weight, 'males, or at any rate English males, tend to regard their weight as given them by God'. So was the finding that among women themselves, attitudes to fatness vary considerably between classes. For the 'socially orientated' woman with a wide circle of friends, 'fatness is likely to be regarded unfortunately. This society will produce concern over slight variations in weight'. But for the 'home-orientated woman' in the 'tightly integrated rural and working-class home there is a rigid distinction between a man's and a woman's social world and little concern about weight'.

What was surprising were a few of the findings which came next as the survey workers probed a little more deeply into the world of rural and working-class female obesity. One startling discovery they made was that a considerable number of women here actually wanted to be fat. 'One woman in the sample,' as the survey reported, 'used her size as a means of regulating her marital relationships with her husband who she knew found fatness undesirable. This was not why she was fat, but her fatness was used to protect herself from her husband's demands.'

Fatness was also thought possibly to 'typify the role of the housekeeper and mother' and 'symbolize robustness' for some people, while for another group the pollsters had discovered, 'the non-competitive housewife', the feeling that a husband would not mind her putting on a little weight was part of her very feeling of security within her marriage. The report quoted one such wife verbatim to back up its argument. 'Once you're married you know your husband. Well, most husbands love their wives, so therefore you're not trying to attract him. You say, he knew what I was like and it doesn't matter. He likes me a little fatter or something.'

Because of all this, the report carried some solemn warnings (which incidentally go a long way towards explaining the failure of slimming preparations to catch on in Britain as they have in the States). For a large number of British women, it thought, the idea of slimming carried with it the idea of a change in social attitude as well as a possible sexual and emotional readjustment within their marriage.

It also conceded that 'many women just like eating', and concluded that 'for some fat women, the very attractiveness of advertisements for slimming, i.e. "be attractive", may be disturbing and in fact actually threatening'.

Once the warnings were over the report proceeded to advise on the likeliest targets the advertising might make for, the people, and predominantly the women, who actually *did* want to get or remain thin. There were women after pregnancy, for instance. Once they had got through weaning their babies they were a sure-fire market, although even here the report had a word of warning about class differences in attitude, 'the hostess or woman who works wanting slimness most'.

The career woman in an organization with relatively high status was perhaps a better target still – 'the greater their relationship with figures of high status, the greater their concern and anxiety about weight increases'. Marriageable girls tended towards the image of 'slim, elegant and sophisticated efficiency'. But it was perhaps menopausal women who offered the slimming preparation manufacturer the best target of all. 'The fears of losing sexual attractiveness combined with fears of ageing combine to give an added impetus to anything which helps them maintain their interest and attractiveness and to deny the awareness of change. This is most acutely experienced by the very socially conscious, particularly by the upper middle class.'

But as far as Limmits were concerned, the comparatively small market of upper-middle-class menopausal women was not where the really big potential sales lay. It would have been easy enough to have mounted a bright, clever campaign to appeal to fashion and status-conscious middle-class women, but this was not the object of the exercise at all. Somehow this advertising had to make an impact on the really large potential market of lower-middle-class and working-class women too. But it had to do this without offending the various emotional working-class female susceptibilities, and also without giving Limmits such a lower-class image that the status-conscious middle classes would rule it out entirely.

Although among AB women it might have been perfectly feasible to play gently upon their feelings of guilt and disquiet at being fat, this was clearly more and more dangerous to do the lower the advertising descended the social scale. For here, if a woman is happily married she does not worry too much about her weight. 'In the more placid, less demanding environment of working-class marriage women are only likely to be motivated to do something when their weight has increased considerably and their clothes no longer fit.' And if she is not happy, her fatness 'is generally equated with lack of sexual attractiveness, apathy, passivity, inability to control appetite and withdrawal from the competitive female situation'.

In other words, among the women in the classes where the biggest potential sales for a slimming food lay, virtually all the heavily weighted sexual or social themes which might have worked with higher-class women seemed to be ruled out.

Instead it looked as if it was going to be far more effective here to stress the purely practical qualities Limmits did possess – the fact that unlike other slimming preparations at that time – it *did* offer something that could be nibbled, and that, unlike more drastic methods of dieting, it could offer something of a substitute meal which the ordinary housewife could eat while the rest of her family was getting on with its everyday food. Above all, just because it seemed a more moderate way of dieting, Limmits could be presented as a less emotionally charged way of cutting down weight. If the advertising was careful it could avoid all those feelings of guilt and anxiety which the more extreme and drastic methods of slimming seemed to summon up. And at the same time there was a chance that in this way women would come to accept eating it as a habit.

So it was that when the campaign finally saw the light of day, it seemed to be going out of its way to be as dull and as ordinary and as factual as possible. There were half-page pictures for the Press showing two biscuits and explaining what they were in a remarkably straightforward way. It was far from a 'creative' campaign. And some of the people in other agencies began to nod knowingly and say that the bright young men of Albemarle Street were losing their touch.

But the strange thing is that, however dull and low-keyed it may have appeared, the product at once became and still remains the largest selling slimming preparation on the market.

'There are times,' said Ramage, 'when an advertising man must realize that the really clever course is not to be clever at all.'

9. Hobson, Bates and Partners—The Unique Selling Agency

As with the best double acts, the two men chiefly concerned seem more different than they probably are. John Hobson – tall, gaunt, with the angular manner of one of C. P. Snow's top civil servants, a precise, painstaking, reticent man, son of a curator of oriental art at the British Museum, educated at Rugby and at King's, where he took a double first in classics. And John Metcalf – solid, fast-moving, a professional coat-off man – literary critic, broadcaster and poker-player, educated at University College School and Downing College, Cambridge, where he read English under F. R. Leavis.

Metcalf is one of nature's welcomers. Hobson has a cautious reserve that has frozen many a new acquaintance into awed silence. Metcalf is a gourmet. Hobson will go to elaborate lengths to avoid having to drink so much as a glass of wine at lunch.

Even their offices seem to have been specially designed to stress how unalike they are. Hobson's is spartan and uncluttered, with black hide chairs and a desk like an operating table. Metcalf has succeeded in banishing all signs of a desk from his and works – also from black hide – in a room full of plants, books and pictures – (eight Nolan lithographs, a Barnet Freedman nude, a Sickert pastel of The Albert, Canning Town) and the only concession the room seems to make to the hard world of advertising is in the telephone and the neat switchboard let into one arm of the sofa so that whoever sits there can buzz any room in the agency with his feet up.

These surface differences are deceptive, for between them, John Hobson and John Metcalf have built up the most thriving new agency to emerge in London during the last ten years. And since personalities are probably more important in advertising than in any other business except politics and the Church, a large part of the success of Hobson, Bates and Partners (the Bates, as we shall see, is an interesting addition that comes later), is due to the way this unlikely partnership has been able to present itself as the advance guard of the new men in advertising, the with-it intellectuals who were to bring 'thinking' into huckstering.

Of course, they were not alone in this claim. The London Press Exchange, for instance, where John Hobson worked as an account man before the war, has always gone out of its way to stress the quality of its 'thinking' and to offer its clients a service that would take into account the whole range of their business. 'I like to regard myself as more of a business consultant than a mere advertising man', one senior L P E executive remarked to us.

But the advertising world is a fashion-conscious world where at least half the secret of success consists in wrapping old truths in new theories, and while most British agencies have been reluctant to adopt the American style of agency 'philosophy', the Hobson men have always gloried in theirs, seeing themselves in the revealing phrase of another agency's director as 'the Marxists of advertising' the dedicated men with the core of inner certainty, the men who really *know*.

And because this is a world where the legend creates the success almost as surely as the success creates the legend, H B P has risen steadily towards the head of the league amid the sweet smell of certainty diffused by its two mandarins at the top.

The way it was done provides the sort of parable of real life success that is so dear to the hearts of advertising men and which would appeal to a twentieth-century Samuel Smiles. It is a classic tale of how to succeed in business by really trying and it begins, like almost all the best stories on the founding of new advertising agencies, with a breakaway.

What divorce is to marriage, the breakaway is to the advertising business. It offers the same tempting promise of a fresh start in life. There can be money in it. It tends to produce the same recriminations afterwards. And like divorce it is a great deal easier in theory than it is in practice. For in theory, all that a frustrated or ambitious advertising man need do to leave the agency he works for and set up on his own is to make sure that when he walks through the door for that last time he takes three of his old agency's clients with him.

Not that he need actually *take* the clients, although this is usually how it is done. He might be lucky enough to find somewhere outside three separate businessmen or advertising managers who are willing to entrust their advertising to him. But a minimum of three accounts every new agency must have if it is to qualify for recognition by the Newspaper Proprietor's Association. Without this no agency is entitled to the standard 15 per cent agency commission for placing its advertisements in the press. With it they can buy space on credit and actually set up in business.

These simple facts of life, every senior advertising man has tucked away somewhere at the back of his mind. They are facts, however, which usually tend to remain academic, for it requires courage and an exceptional combination of circumstances for any agency employee to be able to take advantage of them. For John Hobson and John Metcalf, these circumstances suddenly presented themselves in the summer of 1955.

At this time both of them were employed by Colman, Prentis and Varley. Hobson was 46, and one of the Establishment figures of British advertising. He had been responsible for the standard textbook on advertising media and had launched the Hulton readership survey (by now it had become the I P A readership survey). He was assistant managing director of C P V. He also had a house at Berkhamsted, an income of £6000 a year, and a reputation for integrity, respectability and several of the more unadventurous business virtues.

Metcalf was fourteen years younger. He had already tried making a living as a writer (unsuccessfully) and as a B B C producer (modestly). He had been appointed general manager of Voice and Vision (the public relations subsidiary of C P V) five years earlier at a salary of £700 a year. By 1955 he had built Voice and Vision into one of the biggest public relations firms in London. He had a flat in Marylebone, was just married, earned a salary of over £3000, and was regarded as one of the brightest young men in the business.

Predictably, the two men were not the closest friends. Metcalf himself describes their relationship as that of 'great opponents within the company'. So what was it that brought the two of them together?

Part of the answer lies in the nature of C P V itself. By this time the agency had an unrivalled reputation for its creative work and probably possessed more talent per desk than any other in the country. The work and the politics of the agency centred around the personality of Colonel Varley, who as he himself says, 'picked the liveliest minds he could find and taxed them to the utmost'.

This process could be exciting but also unsettling for the minds themselves. By 1955 Hobson and Metcalf were both showing acute symptoms of being unsettled. And in June of that year, within a matter of days of each other, both John Hobson and John Metcalf happened to have disagreements with the management of C P V which led to their resignation.

What happened then still gets discussed among advertising men. Some insist that in the light of what was to occur, everything must have been carefully worked out from the start. Hobson and Metcalf both deny this vigorously.

At the time of his resignation, John Metcalf had in fact no idea of continuing in advertising and, with his public relations contacts, he was finding no difficulty in setting up his own P R firm, John Metcalf (P.R.) Ltd. (which still flourishes), and which had its original office in his flat in Montagu Square. He had no reason to worry about the future. It was the obvious move for a successful P R man like himself to make, and as he says, 'I was suddenly rather excited by the prospect of being able to turn over ten or fifteen thousand a year working from my own home'.

Hobson had discussed the possibility of Metcalf joining him in his embryonic advertising agency a few days before he resigned, but at this time Metcalf was distinctly cool over the whole idea. 'People seem to think,' says Metcalf, 'that anyone who starts an agency as we did, just has to be a thrusting, bruising, knife-flashing sort of fellow. But what I actually said to John Hobson when he first made his suggestion was, "John, you must be out of your careful, analytical mind".'

'And then, after we had talked several times more during the following weeks I finally said "yes, all right, but it will all be the most terrible failure". I even said, which shows what a calculating chap I was, that I didn't want any shares in the agency, and it was he who replied that if we were going into it together I had to have some shares.'

Certainly, if this is how it really was, Metcalf was being surprisingly naïve, for as Hobson was anxious to point out to him, they had certain positive advantages unusual among men trying to start new advertising agencies. To understand what these advantages really were it is necessary to go back in more detail to the uncomfortable question of why and how John Hobson left c p v.

On the afternoon of June 13th, 1955, Colonel Varley had called a meeting of the directors of c p v to tell them that he had been offered the Pepsi-Cola account for Great Britain and that he intended to accept it. This surprised most of the men around the table. There had been no hint that this was in the air and Hobson naturally pointed out that it would mean giving up the agency's existing soft drinks account for the Lyons-owned Sunfresh Orange business because of the accepted advertising rule that no agency can handle two competitive products.

Hobson was particularly vehement about this. In the first place Sunfresh was very much his account, and since he had been responsible for it at c p v the business had grown until it was billing between £300,000–£400,000 a year. Hobson was proud of this and regarded the Sunfresh account with that proprietary eye which advertising men naturally reserve for their most successful work. He had not heard about Varley's decision to try for Pepsi-Cola until that afternoon and felt that he was being let down in the eyes of his client. He also pointed out that the Pepsi-Cola business in Britain was then worth only a quarter of the Sunfresh account.

Somewhat to Hobson's surprise, Varley refused to budge. At this point he was in the middle of his plan for building c p v into the big international company he had set his heart on, and seems to have felt that the Pepsi-Cola account would be a useful stake in getting into the international field. It was also something of a test of loyalty for the rest of the agency and a demonstration that he meant what he said about internationalism.

According to Hobson there was some hope at this stage that a compromise might still be worked out by convincing Lyons that the Pepsi-Cola and Sunfresh accounts were not directly competitive, and so getting their consent to what had occurred. It was in an attempt to put forward this point of view that Hobson visited Sam Salmon and Leonard Gluckstein of Lyons the following Friday morning. Both of them refused to have anything to do with the suggestion. 'I there and then,' says Hobson, 'on the spur of the moment, asked whether, if I formed an agency, I could have the account. Sam went out, talked to Leonard Gluckstein and came back and said yes.'

Hobson insists that up until this point he had not thought out the matter of starting an agency at all. In his own phrase he had 'pushed at a door and found it to give quite easily'.

'Some attractive possibilities,' he adds, 'lay beyond.'

For in the agency business, rather as in accountancy or the law, a few of the really successful executives come to count for more with individual clients than the agencies they work for. This was so for John Hobson and Sunfresh Orange. It was also so for him and the manufacturers of Cadbury's Drinking Chocolate. For many years now this had been another of Hobson's own special accounts. He had planned the earliest advertising for it when he had been at L P E. The account had followed with him when he moved from L P E to C P V and Paul Redmayne of Cadbury's had long been a personal friend, so that Hobson not unnaturally thought the account might still be his for the asking.

Finally, Hobson had always had extremely strong personal links with another of C P V's big clients, the biscuit firm of Macdonalds. Between them, Macdonalds, Cadbury's and Sunfresh had a combined billing of well over £1 million.

It was at this point that Hobson, suspecting that John Metcalf was on the point of leaving C P V, had called on him at his flat in Montagu Square to make his first suggestion about starting an agency together. He wanted Metcalf to take charge of the creative work and felt that Metcalf's very different personality and experience would make him a valuable ally. 'I outlined my proposition to him,' says Hobson, 'feeling rather like a conspirator.' From then, until he had his own name firmly on the door of his own agency, Hobson was to have to behave like one as well. It was not a role he was particularly good at.

For like many an amateur conspirator before him he was over-anxious to get things cut and dried. The very evening he returned home from his visit to Metcalf, he decided to telephone Willie Macdonald, the head of the biscuit company at his home in Scotland to ask him outright for his support and some business. But he forgot that this was the evening when Mr Macdonald was celebrating his silver wedding, and at this stage this one piece of forgetfulness might easily have cost John Hobson the whole future of Hobson, Bates and Partners. Instead of the encouragement

Hobson was expecting, Macdonald gave him a distinctly frosty reply and suggested that the time and place to discuss such things was the following week at a proper meeting at his office in Glasgow.

This rebuff gave Hobson his first real hint of possible trouble ahead. It made him jumpy, for already a lot was at stake for him, but he went on with his plan and on Monday when he returned to his office at c p v he recruited the next two members of his still embryonic agency – Pat Gierth and Stanley Glockler who had worked on the Sunfresh and the Macdonald accounts at c p v.

As both men were still employees of c p v and had no wish to lose their jobs if Hobson's agency-building came to nothing, their enrolment in the cause was kept strictly secret, although both were offered directorships and a small share in the equity of the new agency if it ever did come into being. Hobson's own position as a member of c p v was clearly untenable by now and so the day after, at a meeting of the directors of the agency, he formally resigned and told Varley that he was going to Glasgow to see Willie Macdonald as soon as he could. He did this next morning and found that Macdonald, far from offering him the business he was counting on, gave him the firmest possible discouragement.

As anyone who has tried it will explain, the setting up of a new advertising agency is an intensely elaborate balancing act, in which a series of unrelated acts of faith must be brought carefully together before the tottering machinery of the new agency can have a life of its own.

The first act of faith belongs to the men who are starting the agency, and involves a sound commercial belief that clients will come and actually entrust them with their advertising. The second must be made by someone with enough money to pay for premises and salaries and typewriters and so make this possible. The third must be made by advertising men who are good enough at their job to inspire the prospective client to entrust his advertising to the untried agency they have joined. And provided everyone – backers, directors, clients and staff – believe that the new agency is going to get off the ground, there is a chance that it actually will. Without the belief of all of them it is doomed before it begins.

This was why Hobson's virtual rebuff by Macdonald's was such a setback. Lack of confidence at this stage from an important potential client could have been contagious and it is more than possible that the whole idea of Hobson's new agency would have collapsed there and then but for an intervention from the most unlikely quarter.

The principal backer of c p v for many years had been a city financier called John Maples, and the day after Hobson returned from Glasgow, Maples called on him at his office in c p v with a proposition. He knew what Hobson was trying to do (as a friend of Metcalf's this was hardly surprising), and he said that he would actually arrange financial support for the agency on one condition – a promise from Hobson not to attempt to take any further CPV accounts apart from Sunfresh, Cadbury's and Macdonald's. In return he said that as well as having his finance provided for, Hobson would actually be allowed to work from his existing office at CPV and to draw his entertaining expenses until the new agency was formed. It was about this time that Metcalf finally agreed to take charge of the creative side of its work.

Clearly Maples was moved partly by the instincts of an entrepreneur and partly by a desire to limit the damage Hobson had already done at CPV. But his decision placed Hobson in an incredible position. He was like some revolutionary leader permitted to carry out a limited *coup d'état* by the head of state and actually given government premises to do it in on condition that he committed the minimum of damage in the process. And to make it more complicated still, Varley was still in a fighting mood. A CPV executive who revealed that he had joined Hobson a few days later was instantly dismissed. Varley personally visited Willie Macdonald to ensure that CPV lost no business to Hobson, and CPV competed strongly against Hobson for the third account he needed for his new agency.

But by the end of July it was clear that Hobson and Metcalf were going to get away with it. Cadbury's had confirmed that the drinking chocolate account was his. Lyons had done the same with the Sunfresh account, and when Hobson and Metcalf heard that they had won the Gold Cup Margarine account as well (despite bidding for it by CPV), they treated themselves to a bottle of champagne in the Rivoli bar of the Ritz to celebrate.

They still had their problems of course. Hobson felt it was hardly tactful to interview applicants for jobs actually under the nose of Varley, so Metcalf's office in Voice and Vision was used for this instead.

The arrangements necessary for financing a new advertising agency in Britain also made things complicated, despite Maples's promise. The difficulty was that by the NPA rules an agency could not raise money by turning itself into a public company (although since then, of course, several have). Ownership had to reside in a working chairman and board of directors so that outside finance needed to come in the form of a personal loan to the Chairman or members of the board.

The original idea of this was to prevent a single large outside firm from taking over an advertising agency and then using it to place all its advertising in the press. In this way the firm would in effect have paid itself the fifteen per cent commission laid down by the NPA as the universal agency fee, and before long the entire agency system might have collapsed. Although the NPA ruling worked to prevent this, there were several disadvantages to the arrangement as well. In the case of

John Hobson and Partners, as we shall see, the initial difficulty of raising capital was only one of them.

In the event, Maples agreed to make arrangements for Hobson to be provided with part of his working capital of £15,000 in the form of a personal loan for £15,000, the rules of the NPA were observed, and when John Hobson and Partners applied for the NPA recognition they needed if they were to get their fifteen per cent from the media owners, their request was granted, and the new agency was in business.

The first eight months of John Hobson and Partners were inevitably the toughest. Hobson calculated that they would use up the capital and loan in the first four months and recoup it in the last eight months of their first year; and this is precisely what happened. At this stage in its life a new agency has to grow or die and the condition of growth requires building up sufficient staff to be ready to take on the fresh work when it appears. And gradually, and then not so gradually, the new work did appear.

'All of a sudden, after about twelve months, people saw that we hadn't gone bankrupt, and the dam broke,' says Metcalf. Suddenly, quite suddenly, John Hobson and Partners began to be spoken of among advertising men themselves as something new and successful in the business. Better and more experienced people began wanting to work for them, and fresh accounts started to roll in. At the end of the agency's first year, billings were up to £300,000, and there was already a hint of a profit in the wind.

But it was now that the Hobson-Metcalf combination showed what it was up to. They had proved that it was still possible to start a new agency from scratch and to run it successfully. With four years of the 1950s advertising boom still to run there is no doubt it could have gone on gathering accounts and being successful in the way of most other small agencies.

This, however, was not their intention. They were interested not just in being a successful agency but in being a successful big one and the way they were going to do it was by being different from the rest. It was now that John Hobson and Partners developed its mystique of 'thinking'. Or perhaps mystique is not quite the right word. 'Our aim has always been to minimize the area of uncertainty in advertising,' John Hobson says; and it was beneath the influence of his unusually precise mind that the men in his agency began treating advertising and all its problems as an exercise in applied logic.

'During the first few years,' says Metcalf, 'the agency stood or fell by John Hobson's reputation as a marketing man.' And part of the reason it did so was that Metcalf spent a considerable part of each working day preaching the gospel according to John Hobson. Most of the work and discipline of the agency during this time originated from Hobson. It was Metcalf's job in his turn to turn this into a tangible legend of the sort that attracts clients and wins an agency a reputation for success.

At this stage there was nothing startlingly new in the actual way Hobson was working. The marketing techniques, the statistical analyses he employed were the standard methods already evolved by the major agencies. What was new was his attitude towards the business of selling – his seriousness, and the sort of standards he demanded from the people round him. 'In advertising there are always a dozen ways of doing any job. We consider them all, one by one, and then test and test and test again until we get the right one.'

This is John Hobson himself speaking and it gives a hint of the central impression John Metcalf was determined to get across to the people who mattered – the idea of this tall, donnish figure who was bringing the same high academic standards to selling cat food or cooking fat that he might otherwise have employed in editing Herodotus or running the Treasury.

Hobson's methods began to get results almost from the start. The campaign for Sunfresh Orange pushed it to the top of the market in a matter of months. And the campaign for Captain Morgan Rum, based on an intensive consumer survey on attitudes to rum drinking, carried this newly advertised product to second place in national sales. There was new business, like 'Bristol' tipped cigarettes ('Today's cigarette is a Bristol'); and a campaign to launch Antussin, a new type of cough treatment based on a drug hitherto not used other than in medicines bought on prescription ('It calms the nerves that make you cough').

But during this whole period the agency's greatest product was John Hobson himself and he was sold as successfully as Bristol cigarettes or Sunfresh Orange.

It was in 1959 that this policy changed, indeed that the whole of the agency changed. Even the name changed. John Hobson and Partners disappeared. Hobson, Bates and Partners took their place. Hobson and Metcalf between them had decided the time had come to accept an invitation to sell out to the Ted Bates Company, one of the largest and probably the toughest advertising agencies on Madison Avenue.

There was general consternation in the advertising world, for it was made clear that the deal was a hundred per cent outright sale. Exactly how much Hobson and Metcalf made out of it has not been revealed and is never likely to be.

All that either of them will say is that the deal involved making them both directors of the main Bates group, giving them a substantial number of its shares and leaving them in charge of their own staff in London. It is this last point which probably provides the key to why the sell-out has subsequently worked as well as it has.

But the sale occurred at a time when the so-called 'American invasion' of British advertising had become a tender topic for most British advertising men. American money as well as American methods seemed to be forcing their way into the London agency business. Now the defection of the most thriving new agency in the country seemed a direct affront to the mood of advertising nationalism which was beginning to spring up.

'It was an act of treason,' George Pope, the Secretary of the NPA told us. 'Moreover, it was done purely for money, purely for money.'

However, there were several other reasons, beside mere money, that made the two men act as they did. And since there has been so much talk recently about the sale of advertising agencies to the States, the story behind the sale of John Hobson and Partners is worth examining.

Late in 1958, John Metcalf was telephoned by a man he had never met called Rosser Reeves. Reeves, as readers of Martin Mayer's *Madison Avenue USA* will recall, was at this time head of the Bates agency and one of the high priests of modern American advertising. He had achieved fame as 'the first man to put a breath claim on a tooth paste', by inventing the line 'it cleans your breath while it cleans your teeth', for Colgate. He had produced General Eisenhower in the controversial spot commercials that helped him win the Presidency of the United States. And he had played a key part in building his own agency into the leading packaged goods agency in the country.

But at this time the Bates organization, unlike most other big American agencies, had no offices abroad from which it could carry out advertising for its clients in foreign markets. By now this had become a serious handicap, and Reeves's visit was intended to do something about it.

Metcalf already had a lunch appointment when Reeves telephoned, but the reputation if not the intention of Reeves had preceded him, and Metcalf told his secretary to postpone his other appointments and hurried across to his favourite corner table at the White Tower to find that Reeves, as he says, 'looked exactly like a younger Harold Lloyd with a hangover. After he had talked for four minutes,' he adds, 'I also understood why this man had captained the 1955 American chess team in Moscow.' In addition he got a very distinct impression that the Ted Bates Company wished to buy John Hobson and Partners.

This should not have been entirely a matter for surprise since Hobson had already been approached by Ted Bates himself during a visit to the States. As Hobson says, 'I admired Bates but I had not been convinced that I should sell. The agency was my company and my name. I did not want to trade either.'

But when Metcalf had his lunch with Reeves the situation had changed and there were three sound reasons for listening to the proposals of the Ted Bates company. The first was that already several other big American agencies had been putting out feelers as to whether the agency was for sale, but none was as interesting or important as Bates. The second reason was that the question of the ownership of the agency was becoming something of a nightmare for both Hobson and Metcalf.

For the same N P A rules which had made it impossible for the agency to become a public company when it began, now operated to keep it part of the personal estate of the two principal shareholders, and a month or so before both of them had had an over-dramatic reminder of what this might mean. At five o'clock one morning Metcalf had been summoned to Hampstead Hospital to find John Hobson unconscious and badly injured after driving his Jaguar into a tree at speed. As Metcalf says, 'for a moment John's life was touch-and-go and I realized that if he died it really was the end of the agency. The Inland Revenue would have assessed his holding in it at its real value as part of his estate and it would have had to have been sold off to meet the death duties. There would have been very little for his widow and the agency itself would have gone bankrupt.' Hobson realized this just as well as Metcalf, and both men knew that if the agency was sold to an American agency (and under N P A rules there was nothing to stop this) its continuity at any rate would be assured.

The third reason that made both Hobson and Metcalf inclined to favour the blandishments of Reeves provide an interesting example of the form ambition can take among the heads of successful advertising agencies. 'Ultimately,' says Metcalf, 'for the major operators in the agency business – as in any other business – advertising comes to take the form of an extremely serious high-level game, in which the bigger the chips you have, the more development there is. In this way it's like poker. Just as you can have a nice game of poker for sixpence a time, so you can have a nice little agency and live very comfortably on nice little accounts. But after a while you want the big chips, and in advertising there are only a certain number of really big clients for the really serious challenging game. By now we knew that the big clients of the future would want an international agency. As far as we could see, joining the Bates Group was the quickest way of becoming this.'

These at any rate are the reasons given for the sale in 1959 of John Hobson and Partners to the Ted Bates Company. The immediate result for the London agency was to bring an additional £1 million worth of billings from Bates's clients selling in the British market. But the London agency also gained something else from the merger – an official advertising philosophy.

For Reeves, in addition to being one of the most successful copywriters on Madison Avenue, had also become in his time one of its most influential dogmatists. In a country that likes its reasons for doing things cut and dried, Rosser Reeves had cut and dried the advertising business into a theory of his own. He called it the U S P – the Unique Selling Proposition.

It was this that in a series of spectacular presentations he attempted to put over to his new British colleagues. And it was this, by the time he had finished, that really turned John Hobson and Partners into Hobson, Bates and Partners – the one doctrinally correct U S P agency in London.

Reeves has explained his theory, with a wealth of incidental detail, in his highly readable credo *Reality in Advertising*. The essence of it is that every successful advertisement should give a reason for buying a product by making a definite proposition to the customer. And the three things this proposition should have are firstly that it should promise a distinct benefit, secondly that this benefit should be unique, and thirdly, that it should actually sell the product.

Certainly for the sort of rapid-turnover, mass-selling grocery products in which the agency had been making its name, the yard-stick which the U S P theory provided was a considerable help towards producing the uncluttered, immediately appealing, functional advertising which was necessary.

After the Reeves indoctrination, it was interesting to see how John Hobson reacted. At first he was uncomfortable about the 'Stalinization' of his agency, and as he admits 'went through a hell of a period for six months'. Then he seemed to emerge as one of the most dedicated U S P men in the business. 'In all our advertising,' he says, 'we believe in logical analytical thinking which will get us to the point where we can distil the major selling proposition for the public. Now this major selling proposition can be almost anything provided it is the one thing your competitor can't say or hasn't said. And it must be a positive sales winning proposition, which demonstrably gets you the maximum sales.'

To start with Hobson, Bates seemed inescapably wedded to the strict letter of this new doctrine of theirs (although even then some cynical outsiders could not always see that the agency's approach was so very different now that they had discovered the U S P from what it was before.)

The agency had been selling Antussin cough treatment pre-Reeves on the line 'It calms the nerves that make you cough' – a classic example of a watertight U S P if ever there was one. It started advertising Cadbury's Bournvita, post-Reeves on the slightly softer U S P 'Helps you relax the natural way'.

Not surprisingly, the U S P was at its most effective where there really was something unique about the product which was straightforward enough to appeal to the common sense of the buying public without too much hidden persuading, and one of the agency's star accounts is for Tuf boots and shoes.

In Britain the boot and shoe market has always traditionally been dominated by the large chains of retail stores. There has virtually never been a successful manufacturers' brand of footwear, and when the small provincial manufacturer who made Tuf boots came to the agency in 1956 offering a £12,000 a year advertising budget, Hobson saw the possibilities at once of applying in this market the theories and methods of modern marketing that apply in other packaged goods trades, and of using advertising to turn the Tuf name into the trade mark of a nationally branded product.

He was able to suggest this because the manufacturing process Tuf used was sufficiently different from that of ordinary boots to produce a harder wearing article than anything else on the market.

Pre-Reeves, the agency worked out the U S P's 'Guaranteed for Six Months' and 'No Repair Bills', for all the Tuf advertising, and on the strength of this the brand has developed until today the Tuf brand has ten per cent of the entire boot and shoe market in the country and has become the leading major brand to force distribution into the big retail chains.

But as anyone who has anything to do with dogma soon discovers, one of the difficulties of attempting to run your life by the strict letter of a theory is that before long it usually becomes necessary to re-interpret it or perish. Currently, this seems to be the point Hobson, Bates have reached with the U S P.

To be fair, John Hobson seems to have been aware of this for some time. As early as 1961 he was explaining to us that, 'if there is not an objective U S P in your product, you had better make a unique virtue out of finding a subjective U S P for it. If there is nothing unique you can say about the product, you must try to make people buy certain satisfactions or combinations of satisfactions associated with it. People,' he added, 'can even be sold the subjective pleasure of buying. Certainly U S P advertising leaves you free to play on people's feelings. That's the advertiser's job.'

The implications of this with its tacit approval of mood advertising, already seem a long way from the strict letter of the original Reeves doctrine. But even so, one of the agency's campaigns, for Double Diamond, with the slogan, 'Double Diamond – the Beer the Men Drink', looks like marking the point at which the U S P has finally been interpreted out of existence.

The man in charge of the Double Diamond account is Michael English, a senior director of Hobson, Bates. English is another Cambridge man, the son of a Lincolnshire school master, who came down with a

First in 1948 and went straight into advertising. He refuses to admit that the new campaign is in any way an abandonment of U S P theory. 'It's nonsense to talk about the strict letter of the Reeves doctrine. That is a complete misunderstanding of what the U S P is about. Reeves's book is a description of how he runs his agency, and why it succeeds. He believes that advertising is a serious business, and his book debunks the hordes of admen whose actions show that they think otherwise.' English stresses continually the need for the examination of facts, for logical analysis in taking a comprehensive marketing view before thinking of an advertising campaign.

'As for the U S P itself it can come from many sources – directly out of a product quality, or a secondary feature such as the packaging, or out of the social circumstances in which it is consumed. Just because the processes are rational and logical, the proposition itself need not be shaped in such a form.'

The Double Diamond campaign seems to be a case in point. The brand was first nationally advertised by the London Press Exchange for Ind Coope after the end of the war and the advertising centred around a little man in a bowler hat for whom, as the copy explained, 'A Double Diamond Works Wonders'. By showing the little man in a number of Walter Mitty-like situations, the advertising managed to convey the inducing idea that this was a drink with something special about it, without ever producing the dangerous, guilt overtones that are anathema in all beer advertising – that it could actually make anyone drunk.

On the strength of the little man and the wonders he worked (together with the rise in power of the Ind Coope group), Double Diamond became Britain's top-selling pale ale.

Hobson, Bates took over the account in 1963 and the area for a U S P that the agency finally hit on was the least objective but hardest wearing of all the claims of beer advertising – its manliness.

The original memorandum Hobson, Bates submitted to the brewers about Double Diamond mentioned the fact that 'the drinker of Double Diamond is middle-aged and middle-class. He is not a solitary man but he is a man's man, a man among men; he has passed through his drinking apprenticeship, his tastes are fully mature.'

So instead of hairy arms on the bar there were tobogganists on the Cresta run and yachtsmen in sweat shirts. Instead of the eight-pint voice of the traditional beer drinker, the commercials ended with a dead-pan announcement, 'Double Diamond – the Beer the Men Drink.' Instead of the maleness of the saloon bar, this was the maleness of men seeing themselves as they would like to be in a world of affluence and jet-age leisure – surfing, parachuting, water-ski-ing, mountaineering.

Hobson, Bates believe that if Double Diamond is to win the sort of place in the mid-1960s that it certainly had in the mid-fifties it can only be done by linking it with the idea of 'the really tough upper-class male', the man who, as they say, 'is so tough that he can drink his beer out of a bottle and far from losing caste, actually gain it.'

10. It's Lonely at the Top

'No one,' wrote Anatole France in a phrase which might almost stand as a motto for the advertising industry, 'gives so much as he who gives hope.' For the adman is concerned with our dreams. One of his surest ways of selling is to enhance the way we see ourselves and to suggest that we become worthy of this enhancement if only we buy his product.

As a rule it is all fairly obvious. The man who drinks Bass, suggests the Bass advertisement, is a manly man and as the Bass drinker reminds himself of that sacred name there is the memory of all those Bass posters with those pink, knotted stevedores' hands to assure him that manliness is indeed the outstanding quality of the man who calls for Bass.

'When a mother cares,' coo the gentle voices of the Persil commercials, summoning up the promise of gentle, caring motherhood for the harassed housewife who picks the right soap powder. The girl who uses Drene shampoo is given hair '*he* will want to touch'. The woman who gives her husband Weetabix instead of a full cooked breakfast is assured that this really does provide 'square meal nourishment', and the mother who puts margarine on her children's sandwiches has her ego soothed with the wholesome picture of the farmhouse world of Summer County freshness.

The psychology behind these dream appeals is fascinating. For it seems that the flattery can be as blatant, the dream-world as unreal as the imagination of the copywriter cares to make it. People can pretend to discount it, and insist that they would never be stupid enough to believe in it, but provided the admen have got our dreams right it appears that we act on them.

For advertisers the late 1950s seem to have been a record time for the dream appeal. The new affluence was finally giving the copywriters something to get their teeth into and as examples of how they began it is instructive to look at two of the most original dream campaigns of all. One of them worked. The other, for somewhat unusual reasons, became an almost legendary failure.

a) 'Top People Take The Times'

Printing House Square, as it used to be in the days before they rebuilt it, had an air of placid invulnerability which exceeded, if such was possible, the air of placid invulnerability in the pages of *The Times* itself. But in the middle 1950s appearances at Printing House Square were deceptive and the calm covered a good deal of managerial activity. For it was clear that there could be a crisis around the corner if something was not done to avoid it.

Since the war all newspapers had been living in the unreal world of newsprint rationing and in 1950 the decision was taken as a matter of policy to cut circulation by 25,000 rather than reduce the size of the paper. Then in 1952 the price had risen from threepence to fourpence and circulation took another jolt, falling from 235,000 for the year 1951 to 230,000 in 1952. By 1953 it was down to 223,000 and by 1955 it had reached 220,000.

All this was bad enough. *The Times* had always prided itself (and sold itself) on the quality rather than the quantity of its readership, but no national daily with the overheads *The Times* had to carry could possibly allow itself to become that much of a minority paper. As a member of the circulation staff admitted, 'if we had allowed things to go on as they were, circulation would probably have levelled out around 200,000 by the early 1960s. That would certainly have affected our advertising rates and threatened the whole economy of the newspaper.'

But as the management of *The Times* knew perfectly well, it was questionable whether the paper would be able to count on even as comfortable a decline as this. Sooner or later newsprint would have to come off ration and a tougher, more competitive era in newspaper publishing would begin.

As early as 1954 the paper had begun to consider what was to be done when this occurred. A survey was commissioned through the paper's advertising agency, the London Press Exchange, to find out the crucial facts of how people regarded *The Times* and what made them buy it. This survey was carried out by L P E's own subsidiary, Research Services, under Dr Mark Abrams, and it revealed a widespread feeling that *The Times* was too expensive, that it was physically too large for busy people to deal with, and that it was dull.

For the management of *The Times* not the least disturbing thing about these 'misconceptions' was that they could not be overcome by any dramatic change in *The Times* itself. It is interesting that sometime before this the *Manchester Guardian* (as it then called itself), had also engaged Dr Abrams and his researchers to discover what their readers thought about *them*, and had remodelled the entire paper on the lines of his findings.[38]

The Times, on the other hand, felt that nothing like this was possible in their case. The editor, Sir William Haley, who had been appointed in 1952, had been giving the staff and the style of the paper as much of a shake-up as was thought advisable. But there were limits to what he could do. Dr Abrams and his researchers might reveal that people thought *The Times* was too big and expensive, but if it was to remain a paper of record, printing tripos lists, law reports, and the detailed results of Oxford and Cambridge college boat races, it always would be rather a handful for a busy man to manage and could hardly become cheaper. They might also show that people thought it was dull, but it is always difficult for a newspaper to prevent at least the appearance of dullness if it avoids divulging the names of its main contributors and correspondents, and no one at Printing House Square was willing to agree to that.

Because of all this, and because they were reasonable men, the management of *The Times* decided that if *The Times* could not be changed, it had at least to be made palatable by the time newsprint rationing ended. They also decided that their best hope of doing this was through advertising and between 1954 and 1956 they and the L P E tried to decide how. The principle was plain enough. Somehow the advertising would have to play up that core of inner knowledge which *The Times* had always prided itself on giving its readers.

But the task was a delicate one for any advertising agency and the pilot campaigns the L P E prepared for *The Times* and tried out in the provincial press scarcely showed the agency at its most inspired.

One advertisement, which only appeared in provincial newspapers, showed two dyspeptic-looking gentlemen staring incredulously at each other above the copy line 'I saw it in *The Times*'.

Another from this period showed a grey top hat and a pair of gloves with the slogan beneath it, "Men who make opinion read *The Times*'.

As one member of *The Times* management put it, 'we felt that campaigns like this were not strong enough to carry us through three years of heavy competition and put on the 20,000 readers we needed.' And by the beginning of 1956 it was clear that these years of competition were near at hand. Sir William Haley had told the management that he felt that editorially the paper was now ready to be promoted and *The*

[38] These included suggestions for a change of typography, for more signed articles, more women's features, more sport, less purely Manchester news, more cultural pieces and more personality articles.

Times itself, to its great credit, had brought the ending of all restrictions on newsprint nearer by its decision to start printing on mechanical paper, which had no restrictions on it, instead of newsprint.

The only problem that remained was exactly how *The Times* should be advertised. It was a problem that became increasingly serious. No one was particularly happy about the suggestions the L P E had put forward and throughout the spring there seems to have been a great deal of discussion about this hypothetical campaign both at Printing House Square and at the L P E, for by now all suggestions were welcome.

But it is hard to believe that the advertising for *The Times* would have developed even remotely as it did had it not been for a chance meeting early in June in the Kardomah café in Fleet Street.

One of the men who had been involved in the advertising discussion from the start had been Stanley Morison, the typographer and historian of the paper in five volumes which he had finished writing some time before. During a long and successful career in Fleet Street he had got to know almost everyone of any importance in the newspaper business and it was natural that when, at the Kardomah that summer day, he ran into a man called Saxon Mills he should have done more than simply pass the time of day with him.

Indeed Saxon Mills was not an entire stranger at Printing House Square since, earlier that year, he had consulted on another matter with George Pope, then Assistant Manager and now Deputy General Manager of *The Times*.

In his time G. H. Saxon Mills had been one of the best of the old school of copywriters in Britain. He had been copy director at Crawfords where he had invented campaigns like Mr Barratt, the bowler-hatted shoe salesman who built up the fortunes of the shoe empire by politely inviting the public to 'Walk the Barratt way'. At Crawford's, Mills had been very much the disciple of the agency's founder, Sir William Crawford and even wrote his biography. After Crawford's death, Mills had moved on to Colman, Prentis and Varley.

But fashion seemed to be against Saxon Mills and his style of copywriting, and when Stanley Morison met him that day he was out of a regular job. It was largely out of kindness that Morison asked him whether he would care to tender some suggestions for the forthcoming advertising campaign for *The Times*. The results were somewhat startling.

Morison sent him the original readership survey, and on July 20th this sad-faced, rather dumpy man in a tweed suit presented himself at Printing House Square with a four-page manifesto on how he thought *The Times* advertising should be carried out. Phrases from this document are still remembered at *The Times*. 'Central advertising themes,' wrote Mills with typical gusto, 'are rarely dignified. We must not emulate the old lady who whispered her wares in the market for fear her friends should hear her. Effective advertising,' he went on reassuringly, 'need never be vulgar,' but, he added 'there must be red blood in it as well as blue blood.'

Encouraged by such fighting talk, the publicity committee of *The Times* sent Mills off for the rest of the summer with the task of preparing a brochure, which could be handed to visitors, showing the sort of people he thought *The Times* should appeal to. The idea of this seems to have been to see what Mills really could produce. By early autumn the outline of his brochure was finished and at the beginning of October the publicity committee of *The Times* met Mills again to discuss it.

For *The Times* this was to be a historic little meeting. One by one Mills passed the pages of his brochure around the table. They showed the sort of people he thought of as reading *The Times* and gave the reasons why they did. There was a youngish barrister, a trade union leader, a woman parliamentary candidate. On each was the slogan in bold letters, 'Top People Take The Times'.

At first a lot of eyebrows seem to have been raised and, although no one actually accused Mills of vulgarity, this was what several of the people who considered his ideas in the days that followed were clearly worried about. But Mills in his canny way had clearly sized up his new clients and had prepared his ground well.

His earlier remarks about old ladies who are afraid to shout their wares in the market-place had gone home, and the management of *The Times* was in a mood to shout as loud as it had to if shouting could produce the readers it needed. Also time was running short, and Mills's campaign was head and shoulders above anything that anyone else, either at the L P E or Printing House Square, could suggest. But most important of all, Mills's theme about Top People managed to crystallize everything that *The Times* and the early L P E advertisements had been trying to hint about the newspaper but had never quite had the courage to say. As George Pope put it with disarming simplicity, 'what Mills was saying was obviously true. Top people, the people who manage the country, really did take *The Times*.'

'Of course it was true,' echoed another *Times* man. 'You only had to look around you and you saw the toppest chaps everywhere and they were all taking *The Times*.'

And so the campaign was mounted. The actual arrangements for it all were unusual in certain ways, for Saxon Mills was engaged by *The Times* to write most of the copy and an office was placed at his disposal in *The Times* building. Stanley Morison advised on the typography, and the L P E engaged the artists, set the copy, prepared the layouts and placed the advertisements when they were ready.

The choice of media was also made by *The Times*, Saxon Mills and the L P E in consultation. 'Remember the type of *Times* reader we were after,' said a member of the paper's circulation staff. 'A sudden increase in casual sales was no use to us. We wanted regular readers. We wanted to sell *The Times* as a habit as well as just a newspaper and we were after members of the public who were about to be recruited into the governing classes whether they were in the universities, the trade unions or whatever.'

Not surprisingly it was decided against using television. 'Television is fine for selling soap flakes but not for *The Times*. The wastage would have been colossal in meeting the sudden demand for extra copies which we would have had to prepare for, with a television campaign.'

Instead, in a campaign the size of which was quite new in newspaper advertising at this time, *The Times* prepared to place its new advertisements in the *Daily Mail*, the *Daily* and *Sunday Express*, the *Evening News* and the *Evening Standard*, the *Observer* and *The Sunday Times*. The *Daily Herald* was ruled out because of what was thought to be the excessive size of its C2, D and E readership (apparently the young ambitious trade unionists Mills was so keen to attract were thought to do their reading elsewhere) and the *News Chronicle* because its readership was too old. £130,000 was set aside for the cost of the first year of the campaign.

The first of the advertisements went up on the hoardings at the beginning of 1957. It showed a success figure to end all success figures, a middle-aged man with the shy smile of worldly satisfaction about to receive an honorary degree and carrying his copy of *The Times* for the occasion. Mills's slogan was underneath in Times Roman to drive the point home.

During the following months the rest of Mills's menagerie made their appearance – the barrister, the scientist, the lady candidate, and the rising young trade unionist. But long before then the campaign seemed to have run into trouble. Everyone was against it. Letters poured in to the editor accusing the advertising of snobbery and lack of taste. Vicky put Top People into his cartoons and there was a skit on them at the London Palladium.

From the outside it looked as if the management of *The Times*, not quite aware of what was happening, had been cajoled by the wily old Mills into a campaign that had then back-fired. In fact, the exact opposite seems to have been the case. In the first place everyone involved in the campaign at Printing House Square was aware of what they were up to and quite prepared for the reaction it got. Even Sir William Haley, although he was not directly involved in promotion, was shown the advertisements several months before they appeared and his suggestions were incorporated in them.

And in the second place, the management seem to have been delighted at the fuss the advertising caused. Now that Mills's old lady had actually got into the market-place and found her voice, she was delighted that people were actually taking notice of her.

But the most interesting thing of all about Mills's Top People idea was that it worked, and that it did so despite all the ridicule and resentment *The Times* seemed to be acquiring in the process. How did this happen?

The obvious answer is that the campaign simply got the paper noticed and that the fuss alone attracted the new readers. This is possible but unlikely. Notoriety alone would hardly have put on the 17,353 increase in regular sales the Audit Bureau of Circulation was crediting *The Times* with at the end of 1957, nor would notoriety have sustained the campaign the seven years it has run since it started.

A more credible answer is that Mills really was doing something more original than it seemed when he invented the Top People campaign and that he was selling this most august of newspapers on its dream appeal as resolutely as if it had been a margarine, a shampoo or a bottled beer. 'The point of the campaign,' said a member of *The Times* publicity committee, 'was to appeal to the latent ambition in all men', and it was doing it by showing a series of situations which had no possible connection with real life. Would anyone who had the remotest connection with the law be taken in by this priggish young barrister being bowed to by his unctuous and elderly client? Could anyone with a grain of humour about himself fall for a copy line which read, 'to take *The Times* every day shows that you reckon yourself a big man. And it may well be the cause of you becoming one'?

But the great value of the dream appeal for the advertiser is that however much people may discount it and pretend to react against it, they often act upon it provided the dream is right. A kind of residuum of persuasion remains when the laughter has died down. It was this residuum which changed the fortunes of *The Times*.

Mills and the management of *The Times* showed great skill in the way they managed this dream of Top People in the period after the campaign had made its first impact. The first advertisements were designed to present the Top People message loud and clear. This was the dream of success at its most unselfconscious and Top People were shown in a sort of cloud-cuckooland of top activity – launching ships, laying down the law and presenting prizes.

Then, very rapidly, the advertising became more stylized, as if the men behind it were admitting that they knew that it was just a bit of a joke, and by June 1957, Jean Carlu had produced the first of the overtly funny Top People ads. From then until 1960 (when the paper suddenly felt the need of a more sober image appropriate to the serialization of

Sir Anthony Eden's memoirs), the Top People campaign was allowed to go on laughing at itself.

It was at about this time that the men behind the campaign had their first real warnings about it. The L P E and *The Times* had been wondering for some time about the paper's reputation among the young meritocrats, the young scientists and dons and rising civil servants Mills had originally seen as the potentially top people his campaign should reach.

Once more Research Services and Dr Abrams were called on to help, and two psychologists were engaged to interview a sample of exactly the sort of rising executives *The Times* was interested in reaching. The sample included administrative grade civil servants, several young economists, university lecturers and several successful young business men. They were interviewed at length in groups of three or four and once the psychologists had discovered what they needed to know about their background, their work and their ambitions, they got down to discussing the heart of the matter – what they thought about *The Times.*

As the discussions went on it was soon clear that the newspaper roused considerable hostility and that almost all of this stemmed precisely from the idea of Top People. The interviewees were chosen from the widest possible range of background but almost all of them registered the same dislike of what they felt was the snobbery and the bowler hat and umbrella image within the advertising itself. At the same time they generally agreed that technically *The Times* was an excellent newspaper.

The findings of these psychologists confirmed *The Times* in their feeling that Top People had had their day and during most of 1960 the campaign was rested. But Saxon Mills's brain-child was too successful to be forgotten in a hurry, and no one seemed able to think up anything which quite equalled it. And so, in one form or another, both we and *The Times* look like continuing to live with Top People for a long time to come.

b) 'You're never alone with a Strand'
'Sunk without trace, I'm afraid. The most memorable advertising campaign in Britain since the war and it failed in only one thing. It just didn't sell the product. Otherwise it was perfect.'

Such is the verdict of John May,[39] formerly copy-chief of S. H. Benson at the time of the campaign which he concocted almost single-handed, for a new cigarette Wills brought out in 1960 called Strand. As a criticism of this curious campaign it can hardly be bettered.

Certainly the whole idea behind the campaign of 'You're never alone with a Strand' is instructive on a number of counts. In the first place it is

[39] John May left Benson's in July 1964 and is now a director of Connell, May and Seavenson.

probably the best case on record of the way a campaign can sell itself so successfully that the unfortunate product gets overlooked in the process. It is also a fascinating example of the odd Pygmalion-like relationship which can grow up between a copy writer and the campaign he creates. And most important of all, it shows what happens when an advertiser tries to sell a product by associating it with a dream but picks the wrong one.

To understand how all this occurred it is necessary to know a little about the man behind the campaign.

In the world of copywriters there are more than enough phoney characters, but John May is the genuine article. He is bird-like, voluble, with bright blue eyes and a blue hop-sack suit with three-inch cuffs. His family was all in the theatre and he used to admit lingering ambitions for the stage himself. In fact his first serious attempt to make a living after the army was to write. It was when this failed that he came into advertising. But instead of conforming to the organization world of a big agency he has managed to remain more than ever himself. He is energetic, highly-strung, married, the sort of man who never puts on weight however successful he becomes. And at thirty-eight John May is very successful indeed.

He is a director of his firm. He owns a house in Pimlico and, quite apart from the Strand campaign, he wrote several of the best campaigns Benson's ever produced. For John May has the knack of personalizing whatever he is trying to sell. There are not many writers who can do it, and at the moment Jeremy Bullmore of J. Walter Thompson is probably his greatest rival at it. It is a difficult technique, and rather a chancy one for its success depends, as Thompson discovered when they created Katie for their Oxo campaign, on picking a character who exactly embodies a wide and seemingly contradictory range of personal and social qualities.

May achieved this most successfully when he invented a woman called Mrs 1970 to sell oil-fired central heating for Shell-Mex and BP. On that occasion he had nine months of concentrated research to draw on before he went out to pick the woman who would personify 'everything we wanted to get over to the public about heating'.

Like the good writer *manqué* that he was, May took immense trouble working out an entire fictional existence for this woman before he had even set eyes on her. She had to live in the suburbs with a decent, appreciative, kindly husband earning a variable but adequate amount of money each week. She had to have two children, 'rising to three when we wanted to show the value of central heating for babies'. She had to be attractive enough for women to want to identify themselves with her, but not so attractive that she would alienate them by over-exciting their husbands.

'Her appeal,' says May, 'had to be as wide as humanly possible, for we had worked out that there were three and a half million owner-occupied houses in the country that were our potential customers. Because of this Mrs 1970 had to be identifiable as a sales manager's wife to the chap living at the top of Wimbledon Hill and as a sales manager's wife to the chap living at the bottom. Her morals had to be above reproach.'

But when May was presented with the task of working out a campaign to sell Strand cigarettes, he had nothing like this time or this research to draw on. It was a campaign that came, almost literally, off his three-inch cuffs.

The idea of the cigarette itself had been in the air for some time. It was a small, fairly cheap filter cigarette selling at 3s 5d for twenty, against 4s 6d for a packet of Senior Service. But it was clear from the start that more than with most cigarettes, the success of Strand was going to depend on whatever aura the advertising could give it. Great attention had been paid to the packet. This was the first cigarette of its price that was sold in the smart, flip-top box that expensive American cigarettes like Marlborough had first introduced into this country. And Wills was clearly out to get the younger age group, the impecunious but fashion-conscious youngster who smokes to impress his friends and show them, by the very way he produces a cigarette, that he (or she) is entirely with it.

'Everyone,' says May, 'was paying a lot of attention to that box – thought it would make it a natural, you see, for the younger market....'

Apparently there was no intention of aiming the cigarette at any particular class. 'What we were really trying to get at,' says May, 'was the younger buyer, the immediate school leaver, although mind you, officially it was no part of our job to persuade the younger generation to smoke.'

Benson had had some time to prepare the campaign, which they did along fairly conventional cigarette advertising lines. But it seems that for this particular cigarette Wills was looking for something more than conventional cigarette advertising. As things were to turn out they certainly got it.

What happened was that almost at the last moment Wills, exercising that capriciousness which is the inalienable right for every advertising client, turned down the campaign Benson had prepared. A launching date had been fixed. The tobacconists had been prepared and, somehow, something had to be done.

It was precisely the sort of situation in which a person like John May excels himself, and between lunchtime when the campaign was rejected, and the next when he was due to meet the agency account handling group to discuss what was to be done, he dreamt up the outlines of the most notorious campaign of his career. And because Wills really was looking for something new this time, which might conceivably hit the jackpot of the teenage market, they accepted. For the first time in the history of advertising, someone was actually going to try selling a product on the mass market by associating it, not with sex or manliness or social success, but with the loneliness and rejection of youth. The slogan May suggested was, 'You're never alone with a Strand'.

The whole idea was a hunch, and a last-minute hunch at that. But then far more of the successful campaigns than the agencies like to admit are hunches, and behind this particular hunch lay a considerable body of reason, experience and common sense. For, as May says, he already had a fairly good idea of the mood of the young people he was appealing to. 'Such assessments are inevitably subjective, but I thought that the mood of the young was not all that different from the mood of the late 1930s I remembered from my own childhood. They have the bomb to worry about. We had the threat of war. But the keynote of both generations is insecurity. The only difference is that whereas, before, this exploded into a hypermanic jollity, this insecurity now seems to be producing a hyperconscious (his word) loneliness, along with a slightly vicious and entirely independent way of living.

'Translate that into a television commercial, wed it with your product, and by all the laws of logic you have got your advertisement centred exactly where you want it. Theoretically at any rate, you should have an advertising mix that should sell you an awful lot of cigarettes.' It was a theory which he and Wills were prepared to set about turning into reality.

To do so, they made no use of research, 'apart from the purely statistical stuff about the state of the market'. This seems to have been partly because of time, partly because of the nature of the campaign, and partly because of May's own slightly unfashionable ideas on the value of motivation research to the copywriter. 'No doubt,' he says, 'if you grill a married woman of thirty-seven with two children and an income of £650 a year for three hours on the significance of the baked bean, you will get some pretty strange results before you are finished, but these are not necessarily the reasons that make a housewife buy baked beans when she goes to her grocer.'

Instead he set out to personalize the whole idea of loneliness. 'This,' he says, 'is the age of personality, so naturally I tend to personalize my copy wherever I can.' And just as he had attempted to create an ideal woman to express all the virtues of central heating for his Shell-Mex advertising, so he now set about making a fictional hero for Strand cigarettes who would embody the maximum appeal to lonely youngsters.

It did not take him long to find what he was looking for. He had always watched a lot of television and was a keen cinema and pop music

E

fan. Everywhere he looked he saw the same sort of character emerging as the new style hero of the young. He was James Dean and the early Marlon Brando. He was John Cassavetes playing Johnnie Staccato in the television serial. He was the Frank Sinatra he saw staring at him from the sleeve of the LP of *Only the Lonely* – 'a lonely, rejected, beat figure who seemed to be becoming the idol of the young'.

'Sinatra was the prototype of the man I had in mind. Loneliness had made him a millionaire, I didn't see why it shouldn't sell us some cigarettes.'

Having made up his mind over the sort of character he was looking for, May's next job was to find him in real life. This took some time. It had been decided that the campaign was to run primarily on television, so that he needed an actor rather than the normal run of advertising male model and after several weeks of auditions and rejections, he picked on a twenty-eight-year-old actor called Terence Brook to play the part he needed.

In appearance at any rate, Brook fitted the bill to perfection. He had an uncanny resemblance to the late James Dean. He could look tough yet lonely, rejected and still defiant, innocent but with the air of a young man who has had it all.

It was now that May really began to enter into the part he had created. He is understandably diffident about the extent to which he modelled the situations of his lonely man on his own experiences. But he admits that he put a great deal of himself into the commercials he wrote.

'In those days I had got into the habit myself of walking around London late at night, and the loneliest thing that ever happened to me was to find myself along by Gloucester Road Station at about three o'clock one morning, and suddenly hear music coming from a lighted basement window where a group of young things were having a ball.'

This formed the basis of one commercial in which Brook was filmed in battered hat and weatherproof, leaning against the wall of Chelsea Embankment watching a lighted window on the other side of the street. In his loneliness his one inseparable companion was his Strand cigarette.

May then remembered another time when he had felt very lonely on Brighton Beach. 'Sea, you know, is a terribly lonely thing,' and another commercial was shot there. 'I soon began,' he says, 'working on the principle that the loneliest place of all is the place where other people are enjoying themselves.'

And in all these situations, Brook was seen lighting a cigarette. 'The cigarette is part of his loneliness and lighting it is his symbolic act of independence.'

By cigarette market standards, the Strand campaign was of strictly marginal importance (Player's at that time were selling around 350 million a month against roughly 15 million of Guards, which were Strand's nearest rival). But from the moment the first commercial was shown, the reaction it got was out of all relation to its importance. May's hunch about the impact of his hero was soon proved to have erred on the side of caution. Terence Brook was a wow.

Before long he had a fan club of his own. Letters arrived in batches offering him marriage 'and several less respectable forms of enjoyment'. Pye Radio asked him to make a record for them and when the *Daily Mirror* held a poll among teenagers for their man of the month, the man with the Strand came out at the top.

In terms of audience reaction John May had probably created the most successful advertising campaign since the war, but nobody bought the cigarettes. Or perhaps this is a slight exaggeration – quite a few people bought them at first and went on buying. According to one worldly-wise old marketing man Strand had its greatest sales among the ranks of middle-aged, childless women who felt an overpowering urge to mother this lonely young man in the commercials. But the young people, for whom the cigarette had been produced and who responded to Brook with such enthusiasm kept their distance and stuck firmly to their Woodbines, Senior Service and tipped Gauloises.

The commercials ran for several months, and then were not renewed. Some press advertising was carried on 'in a somewhat lower key', and then petered out as well. The campaign died, although the cigarette is still being made, and you still occasionally see a display bill of lonely Mr Brook and his Strand cigarettes in the windows of the sort of small tobacconists which are kept by old ladies in the dingier parts of South London.

But why did it happen? What went wrong? For John May, the untimely death of what is undoubtedly still his favourite campaign is a matter of mystery as well as of personal sadness. 'I still think it *should* have worked,' he says ruefully. 'After all, the lonely man really was the idol of the young. They dressed like him, tried to behave like him. Why shouldn't they have smoked the cigarettes he smoked as well?'

There are several possible explanations. One is that however much the young may admire rejection in the abstract, very few actually want to label themselves as rejects in the eyes of their friends. Another is that the idea was too unsubtle for a generation which has grown a good deal subtler in its personal ideals than the older generation often believes. Another is that beneath the show of rebellion and rejection, the young are good conformists at heart. The fact that at the time of the Strand campaign the current orthodoxy happened to be centred on the rebel without a cause did not mean that they were all longing to be outcasts and rebels themselves.

Or perhaps the real answer is that given by one of the few teenagers we could find who had actually smoked a Strand for himself. 'Perhaps,' he said cautiously, 'it just wasn't a very good smoke at the price.'

11. 'The most prosperous agency'

Only two of London's big agency bosses favour monogrammed shirts. One is Patrick Dolan. The other is Jack Wynne-Williams, chairman of Masius International, managing director and controlling shareholder in Masius, Wynne-Williams (known till July 1964 as Masius and Fergusson).

The resemblance does not end there. Like Dolan, Wynne-Williams is pre-eminently a salesman – and a salesman of a particularly dedicated type. 'I wouldn't smoke cigarettes advertised by a rival agency,' he once said. 'They would not taste right.' This dedication has brought him, among other things, a Rolls, a 600-acre estate in Suffolk, a flat in Down Street and a collection of fine paintings which includes three Epsteins.

His agency, situated south of Piccadilly in St James's Place, has a top executive floor which is furnished with an opulent elegance not even Dolan can match. And Wynne-Williams has Dolan's thoroughbred toughness, as evident in his size (he played forward for the London Irish, boxed as an amateur heavyweight for the Belsize and used to act as a steward at some of Churchill's political meetings before the 1931 election) as it is in his manner.

Yet Wynne-Williams is also the one big agency boss who has run contrary to the tide of American take-over which Dolan typifies. He went into Masius and Fergusson at a time when it was controlled by an American, Mike Masius, worked for him for ten years, and when Masius died Wynne-Williams succeeded him. What is more, he has been a good deal more successful than most of the American invaders; Masius, Wynne-Williams is now one of the fastest-growing advertising empires in London.

There is a monolithic simplicity about Wynne-Williams' own career; he has spent his entire business life selling things to people. From Stoneyhurst he went first as a trainee to a Shell company, Asiatic Petroleum, and then to J. Wix, the makers of Kensitas cigarettes as a van salesman. Soon he was boss of the company's London district. It was while he was with Wix that he first met Mike Masius. They became life-long friends. This, of course, was long before the days of Masius and Fergusson – Masius was then Albert Lasker's man in London as head of Lord and Thomas's European business. Because of the kidnapping scare which swept America in the mid-1930s, Lasker sent his son Edward out of the country to do his sales training. Edward came to London and it was Wynne-Williams who trained him.

Both connections proved useful. Wynne-Williams soon turned to Masius for advice and help in finding a better job, and Masius told him that Pepsodent, whom the agency served, were looking for a new general manager. Though he was only twenty-three, Wynne-Williams got the job, was made managing director a year later and stayed with the company until 1946.

Lever Brothers had bought out Pepsodent, and Wynne-Williams – 'I'm not a big organization chap by nature' – left. There were plenty of opportunities, but Wynne-Williams had begun to think that he should raise enough capital to go into business on his own account. A friend was pressing him to go to Brazil to manage a department store there, and he was prepared to pay handsomely. He offered Wynne-Williams £5,000 a year, then £10,000 and was twice turned down. But he was persistent; what would persuade Wynne-Williams to go, he asked? Wynne-Williams put up what he imagined were impossible terms –'a percentage of the profits, a sizeable proportion of the equity and a very big salary' – but they were accepted. So he went to Brazil in January 1946 for five years, with the idea of making enough money to buy his own business.

By 1951, Mappin's store had become the biggest in Brazil with an annual turnover of £4 million, and Wynne-Williams had made himself a small fortune. He came back to London, bought a 15 per cent share in the agency from Masius, who himself had bought out Albert Lasker in 1942, and accepted a salary which was less than a tenth of his income in Brazil; when Wynne-Williams arrived at Masius and Fergusson in 1951, their billings were only £850,000 – and 60 per cent of that came from one client, Colgate. By 1964, the firm was spending £11½ million a year on behalf of their clients.

But building the business was not to be Wynne-Williams's only problem; he also had to deal with problems which affected the future existence of the agency. Mike Masius, a sick man, was anxious to keep the organization going and to pass on control to Wynne-Williams before death duties could destroy the agency. Wynne-Williams remembers talking to him as early as 1953 – at a pre-Coronation party – about how the withdrawal of Masius' capital could be achieved without destroying the agency.

At that time, Masius had control by virtue of owning 35 per cent of the 'A' shares, each of which carried double-voting powers. He wanted to retain his control *and* to realize the capital value of his investment in the agency.

Wynne-Williams's solution to this tricky problem was to go to S. G. Warburg, the merchant bankers, for help – he had known one of their top executives, Eric Korner, while he was in Brazil. Out of their conversations with the merchant bankers came what is now known as the Warburg Deal. It took four and a half years to carry through, but out of it Mike Masius got exactly what he wanted.

The details of the Deal are complex and a little obscure, but the stratagem used was simple and perfectly legal. Put crudely, it consisted of draining Masius and Fergusson of its liquid value by discontinuing the company and selling its assets to Warburg, and then creating a new company which could carry on the business with a small initial capital. Masius thus extracted his money *and* kept his agency.

The first step was to create a new, service company – with the name of Maspar Services – which took over all the assets of Masius and Fergusson. All the shareholders in the agency (who thus became shareholders in Maspar Services) then sold their shares to Warburg for £750,000 – and the proceeds were divided among them according to their holding. Masius took £263,000, Wynne-Williams, Hackett, Risdon and his other colleagues divided the rest. Maspar Services operated from the same premises as Masius and Fergusson in St James's Place. That was stage one complete; Masius had capitalized his investment.

The next move was the formation of a new company, carrying the old name of Masius and Fergusson and being in essence exactly the same thing as the old agency, minus the services which Maspar provided. The new company, however, had a capital of only £10,000 in 5s shares, and Masius needed to re-invest only a very small proportion of his money to remain the majority shareholder. At the same time, however, he gave Wynne-Williams an option on his shares at £1 each should he retire or die.

The reason the Deal took four and a half years to complete was not any doubt about its legality, but the fact that what Wynne-Williams calls 'the alphabetical chaps', the N P A and the I P A, were very reluctant to grant recognition to a new agency formed in this way. The N P A's opposition, in particular, was the factor which held things up for a long time. Finally a compromise was worked out, the N P A recognized the difficulties of the death duties situation and agreed. This was, of course, before the days when agencies could go public.

Both Masius and Wynne-Williams went through some anxious

moments as the years went by. There was the possibility of selling out to another agency, and at least once this escape route seems to have been considered. They received many bids: Bates was one, Dolan another, but accounts differ as to how far these negotiations went. Dolan says he met Masius, told him he could find the money to buy, got the backing of Jocelyn Hambro for the deal, and that the two agencies actually exchanged balance sheets through their accountants.

Wynne-Williams, on the other hand, does not think things went so far. He remembers Masius telling him that Dolan had a proposition to put to them, and going to dinner at Dolan's South Street house. Hambro was also there, and after dinner – when Hambro had gone – Dolan said he would like to buy Masius and had Hambro behind him. But Wynne-Williams says that there was no meeting of minds because Dolan was doing less than £1 million a year, and that most of his profitability lay in his P R company, Patrick Dolan Associates – 'more important,' Wynne-Williams adds, 'our approach to advertising was fundamentally different.' Whichever account is true, the N P A made the overtures irrelevant by giving recognition to the 'new' agency.

Meanwhile, Masius and Fergusson grew with astonishing rapidity. They acquired the Aspro account and later were given Rennies, helped start the boom in pet foods – they had handled Kit-E-Kat and Pal meat from the beginning – and then picked up one big consumer account after another – Mars Bars, Maltesers, Ajax, Weetabix, Libby. They helped launch Babycham, which opened up the female drink market, and Wills's Embassy, which started another phase in the cigarette coupon war. There were losses too, Quaker Oats (1953) and Pepsi-Cola (1955) among them (Wynne-Williams recalls with horror one black Saturday morning when he lost £1½ million worth of business) but despite them the agency's billings soared. More recently Masius have picked up Bisto, Cerebos, Nescafé and Hoover Keymatic among others.

Yet Masius still only has twenty-three clients. Five of them, however, are £1 million accounts and most of the twenty-three have become considerably more valuable with the years. Colgate, for instance, who were spending £750,000 in 1958, were worth £1½ million to the agency by 1962. Wynne-Williams insists that it is dedication to existing clients rather than the hunt for new business which has kept Masius prosperous. 'Our interest is in one thing,' he said. 'Market leadership for the products we have.' He then proceeded to reel off the list of firsts – 'Kit-E-Kat, the top cat food; Pal, the top canned dog food; Trill – 50 per cent of the bird seed sold in Britain; Colgate – the top dental cream; Ajax – top scourer with over 60 per cent of the market. . . .'

Masius, Wynne-Williams still do not have a new business department nor, according to Wynne-Williams himself, do they have anyone on the payroll whose job it is 'to list every major advertiser, to know the managing director, who his sister is, where he plays golf and so on'. His answer to the agency's failure to get the Ford business is simple: 'We didn't really try at the time.'

Talking about his successes in his splendidly appointed office, Wynne-Williams is all plain man as he looks at you over the top of his horn-rimmed half-spectacles. He attacks the 'chi-chi' in the advertising business: 'We don't have modern Argentinian artists doing paintings for us. We tell an agreed message strong and hard. It stands to reason that anything *avant garde* is too abstruse for advertising. Advertising is not paid to educate cultural tastes. It is paid to sell. Our creative people don't create for their own amusement.' As for himself, 'I have learnt little since I was a van salesman.'

The furniture in the room – the half-moon period desk, the superb Regency chairs, the Sheraton bureau crammed with Wynne-Williams's collection of miniature drink bottles, the mahogany case filled with his collection of crown pieces – clash curiously with this stark attitude and seem to suggest that any good van salesman should be able to make a fortune at advertising.

Yet despite Wynne-Williams's dislike of talking about advertising philosophies – 'we believe in getting on with the advertising' – the success of his agency is based on a very clear-cut philosophy, so clear-cut in fact that it amounts to immutable divine law.

Wynne-Williams describes this philosophy as 'the joint client-agency search for the Most Fertile Area, for what we call the prime benefit of the product'. The M F A, he admits, bears a strikingly close relationship to the U S P – Unique Selling Proposition[40] – philosophy first enunciated by Rosser Reeves of the American agency, Ted Bates, but he adds that even the U S P was only a restatement of the old prime benefit doctrine of Claude Hopkins.

How does the M F A work? 'If you study any product deeply enough,' he explained, 'you will find what it is that people want from it. It is this and this alone that you must play on. This is not always as easy to find as you might think, and even when you have found it, it is not always certain that your product will have it. If it hasn't, then the client has to reformulate his product.'

He illustrated the point. 'A simple case was Pal meat, which started life under the name of Meet. We wanted to call it Huntsman, but somebody else already had that. At that stage it was just chunks of meat in gravy – natural food for a dog, but after a while the sales levelled off. We thought the problem through and did a lot of research on what people feel about their dogs. Finally we decided that people wanted Pal to have something which made them feel they were doing their dogs

[40] See page 116.

good when they fed them. Our client added marrowbone jelly and the sales went up again.'

Client and agency applied the same principle to selling Trill. Research showed them that many people who own caged birds have a deep guilt feeling about keeping their pets indoors and starved of sunshine. So again, the client was persuaded to add Vitamin C to the birdseed – the so-called 'sunshine grains'.

Often, the M F A seems to be a good deal less subtle. The agency had the job of doing advertising for Brolac paint, but felt that what other agencies were claiming for their paint products was often self-evident. 'Just a waste of money to talk about colour,' said Wynne-Williams, 'like telling people that sweets are delicious, that toothpaste cleans, that soap removes dirt – these benefits are presumptive.' The most significant thing they could find out about painting – the M F A – was that when people have painted a room, they don't want to do it again in a hurry, 'Ergo,' concluded Wynne-Williams, 'the best thing you can say about paint is that it lasts and lasts and lasts – and that is what we said for Brolac.'

This single-minded search for one M F A has led to the charge that Masius's advertising tends to be unsophisticated, even banal. Wynne-Williams answers the charge with case-history after case-history. He also reacts sharply to the charge that Masius is not a creative agency. 'Our clients pay us to sell,' he said, 'not to win Layton awards, and we create ads that convey a carefully planned message. Our creative people can't come up with irrelevant jokes, however amusing, or art for art's sake. I don't know if it's good for creativity, but a lot of great art has been done under equally stringent conditions. We have some of the best creative minds in the business, but their value to us lies in their ability to keep both feet on the ground while indulging in flights of fancy. Don't forget that a lot of agencies fall foul of their creative departments. When David Ogilvy put one patch over the eye of the man in the Hathaway shirt, he put two patches over the eyes of a lot of advertising people over here. They're just looking for gimmicks all the time.'

This, then, is the lean, hard shop which Wynne-Williams runs so successfully. He is a professional in a world of amateurs, a man who sees himself as the Bradman of the advertising world. He runs a salesman's agency which prides itself on its lack of frills but which he calls 'the most prosperous agency in London'.

12. Obiter Dichter

Dr Ernest Dichter, president of the Institute for Motivational Research Inc. (headquarters: Croton-on-Hudson, New York, and twelve other offices – including London and Johannesburg) has never been quite so successful in Britain as he is in the United States and some other European countries, particularly Germany. This is partly due to the fact that motivational research has always had a rather sinister ring here; but, more important, the image of Dichter created by Vance Packard's *The Hidden Persuaders* put off a lot of British manufacturers.

The result is that though he states that he has an international turnover of roughly $1 million a year, only £30,000–£50,000 of it is earned in Britain. In America he can still ask – and get – $1000 a day for his personal advice. He is, however, also consultant to a number of important companies and agencies at a somewhat smaller fee.

Dichter first set up shop here in 1959, and he now has offices in a side-turning off the Tottenham Court Road. It is a new-looking and rather lonely outpost of the psychological advance. Ernest Dichter Associates employs eight psychologists, one psychoanalyst, and an interviewing staff of 150 – fifty of them qualified depth interviewers. Dichter himself, a squat, balding man who has still kept his German accent, only drops in for short visits every few months: at 55, he is still globe-trotting at the behest of clients who want Dichter or nothing.

In its five years in Britain, the consultancy has completed about a hundred surveys, ranging from an examination of why Englishmen polish their cars to a study of our attitudes to the use of contraceptives.

The purpose of the studies is always the same: to produce 'a really persuasive copy platform' for the client's advertising agency to work on. One of Dichter's associates added an interesting explanatory gloss: 'We are really undressing people in terms of their attitudes. We are undressing them of their rationalizations.'

According to Dichter, the rationalizations lie thicker on the ground in Britain than in most other places. 'This,' he said, 'is the most puritanical country in the world.' (Dichter's concept of puritanism sometimes seemed to be equated with a refusal to buy the goods he is trying to sell.) He cited as an example the average British woman's attitude to cosmetics.

'They're just not yet sold on the desire to stay young,' he declared ruefully. 'For the older generation here, it's still immoral to change nature. Do you know, you've got the lowest figures for the use of nail polish? The women say "that's OK for loose women, but not for me".' A study of British attitudes to central heating revealed the same characteristic: 'there was resistance to the idea because people thought it was soft.'

Britain's very high consumption of sweets and chocolates did not quite seem to match the thesis, but Dichter sees this as a major outlet for all our suppressed emotions. 'It's probably due to a higher degree of frustration,' he said. 'People canalize their vicious tendencies into candy-eating. That's why the British are the biggest sweet-eaters in the world. You're administering love to yourselves in the form of self-indulgence.'

He still does not think the British eat enough chocolate, however, and has advised one company (he does not say which – he seldom names his clients) how to boost their sales. The first thing, he believes, is that chocolate still has too high a status, that is to say it is considered as a special reward and not as a regular dessert. 'Let's take the status out of it,' he says, 'and always have a dish on the kitchen table.' (At least one company, Rowntree – though the policy may not be based on Dichter's advice – has used this line with their 'Always keep a cupboard full of Kit-Kat' campaign.)

The other recommendation Dichter made was that 'chocolate should be given a more masculine image'. Men don't eat it, he says, 'because it is thought of as feminine and not manly'. His answer – it should be shown in the context of masculine sports, hunting, fishing and the like.

Dichter found what he thought were more hopeful signs when he did a survey of the use of contraceptives in Britain. People, he discovered, were not just after freer sex, but were actually making positive efforts to find pleasure in it. For this reason, he saw a great future for pills and female contraceptives. And while he found there was still puritanism among older, middle-class folk, among the working-class and the young it was much less marked.

The manufacturers of contraceptives were not particularly happy about one aspect of Dichter's report, however. This showed that a high proportion of the contraceptives used were bought by unmarried people.

Part of Dichter's usefulness to clients is that he has had considerable international experience. 'The great advantage we have over most British firms,' said one of his associates, 'is that in the U S A we've been at it for over twenty years and the sort of problems we face are not specifically American problems, but those common to all affluent societies. We have a tremendous library back at Croton-on-Hudson, with three or four million case studies stacked away. I can usually look at a problem and say, "this is just the thing the American market faced back in '43".'

For instance, Dichter has advised public utility companies in America how to fight off impending nationalization. 'We found that saying that nationalization meant loss of freedom didn't impress the American public,' he said. 'So we utilized the fact that, once the companies were nationalized, the public wouldn't be able to exert any power over them. The loss of one's importance proved to be more frightening than the loss of one's company.'

Consequently, Dichter felt he could have offered some useful advice to the steel companies in Britain, and was critical of the way the campaign had been fought. 'My advice to your steel industry,' he said, 'would have been to give themselves a face. After all, people can't identify themselves with the power of industry. What they should have had in their ads were the very personal things made out of steel – a pocket-knife, hairpins, or – even better – a key. A key gives security, you see, and then you *can* say effectively that this is what the steel industry means to you.'

Dichter also thinks it is about time Britain's giant banks and corporations 'personalized' themselves in the same way as Betty Crocker has personalized the General Mills company in America. 'Why,' he said, 'just look at Germany. There they say "our Krupp"; here your people still say "those villains". And your banks have got much too stand-offish an image. They ought to create an uncle-figure for themselves, somebody anyone could go to for help. And why couldn't a company like B M C find a personality with whom people could identify themselves?'

In Germany, where he now has four major agencies, Dichter has fought a number of campaigns of which he is particularly proud. One was for the motor manufacturing firm of N S U, who had the problem of a declining demand for their mopeds. 'They considered the market of ten million bicyclists as their national target,' recalled Dichter. 'They promised the cyclist an effortless ride with a ten-year guarantee in their advertising, but all to no avail. We were asked to find out why. So we asked the German what he was dreaming about, and of course almost everyone wanted a car. So, to promise him a moped which would last him ten years was the last thing he wanted, and we advised them to get rid of the idea. Why not make half a car out of the moped, we said, and offer a trade-in allowance towards an N S U Prinz. We also put a horn rather than a bell on the moped – and the sales went up.'

The other triumph was a piece of research Dichter did for the German Laundry Association. The laundries wanted to increase their trade, and hired Dichter to find out why they were not doing so. 'Their basic mistake,' said Dichter, 'was that they said in their ads that your wash will get personal care and will be personally inspected. We found that German housewives didn't want anybody to see their dirty wash – they were ashamed of it. So we changed the ads – and said nobody will ever see your wash because it is electrically, automatically done. Only then will it be personally inspected.'

Not all Dichter's clients are so secular. He was hired by the American Jesuits to help them in increasing their recruitment figures. Dichter's advice: 'don't offer them a life after death, but a full and satisfying life on this earth – the same thing as industry.'

The only thing Dichter is defensive about is the charge which has been constantly levelled against him – that his research is never thorough or conclusive enough, and that such results as he has achieved have been based on his sharp intuition. 'Look here,' he said. 'I have an interviewing panel of between 2500 and 3000 in America and I spend $200,000 every year on research.' Whether he is a brilliant researcher or merely a clever advertising man with a psychologist's expertise, Dichter has revolutionized the techniques of the advertising game.

13. Hunting the Masses

'We,' said a media group head in one of London's biggest agencies, 'are the only people in advertising who think in terms of masses. The creative people work on the basis of the ideal consumer.' Thinking of masses is, no doubt, a grandiose function, but they are apt to be an elusive target, and since the ammunition is so expensive – in October 1964 a full page in the *News of the World* cost £9000 and thirty seconds of A T V's air-time during peak viewing hours on a Sunday £1500 – the media planners can hardly afford to miss. They are the marksmen of the agency business. The marketing men indicate the target; the creative men provide the ammunition; the media men are left to do the shooting.

As the advertising business has developed, hunting the masses has become an immensely complicated operation. In the years before the war, space was cheap enough and information about the target scanty enough for media men (who were then known simply as 'space-buyers', which put them just one step above the accounts department) to spray their shots in what they felt to be the right general direction. They did most of their space-buying very congenially in the bars and clubs around the agencies, where they held court and graciously received the favours of the space-sellers from the newspapers and magazines. ' "I understand you're buying space for Quaker Oats", interlocked with "What are you having, old boy?", that used to be the form,' one old space-buyer recalled.

But as space became more expensive after the war, agencies had to find out how to pinpoint the target more precisely. Clients who had spent £20,000 on the strength of a space-buyer's know-how wanted a more specific analysis before they laid out £500,000.

Media departments, like research, flourished and expanded (Masius, Wynne-Williams have fifty-two media men out of a staff of 400, Thompson 114 out of 850) and a flood of figures describing the market began to pour in during the early 1950s. Now they have to be meticulously scrutinized and assessed before any money is spent. The result is that the media men have become the boffins instead of the bar-flies of the agency game.

The trend was confirmed by the appearance in 1955 of commercial television with its attendant cloud of statistics and its sophisticated techniques of audience measurement. Between 1956 and 1959, most agencies merged their Press and T V departments, and the agonizing reappraisals which followed left research kings in command at most of the big firms. The old space-buyers, whose merit lay in their knowledge of the market and their ability to drive a hard bargain with the space-salesman, sank almost without trace.

The change-over represented a profound revolution in advertising practice. Whereas the old space-buyer would have looked at the national daily newspapers and decided on instinct and long practice which were the ones to use, today's most progressive media boffins calculate that there are 511 different ways of permutating the nine national dailies into a media schedule, and then let a computer tell them which is the best combination.

The object of the exercise is simple enough. If the agency wastes £1 million hitting the wrong target or no target at all, they presumably lose clients. Yet, despite the aura of science and precision, millions are still spent on hunches. 'There are still no tables from the mountain in this game,' said the director of a very large media department. 'One has to use one's wits to rationalize advertising expenditure. The skill lies in persuading the client of its effectiveness.'

The media men can certainly muster an astonishing collection of statistics describing the British market. They know that (at the end of 1962) there were something like 52½ million people in Britain; that just under 40 million were adults (i.e. over 16) – 18,824,000 men and 20,864,000 women; and that 17¾ million of the women were housewives, their prime target for most fast-moving consumer goods.

These figures can be further broken down by class. In the media man's

Bible – or at least its Authorized Version, the National Readership Surveys published regularly by the I P A on the basis of a nation-wide sample of over 16,000 adults[41] – there is a breakdown of the population into the standard AB, C1, C2 and DE groups. At the end of 1962, there were 4,837,000 ABs (12 per cent of the population), 6,518,000 C1s (17 per cent), 14,870,000 C2s (38 per cent) and 12,475,000 DEs (33 per cent).[42]

At least one agency – Thompson – is dissatisfied with this method of class breakdown. 'We think it's probably not enough to look at earnings and the sort of house people live in,' said Christopher Higham, the media director. 'What we did for one of our accounts was to split the spectrum into three – upper, middle and lower – using the number of children in a family and their age as a vital distinguishing factor. Disposable income is the thing we want to get through to. So, we took the man's job and the terminal age of his children at school, put them through an I B M computer on cards, and came out with what we think is a more meaningful AB group. Only one client has so far accepted this concept.' Thompson have also tried to pin-point the importance of 'heavy buyers' in different product markets. They came up with a number of predictable conclusions – one of them that households earning over £25 per week are 27 per cent of the national total, but that, while they spent 30 per cent of the money spent on margarine, they account for 55 per cent of expenditure on vehicles.

The National Readership Survey also breaks the population down into age-groups. It calculates, for instance, that there are just over six million people between 25 and 34, and over seven million in the 45-54 group. This kind of division can be critically important in markets like cosmetics where lipstick and mascara are aimed precisely at particular age-groups. Ninety-six per cent of the 25–34 group use cosmetics of one sort or another, but only 65 per cent of the 45–64s.

If combination of the sex, class and age divisions are needed – as they often are – a little extra effort on the part of the media men can produce the number of AB housewives between 25 and 34 who use mascara and read the *Daily Express*.

Division by region can be equally important. For instance, it is well known that the Scots keep a very small proportion of the 8,479,000 cats in Britain, so there is little point in saturating the country with advertise-

[41] Interviews are conducted in 160 different Parliamentary constituencies four times a year. Questions are asked about ninety different publications.

[42] It is interesting to note that in the first major study of the British market in 1934, (*The Home Market – a Book of Facts about People*), Mark Abrams calculated that 5.3 per cent of the population were As and 21.3 per cent Bs. The standard of judgment was, however, somewhat different. In 1934, ABs were anyone who earned more than £4 a week, and, for that matter, 67.6 per cent of the population earned less than £3 per week.

ments for Kit-E-Kat. Similarly very few Scots smoke Bachelor, and the sales of Horlicks are low. On the other hand, the consumption of soup north of the border is twice the national average. Other regions have their own deviationist tendencies.

The National Readership Survey also estimates the size and shape of all manner of specialist consumer markets. 12,865,000 men smoke – and 7,905,000 women:[43] 9,362,000 men drink beer, but only 1,161,000 drink wine: 7,598,000 women own a washing machine: there are 12,797,000 members of car-owning households (3,536,000 of them ABs), and 5,521,000 petrol-buyers. Besides the 8,479,000 cats, there are 9,959,000 cage-birds, and 9,443,000 dogs in Britain – and 18,955,000 do-it-yourself enthusiasts, 8,522,000 of them women.[44]

These are just a handful of the cruder statistics which are available. They describe a few of the thousands of different masses which media men have to aim to hit. Usually, if a client is progressive, the agency will nowadays be given much more detailed information about exactly whom the manufacturers think they are selling to. (In the bad old days, the agency was lucky if they got the company's sales returns. Now, they are frequently entrusted with detailed profit figures.) Nobody is left in any doubt as to the prey: the difficulty comes in hitting it cheaply and effectively.

Despite the inroads of television, newspapers and magazines still earned more from advertising business in 1963 than the commercial T V contractors (£176 million compared with £81.5 million, including the tax on television advertisements). But their proportion of the total business had fallen badly. In 1954, the last year before the appearance of commercial T V, the Press had claimed three-quarters of the advertising cake: in 1962, it took just over half.[45]

[43] The figures come from a 1962 Survey.

[44] The vast mass of information asked of the readership panel (180 questions about readership, apart from this mass of other queries about their habits) has thrown some doubt on the accuracy of the N R S figures. Dr Belson, of the London School of Economics, asked by the I P A to make a study of the interviews said that respondents tended to suffer from fatigue, during the prolonged barrage of questions.

[45] Of the three other types of media, outdoor advertising is the most important (£20 million in 1962 on posters, signs and transport advertising etc.).

The *poster* industry still takes a significant percentage of the total advertising cake, despite a fall in the number of sites. In 1935 there were about 400,000 normal-size poster panels (16-sheet) for hire; in 1962, only 150,000 panels of all sizes, less than 100,000 of them 16-sheet. The result of this is that booking for a comprehensive campaign can be difficult, particularly since nearly 70 per cent of the sites are held on long-term contracts, primarily by the beer and cigarette empires. The north of England has over one-third of the available panels. Prices vary enormously, according to the position of the site, ranging from 7s to 60s a

There are at present nine national dailies (*Express, Financial Times, Guardian, Mail, Mirror, Sketch, Sun, Telegraph* and *The Times*) and eight national Sundays (*News of the World, Observer, People, Sunday Citizen, Sunday Express, Sunday Mirror, Sunday Telegraph* and *Sunday Times*). In addition, there are 136 provincial dailies (62 mornings and 74 evenings) and something like 1350 provincial weeklies.

Why do media men use newspapers? In terms of cost, it is almost impossible to say whether the Press is a cheaper medium than television. For instance, it cost (in January 1963) 8s to reach 1000 of the London T V audience in peak viewing hours on weekdays with a thirty-second spot.[46] At the same time,[47] it cost 12s 11d for a full-page advertisement in 1000 copies of the *Daily Mirror*, and 23s 9d for the same coverage in the *Daily Express*. But since the Mirror has an average of over three readers for every copy of the paper, direct comparisons are very difficult. Even if one takes the cost of reaching 1000 *homes* in the London television area – 18s in peak viewing hours – the complex riddle of which has the greater impact on the greater number of people is still unsolved.

---

week for a 16-sheet space. Eighty per cent of 16-sheets would cost somewhere between 10s and 15s – and a well-selected coverage of Britain with say 4,000 16-sheet panels would cost £72,000 for a twenty-six-week period.

Cinemas have apparently had less and less to offer the media men. In 1956, weekly audiences were running at 22 million; by 1962, they had fallen to just over seven. Nor are they strong any longer in terms of AB coverage or any kind of specialized audience. Nevertheless in 1962, cinema advertising topped £5 million for the first time. The maximum length of film allowed is two minutes, and the cost of running a one-minute film can vary from £2 5s to £30. Assuming a 25 per cent audience, and using all types of cinema, the cost-per-thousand works out at roughly 14s 2d.

Commercial radio advertising has never risen much above £500,000. In 1935, there were six stations which could be received in Britain – Luxembourg, Paris, Monte Carlo, Toulouse, Radio Normandy and Athlone – and Radio Luxembourg had a top Sunday audience of 7 million, while Radio Normandy could claim 3½ million. Of them, only Luxembourg has survived, with an average audience for a winter evening in 1962 of 5 million (less than 1½ million adults), but it has recently been joined by Radio Caroline and Radio Invicta, among others.

Commercial broadcasting may not exceed 1½ minutes in any quarter-hour period. A minute during peak hours in the winter costs £193, 7 seconds in off-peak summer time only £17. Sponsored programmes can also be booked – with the sponsor allowed 200 words for each 15-minute period – at a top price of £100 for each 15 minutes taken.

[46] European Media Information Programme: J. Walter Thompson media department, April 1963.

[47] These calculations are based on circulation figures for July–December 1962.

But media men have evolved a rough set of principles which indicates whether newspapers or television is going to be the ideal first-strike weapon for their particular purpose.

The first rule of the media business is that advertising must dominate the chosen medium at some time or other, and preferably all the time. That being so, a small overall budget can rule out the use of television. 'Suppose you'd £100,000 to spend throughout the year and you'd got to reach all parts of the country,' said Michael Firman, one of Masius, Wynne-Williams media group directors. 'If you went on T V, the few spots you could afford would be swamped. If you've got £100,000 to spread evenly over the whole year, I'd probably go for big impact in two top-circulation national dailies.' Firman thought an agency needed to have upwards of £300,000 to run a successful T V campaign on television throughout the year, or perhaps £175,000 for a winter campaign. But he added that short-period campaigns on smaller budgets could be mounted.

The sex of the target is another factor. Television's main claim to the agency's money is that it is the most effective way of hitting the house-wife. There are usually more women in an I T V audience than men. Most of the national newspapers, on the other hand, claim more male than female readers (the exceptions are the *Sunday Express* and the *Daily Telegraph* – 50 per cent of each – and the *Sunday Times* and *Observer* – both 47 per cent male, 53 per cent female). For products aimed at a purely male audience – shaving lotion, for instance – newspapers are generally considered the best bet.

There may, of course, be other considerations. The agency's creative men may decide that they have a long and complicated story to tell, or a complex, expensive and glamorous product to display. This generally rules out television. The vast majority of car advertising, for instance, goes to the newspapers because the motor manufacturers know – first of all – that they are selling to a largely male audience, and, secondly, feel that they cannot tell their story so successfully in a short T V spot – possibly sandwiched between a detergent and a cat food.[48]

And finally, the quality newspapers are the natural choice for 'prestige' advertisements by big companies. They are interested in hitting financial and commercial top people, not housewives.

Having decided to spend money on print (and most schedules in fact contain a judicious mixture of Press and television), the media men have to decide *which* newspapers to use. With rising costs, the choice has become much more difficult. 'In the old days before the war,' said

[48] Television *is* used for cars, of course, particularly to heighten the impact of a new model, and at least one big company (Ford) have for some time been conducting experiments on the impact of TV commercials.

Teddy Roberts, who has been in the L P E media department since the 'twenties, 'we'd be able to get fifty papers on an average schedule. Now we can generally only afford ten at the most.'

He opened his top drawer and produced some tattered sheets of paper. They turned out to be a three-month schedule for Wolsey underwear, vintage 1930. It included the front page of the *Daily Mail* (then the premier advertising space, costing £1400) and nine 8-inch double column advertisements in the same paper, half a dozen 11-inches across three columns in the *Daily Express*, similar spaces in six other national dailies and about twenty leading provincial papers, not to mention half-pages in all the top magazines.[49] The total cost was £16,000.

Today, things are different. 'If,' said Roberts, 'we take an 11-inch triple in the *Mirror*, *Express*, and *Mail* once a month for a year, that's £36,000 gone for a start. The result is that we can seldom include more than two dailies, two Sundays and two women's papers. We've got to be very selective and we have to rely on statistics to guide us – everything is so marginal.'

Heavy costs have, by and large, driven media men more and more towards the big-circulation dailies and Sundays, which they can use to hit almost everybody. 'My blanket paper,' said Roberts, 'that's what I call the *News of the World*.' On a crude cost-per-thousand calculation, papers of the *News of the World*'s size have an obvious advantage. It provides a circulation of roughly 6¼ million, at a cost of 28s 11d per 1000 on a full-page advertisement. *The Sunday Telegraph*, on the other hand, offers 660,635 readers – cost per thousand 79s 10d. The margins between the dailies are sharper still. A full page in 1000 *Daily Mirrors* costs 13s: in the *Financial Times* (circulation 152,351), it costs 208s 5d.

And although the *Financial Times* can claim a very special type of audience, most of the provincial papers cannot. Even so the *Birmingham (Evening) Mail* costs 63s 9d per 1000, the *Manchester Evening News* 52s 8d and the *Belfast Telegraph* 60s 6d.[50]

It is the provincial papers, in fact, which have taken the hardest knock from rising costs. In part, this is because they have lost their special *raison d'être* on media schedules. An L P E survey in 1934[51] showed that 60 per cent of Scots did not read any of the national dailies – and that even in the north of England, one-third read only provincial papers. Products which sold heavily north of Birmingham simply had to advertise in the provincials.

[49] The religious magazines of the day were included – 'to appeal to an older public'; so were the medical press 'because doctors would recommend wool'; and the motoring press 'because it was cold in those open bodies'.

[50] Costs based on the circulation figures for January–June 1964.

[51] 'A Survey of Reader Interest in the National Mornings and London Evening Press, 1934'.

But as the big national dailies began to modernize their distribution, the provincial Press became less important to the agencies. The war, however, kept local papers in an unnaturally buoyant position. Because of the shortage of newsprint (and therefore advertising space), media men dashed to the provinces and took everything they could lay hands on.[52] When newsprint rationing came to an end the national dailies strengthened their grip again.

Christopher Higham summed up the feelings of most agencies: 'The provincials are not efficient in cost terms. On a cost-per-thousand basis, their display ad rates are two to two and a half times as expensive as the nationals – and even then you've not got the same power. After all, when you're thinking of the sales force in any particular area, it's the ads in the nationals which give them prestige with wholesalers and retailers.'

Other media bosses do not like to see their products advertised cheek-by-jowl with what they call 'Jerry Bloggs's local stuff' and they frequently complain about the quality of the reproduction of some provincial printing presses.

But equally they would qualify their reluctance to spend in the provinces when it comes to the good provincial evenings and weeklies. (Outside London, 53 per cent of all adults read an evening paper.) Indeed, classified advertisements frequently boost the important provincial evenings to fifty pages (more than twice the size of their London equivalents) and if agencies suddenly try to take space on Friday nights – to catch the heavy weekend shoppers – they are frequently turned down flat. Some provincials, in fact, are able to charge a 10 per cent premium for Friday spots.

Higham believes that the regional evenings and weeklies *could* easily become a third major press medium (in addition to the national papers and the magazines) if they were ready to join together and do some syndicated space-selling. 'Suppose, for instance, you wanted to hit Yorkshire, then you could prepare one advertisement block for all the Yorkshire weeklies and evenings, and at a reasonable rate compared to the Nationals. That's what could happen, but at the moment, it doesn't.'

Some of the proprietors have actually joined together in the Evening Newspaper Advertising Bureau with something of Higham's strategy in mind. They have so far collected support from about 75 per cent of papers – Thomson Newspapers, the Westminster Press and Allied Newspapers are all members, but Northcliffe remains outside although Provincial Newspapers have been in membership since 1964.

The most progressive of the provincial groups have fought to hold their advertising by pushing their special virtues before the agencies.

[52] The largest advertising space available anywhere was a 5½-inch double column.

Nobody has tackled the job more thoroughly than Thomson Newspapers. For instance, a readership survey of Wales, published in November 1961, claimed that the *Western Mail* had 62 per cent more readers in the ABC1 groups than all the quality national dailies put together.[53]

Similarly the group's *Aberdeen Press and Journal* was found to cover 64 per cent of the adult population of Northern Scotland, with the *Scottish Daily Express* a poor second on 36 per cent. The Thomson surveys also aim to give the kind of specialized information about local markets which agencies might want to have. The survey of Northern Scotland, for instance, gave figures for membership of the Co-op, for regular home bakers and for ownership of vacuum cleaners, and a similar survey of the northern English counties gave statistics for households which included shift-workers and homes which employed domestic help.

As far as the national newspapers are concerned, the IPA's National Readership Surveys contain a mass of information. They tell the agency's media men how many people read the paper, how old they are, what sex they are, how many are housewives, what social grade they belong to, what areas the paper is strongest in, how many readers own dogs, cats or birds, how many have washing machines and so on. These vital statistics are known as the paper's 'Readership profile'.

For instance, the two top-circulation dailies which often serve as 'bankers' for the media planners – the *Daily Mirror* and the *Daily Express* have very different profiles.[54] The *Mirror* audience has a slightly higher percentage of women, it is younger than its rival, but 83 per cent of its readers are C2DE. Thirty-three per cent of the *Express* readers, on the other hand, are ABC1. Regionally, the *Express* tends to be stronger in the north of England than the *Mirror*, but considerably weaker in London and the south-east (it covers only 28 per cent of the population in the area, compared with the *Mirror's* 44 per cent).

The 'quality' nationals, daily and Sunday, play hard on their high AB readership. Most of them can claim between 40 and 60 per cent AB readers, and one of the big Sundays is so jealous of its high ratio that it does not welcome new CDE subscribers. Such journals generally parade

[53] It went further by cutting across the traditional class divisions to create a new kind of person – the 'Active Leader'. The 'Active Leader', it said, was a person 'with a high degree of leadership ability who was also in a recognized position to influence the community'. The 'AL' was first judged by the number of official positions in organizations which he or she held, then double-checked by a series of standard personality tests measuring 'dominance' and 'sociability'. Half of the 'AL's turned out to be working-class, and 34 per cent read the *Western Mail* – more than any other paper in the area, local or national.

[54] All the statistics from the National Readership Survey which follow come from a 1962 issue.

their high-class clientele under a cloak of humour. *The Times* claims to be read by three-quarters of the country's top clergy, but says so with cartoon posters. *The Sunday Times*, in another gay cartoon, invites media men to 'Pick from the Top of the Tree', where 'the fruit is sweeter, the rewards richer. It (*The Sunday Times*) offers you more readers in the top socio-economic classes than any other quality paper, daily or Sunday.' What the advertisement does not say is that both the *Daily* and *Sunday Express* have more AB readers (though the *proportion* is smaller) than *The Sunday Times*. *The Express*, of course, can be relied on to say that for itself.

In the space-selling war – on the outcome of which the life or death of newspapers directly depends – every blow counts. *The Times*, for example, took a hard knock when *The Economist* did a survey on top businessmen's papers in 1962. This stated that 39 per cent of this select band read the *Daily Telegraph* and only 21 per cent *The Times*. This confirmed what some agencies had already been thinking. 'In the past,' said one of Thompson's media planners. '*The Times* was *the* paper in which to advertise to chairmen and directors, but we felt that a revaluation of the *Telegraph* was necessary, so we did our own study – using terminal educational age and isolating businessmen from the AB group.' The results confirmed *The Economist* findings.

The media men in the agencies are, of course, constantly besieged by space-salesmen from the newspapers and magazines. In some of the larger agencies, particular media planners are told off to act as contact men to whom the advertising representatives can put their case. If ample lunches are sufficient reward, most contact men can count themselves well repaid for their trouble. Others who refuse the lavish hospitality try to keep the numbers who visit during office hours down to a decent level.

But it is true that media-buying decisions are often made on a curious mixture of statistics, hunch and plain prejudice. It may even be a battle of prestige between two big companies, with one taking full-page advertisements simply because its rival has already done so.

Quite often the deciding factor is whether the agency thinks the newspaper has the right 'atmosphere' for the product. At Thompson, for instance, the comparative cheapness of the *Mirror* is not always preferred to the *Express*. 'Suppose for instance, we were advertising a quite high-cost durable consumer product,' said Christopher Higham, 'we would probably choose the *Express* because the particular editorial approach of the paper, the feature-writing, was right for the age and class we were aiming for.'

The same consideration sometimes leads the agency to prefer the *Sunday Express* to the *News of the World*.

The product must, of course, be planted in the most fertile soil available. For that reason, almost all fast-moving consumer goods – cigarettes, chocolate, foodstuffs – tend to be advertised in the daily papers on Thursday, Friday and Saturday, to catch the weekend shoppers. The Sundays, on the other hand, are favoured for what a media group head at one big agency called 'cheque purchases rather than purse purchases'. The theory behind this widely-held assumption is that Sunday is a day when the family are together and in the right frame of mind to make big decisions. There is always, for instance, a good deal of car advertising in the Sunday papers – though Ford in 1964 spent a lot of their appropriation in the *Daily Telegraph*, the *Daily Express* and the *Daily Mail*. Their research suggested that these were also papers where new-car buyers were likely to be found.

A variation on the same logic leads many media buyers to regard the popular Sundays – often more particularly the *News of the World* – as the best place for patent medicine advertisements. 'They're in the house all day long,' said one. 'People are lying in bed, or sitting in an armchair – they're receptive to cures. What you want with patent medicine ads is the constant drip of continuity at the right time.'

Other, more sophisticated cure pedlars, tend to be more selective. 'With an analgesic, yes, we would look for large circulation without any particular bias,' said a media planner in another big agency, 'but for rheumatic sufferers, we'd want a bias to working-class in industrial areas, because a very high proportion live in mining districts.'

Both within, and between, agencies there are plenty of fierce arguments about the right choice of media. Most agencies boast as a matter of standard practice that they are smart enough to get £1250 worth of advertising for £1000.

Agencies with a claim to sophistication in their approach to media attach varying degrees of importance to sheer economy. 'We *do* head-counting,' said Thompson's Christopher Higham, 'but we take it beyond that. Knowledge of the product might easily lead you to reject cost-per-thousand.' Christopher Nuttall, who is the Campaign Planning Director at L P E, thinks marketing planning is more important than cost or numbers – 'knowing who you're going for and hitting them in the right environment. The editorial climate is far, far more important than the cost of a number of readers.' 'People just don't walk around in batches of a thousand,' as one agency media boss put it. 'A thousand what, anyway?'

But Masius adhere much more closely to the cost-per-thousand baseline. Michael Firman believes that 'advertising has gone from no science to too much science. Too much theory in a practical world only leads to a mass of suspect figures. Our clients are not interested in academic exercises which are inconclusive.' The agency uses Gallup to do studies on the number of people who read and note particular advertisements.

The debate often, in fact, resolves itself into an argument between agencies which spend a lot of money on research into more effective ways of media-buying, and those who don't. (The debate goes on, *a fortiori*, in the television field, but more of that later.) The anti-research agencies contend that it is little more than a sales gimmick, and that they can get value for money without long-winded theses. The firms which lay out hard cash on research studies, on the other hand, think they are the only way of reaching the millenium – i.e. proving that advertising is effective.

Thompson, for instance, are spending a good deal of money trying to find out whether advertisements get more attention on right-hand pages than those on left-hand pages – and whether large spaces and advertisements in special positions are worth the premium rates which newspapers charge for them. (Special positions can cost up to 80 per cent more than basic rates, large sizes anything between 10 and 25 per cent extra.)

The evidence they have gathered suggests that, for a given half-page advertisement in a national daily, 20 per cent of the readers will not even look at the page: 50 per cent *will* look at the page, but not the advertisement; and 30 per cent will look at both. They are planning to measure more precisely the impact of the space they buy by feeding this data into the computer which they already use to assess the coverage and profiles of their media schedules. 'Suppose we know that, say, 20 per cent of people read the *Daily Mail*,' said Adrian Sycamore, an ex-Cambridge scientist who is now one of the agency's media research men, 'and that 80 per cent of them, on average, read the woman's page, and that a third of *them* recall seeing a half-page advertisement on it, then we can use these figures and similar ones to construct a mathematical model which will predict more of this type of data; the mathematical relationships incorporated in this model may allow for the copy of the ad, its position on the page, the fact that it was in colour or black and white, its position in relation to other ads and so on.'

L P E, too, spend a lot of money on expensive research projects. John Caffyn, their Communications Research Director, says L P E lays out anything from £20,000 to £40,000 a year on various studies. The theory he is pursuing most intensively at the moment is that since word-of-mouth is one of the most important routes by which goods are sold, it is essential to find out *how* it works.

The agency has also made clear how many unanswered questions remain in the apparently simple matter of assessing newspaper readership. In a paper published in 1962, Christopher Nuttall set out some of them. What, he asked, did the high 'readership' figures given for papers mean? (Daily and Sunday papers have a 'readership' of between 2.8 and 4.7 readers per copy.) How intensely did the second, third, and fourth readers look at the newspaper? And, in any case, how long did people spend with their paper? Nuttall quoted a study which Research Services had done for 'a newspaper' comparing the amount of time spent with a quality Sunday and a popular Sunday. This showed that, while only 3 per cent of the popular's readers spent over an hour with it, 43 per cent of the quality's readers did so.

Nuttall raises a score of other problems which are extremely relevant to the space-buyers. How *did* people read newspapers – page by page, or merely turning to specific items? How many 'readers' are regular and how many irregular and is there any difference between them? (Here Nuttall quotes a study examining the two types of readers for a quality Sunday which shows a very wide divergence. Forty-seven per cent of the regulars, for instance, were AB, but only 14 per cent of the casual buyers.) And *when* is the paper read? Another Research Services survey had shown that more readers of 'popular' papers read them before and during breakfast than the readers of quality dailies. And when are readers most likely to notice advertisements?

These are the sort of questions which some agencies are prepared to ignore while others spend thousands trying to answer them. Even the fact that they are being asked shows how much space-buying is still an art rather than a science.

In addition to the newspapers, national and provincial, there is a huge collection of magazines. Altogether there are about 800 consumer magazines in Britain, with another 1,600 trade, technical and professional publications.[55] Only ninety magazines, however, are considered important enough to have their 'profiles' done by the I P A Survey.

Media men go to the magazines for a number of reasons. They are a very useful second shot in a campaign which puts most of its money into the newspapers or T V – the Oxo campaign is a perfect example. The big-circulation women's weekly magazines may even be used as a first-string by agencies – like Thompson – who sometimes prefer them to the dailies for food products with a strong sales story for housewives.

The women's weekly magazines are undoubtedly the most important group. There are five with circulations of over a million. (*Woman, Woman's Own, Woman's Weekly, Woman's Realm,* and *Woman's Mirror*). Of these, *Woman* (circulation 3,328,000) and *Woman's Own* (2,215,000) are easily the biggest, and they are the most likely 'bankers' in any campaign designed to hit the housewife. (*Woman* alone covers more than 40 per cent of all British housewives.) They are not particularly expensive – a full page in *Woman* costs 17s 5d per thousand readers, a full page in *Woman's Own* 18s.[56]

There are, however, additional difficulties for the media men in book-

[55] Some trade papers, like *The Grocer* (circulation roughly 60,000), are of considerable importance to advertisers.

[56] Figures taken from a 1962 I P A National Readership Survey.

ing space in them. One is that some of them require as much as six months' notice, and they are popular enough to be overbooked at times. In any case, the big weeklies only give about one-third of their space to advertising (in the case of newspapers, it is usually about 45 per cent, for monthly magazines as much as 50 per cent).

The weakness of the woman's weeklies from the agency point of view is that they carry the bulk of their readership in the C2DE social grades. From this point of view *Woman* – with 30 per cent ABC1 – is the best. This is where the high-class women's monthlies come in. *Vogue, Good Housekeeping, Woman's Journal,* and *Flair* all claim a better than 50 per cent ABC1 readership.

There are three other general magazines which agencies particularly favour. One is *Reveille* (circulation over 1½ million) which is reckoned to be ideal for mail-order advertising. Then there is *Radio Times* (circulation around 5¾ million), also favoured for the mail-order business. The *Radio Times* has special virtues because not only is a nine-day life claimed for it, but it is also in frequent use.

Finally, there is the *Readers' Digest,* the leading general monthly magazine (circulation, well over one million) which some agencies choose for their patent medicine advertising. Nuttall at L P E called it 'a look-after-yourself magazine'. Other media men like the *Digest* because it provides thorough statistics about the nature of its readership and is a useful addition to any general schedule. They say its only weakness is that, being a monthly, it is slower-working than the weeklies.

There is a good deal of detailed information available about top magazines. For instance, the National Magazine Company, which owns magazines like *Good Housekeeping, Harper's Bazaar, House Beautiful* and *She,* has sponsored a very detailed analysis of the 'readership characteristics and habits' of twelve of them. It unearthed a fascinating catalogue of contrasts between the various magazine audiences. In the cosmetics field, for instance, while 54 per cent of *Harper's Bazaar* readers used mascara, only 37 per cent of *Vogue* readers bought it. *Queen,* on the other hand, had the highest proportion of readers with expensive refrigerators – 12 per cent had paid over £100 – but (and here one can see the refrigerator-makers cocking their ears) 41 per cent of them were over four years old.

The study also tells media buyers how many of each magazine's readers bought sandals, brassieres, pyjamas, slacks and so on during the previous four weeks, how many of them read the magazine at the hairdressers, how many bought it for themselves and there are all kinds of odd bits of information. Readers of *Honey,* for instance, 'have a marked tendency to own gas cookers rather than electric cookers'.

There is also a section on readers' confidence in the magazine's advertisements. The results must have come as a shock to people who believed that the quality image of the magazine would rub off on the advertisements. *Honey* had the highest percentage of readers with 'a lot' of confidence in their advertisements, 30 per cent, *Queen* the lowest with 11 per cent. However, when the sample was asked whether they had special confidence in the advertisements of any of the twelve magazines being studied, *Good Housekeeping* got twice as much support as any of the others – 33 per cent.

Then, after a section on readers' interests – 62 per cent of *Honey* readers were interested in looking after children, only 38 per cent of the devotees of *House Beautiful* – the researchers tried to establish a 'brand-image' for each magazine, with ten dimensions – sophistication, warmth and friendliness, liveliness and excitement and so on. *Vogue* was top for sophistication (95) *Honey* bottom (27.6); *Good Housekeeping* had highest marks for influence and prestige (98.1), *She* lowest with 80.2; *She*, on the other hand, went to the top for liveliness and excitement (90.7), *Good Housekeeping* sank to the bottom (58.6). All these rather nebulous dimensions are supposed to help media men gauge the 'atmosphere' of a magazine.

Yet, despite this volume of information, even more questions are being asked about the validity of readership figures for the monthlies and weeklies than are asked about daily newspapers. A study, done for the IPA by Dr Belson of the London School of Economics, into the accuracy of the National Readership Survey in 1962,[57] suggested that the figures for daily papers were fairly accurate; that, on average, the figures for Sunday and weekly papers were not far from being accurate, though in the case of some there were appreciable errors (for instance, *Reveille*, Benson thought, was given readership figures considerably below its actual level); but, in the case of monthly publications, he discovered a wide margin of error. He thought they were seriously under-estimated. (Harry Henry, the marketing manager of Thomson Newspapers, thinks on the contrary that the IPA figures are a serious *over-estimate* because when a respondent is asked if he has read a particular magazine, he answers 'yes' even if it is an old copy. Henry called this 'replication'.)

The IPA has not, so far, been able to do anything about implementing the recommendations Belson made on amending the methods used in the National Readership Survey; and very few people in the media-buying world are particularly happy about the figures they now have to go on.

[57] *Surveys in Readership*: William A. Belson: Bunner Publications, 1962.

14. Hitting the Housewife

The arrival of commercial television in the London area in September 1955 turned the media business upside down. It was the first new medium the agencies had had to cope with for a quarter of a century, and that in itself was enough to send some of the smaller ones scuttling off to learn how to make TV commercials; but – and this was the point – advertising on television was, in more senses than one, shooting in the dark.

The media men had very little idea who they were shooting at through the glamorous screen, and not the faintest clue how many of them were going to be hit. (They are still trying to fathom the answer to both problems.) After all, at the flick of a switch, a million viewers could (and did) depart – moved by sudden boredom or a momentary revulsion – and as the audience fell, the cost-per-thousand rocketed upwards. The media men were suddenly cut adrift from the comfortable world of the newspapers and magazines, where circulation figures were so comparatively steady that they were only published for six-monthly periods, into a world where anything could happen from one minute to the next. TV, in fact, took all the predictability out of the business.

The upheaval could hardly have come at a worse time. Most media departments were still passing through a period of intense unrest and rapid reorganization. The new arrival kicked the bottom out of an already shaky situation.

Commercial television did, however, take some time to get under way. On opening night, there were only 200,000 sets which could take the new service, and no more than 500,000 by the end of 1955. (There were already 5 million sets which could receive BBC programmes.) The agencies, for their part, viewed the whole enterprise with what now seems like astonishing caution. Very few were even ready to bet on commercial television's ultimate survival, and while some – most of them American-owned – jumped in quickly and bought air-time, many sat back and waited. 'After all,' recalled one media planner with a cynical smile, 'at that time you could reach more people with ads on the backs of tram tickets.'

Even agencies like Masius – now very heavily committed to TV – sat on the sidelines, and worked on the principle that clients should have television only when it became economical.[58] Advertising spots were easy to book, partly because of this widespread caution and partly because costs were high. In January 1956 it cost 25s to reach 1000 homes in the London area (peak time, 30-second spot); by 1963, the price was down to 14s.

Nor did 1956 bring any startling changes of attitudes. The Midlands, Lancashire and Yorkshire all opened up to commercial T V, and by the end of the year 2½ million homes could receive it, but so far as the media men were concerned things hadn't altered much and it was still very much a buyers' market. You could book spots whenever and wherever you wanted them.

Then, in 1957, the T V boom began. Quite suddenly, the potential of the commercial screen bore in on the agencies as audiences grew, and sizeable T V appropriations crept into a lot of the big schedules being prepared in the spring of 1957 for the coming winter.

Michael Firman noticed the abrupt change, because he had joined the Masius T V department in May 1957. At that time there were five people, including himself, in the section. 'I started off with the usual system,' he recalled. 'You made a handful of telephone calls to the contracting companies in London, the Midlands and the North, and got what you wanted. Then, within four or five weeks – starting from the beginning of July – you couldn't buy anything.

'Overnight we had the worst possible sellers' market. You made your usual phone calls, but suddenly it was "Sorry, you can't have those dates. We've got Thursday, but not Friday. We'll put you on the waiting-list, and if there are any cancellations. . . .".'

And of course, commercial television could not, like the newspapers, put on extra advertising space, just when it wanted to. The companies were strictly rationed, not by the Television Act of 1954, but by the Independent Television Authority.[59] So from the summer of 1957 until the spring of 1961, when the Government imposed a tax of 11 per cent on all television advertising, the agencies had to contend with a sellers' market.

Worse was to follow: the B B C began to fight for mass audiences. So far as the media men in the agencies could see, the Corporation's first reaction to commercial television had been to ignore it. This left the advertisers sitting pretty, because the commercial stations played hard

[58] In the first six months, over half the television time bought was accounted for by ten companies. Unilever alone accounted for 20 per cent.

[59] The Television Act did not lay down any specific limitations on the amount of advertising which the companies might take, but the I T A prescribed a maximum of six minutes of advertising an hour, averaged over the day's programmes, with a further limitation restricting the maximum to seven minutes in any single hour, i.e. 6–7 pm, 8–9 pm.

for mass audiences and often got them. 'In those early honeymoon days,' said one media planner wistfully, 'the knobs seemed to be cemented to the commercial channel. They switched on in the early evening and stayed with you all night.' Under these circumstances, the media men could reasonably afford to guess the size of the audience even six months ahead.

But then – and media men generally date the change from the beginning of 1958 – the B B C began to compete. 'I first realized what was happening,' said Firman, 'when I heard they had bought a packaged deal of R K O R A D I O films. I saw then that they had 100 feature films which they could put on with very little warning and which could take away anything between 10 and 30 per cent of the commercial audience.'

And since nobody in the agencies knew what programmes the B B C would run even the following week until the appearance of the *Radio Times*, booking T V spots six months ahead became an extremely risky business. In one case, the spot might finish up opposite *Macbeth*, in which case the commercial audience would be huge; in another, against a top boxing match, in which case the audience might be tiny. The agencies could not begin to guess what they would get for their money.

They reacted in a number of ways to this new crisis. First of all, they began to try to ferret out in advance what both the B B C and the commercial companies were planning for the future. A sort of underground espionage organization grew up, with the agencies trying to tap contacts in both outfits for useful titbits of information.

They found the B B C a very hard nut to crack. Indeed, the sort of information which their contacts in the Corporation have been able to throw up has often reduced top agencies to deputing media men to disguise themselves as 'interested viewers' who ring up the B B C for more information about forthcoming series.

They appear to have an easier time with the commercial companies, which is perhaps not surprising. For instance, when *Coronation Street* – the darling of the agencies because of its consistently high audiences – changed its time during 1963, the fact was common knowledge among the sharper media men long before the news became public. In fact, by the time the change was announced, some of the agencies had already moved their spots accordingly.

There was, in any case, good reason for some of the I T V companies to be forthcoming. A B C, for instance, which provided programmes for the Midlands and North at the weekend, had to sell their air-time hard during the buyers' market and gave a three-month advance schedule as an extra service to agencies. Associated-Rediffusion – which served London during the week – were less forthcoming, simply because they didn't need to be. All the agencies bought time in London whether or not they knew in advance what the programmes would be.

The 'spy' network took some time to build up, however. Meanwhile agencies set about hurriedly reorganizing their media departments. Some joined the hunt for such T V 'specialists' as were to be had, others took on graduates from the universities for training. In most agencies, however, the arrival of commercial T V merely helped the rise of the boffins to power: half of Masius's media planners are now graduates.

At the same time, agencies had to persuade their clients to give them much more say in how and when their money should be spent. Clearly, in this situation, it was impossible to hand out a firm schedule for a year ahead – as was perfectly feasible in the case of newspapers and magazines – and Masius, for example, asked clients to accept a month's advance schedule, but even that had to be subject to last minute alterations.

The whole field of T V buying was (and is) one of frightening complexity. There is, for one thing, the sheer volume of work involved. A big agency, like Masius, has to book 600 different spots a week with fourteen different programming companies all over the British Isles. Each of the fourteen has different audiences, different rates, different discounts, and there are all kinds of special prices for things like 5-second slides, 7-second slides and 'live' commercials. This apart from any late alterations which may need to be made for spots already booked.

Each of the companies issues its own rate-card. They offer cheaper rates for spots booked early in the afternoon or late in the evening, but because of the enormous demand for air-space in peak-time, they have been able to charge peak-time rates for a vast segment of the evening. The peak-time segment on A T V for London on Saturday nights stretches right from 6.25 to 11.5 p.m.; Scottish Television, on the other hand, only charges top rates from 9 to 11 p.m. on Saturday evening.

This extension of the peak-viewing segment has also been used to bring in extra revenue in another way. If agencies want their spot to appear in one particular break during the segment, they have to pay a fixing surcharge of anything from 10 to 20 per cent on top of the basic rate. If they want a special position *within* a particular *break*, then they probably will have to lay out an extra 5 per cent. Since both the agencies and the commercial stations know that the size and the attention of audiences vary hugely at different times in the peak segment, this is simply another way of adding to basic costs for people who want to catch the greatest number of viewers.

On the other hand, if agencies are prepared to spend large sums of money, most companies offer volume discount to the tune of 2½ per cent for every £50,000 spent. (Smaller stations give more – Westward Television offers 5 per cent for £50,000 – as an added inducement to time-buyers.) One company – Associated Television – give what they call a 'research discount' of 3 per cent, but there are strings attached, in that the money must be spent with Schwerin, a company which tests the impact of T V commercials.

What, in any case, are the agencies getting for their money? The controversy is still going on. Their best guide to the audience they are reaching is provided by T A M ratings – the television equivalent of the I P A's National Readership Surveys. Television Audience Measurement began operations in April 1955 to get ready for the launching of commercial T V. At about the same time Art Nielsen, the American head of the A.C. Nielsen company, the world's largest research firm, arrived in Britain. He announced that his company, which already did the most widely accepted television audience rating in America, would provide the same service in Britain.

Bedford Attwood, the T A M boss, had no intention of letting Nielsen steal his pitch, however, and in 1957 T A M was given a contract which made it the official service to the British commercial television industry. In mid-1959 Nielsen, who by then was losing a lot of money, merged his interests with T A M.

T A M's current contract with J I C T A R (Joint Industry Committee for Television Advertising Research) is worth about £475,000 a year. For this they provide basic audience statistics to agencies and advertisers as well as to the programme contractors. T A M claim that, since all sides of the advertising industry are parties to the contract, they cannot be accused of producing the kind of viewing figures which the companies – whose bread and butter depend on them – would like to see.

T A M's research methods are worth a brief explanation. The device they use to give them information about the likely size of the audience looks like a clock and is called a Tammeter. The Tammeter is connected to the back of the television set and when the set is switched on a tape inside the measuring device records how long the set is switched on for, and the channel to which it is tuned.

The new J I C T A R contract (signed in 1964) provides for 1975 homes in the eight most heavily populated I T V areas to have Tammeters installed.[60] They represent a cross-section of the 12½ million homes which can receive the commercial network – divided by social class, size of household, age of housewife and by the presence or absence of children in the home. There are 400 Tammeters in London and in the North, 275 in the Midlands and 150 or 175 in each of the other regions. (Under the previous contract there were only 920 homes in the scheme.)

The instrument simply records the period for which the set was

[60] I T V areas with small populations are measured with Recordimeters, a metering device which is cheaper to run and merely shows how much the set is used, not even which channel it is tuned to. The log which is filled in by the family obviously becomes more important in this situation, and a light comes on every half-hour on the T V set to remind the viewers to fill in their Diary.

switched on. It says nothing about *how many* people were viewing – and it obviously cannot measure the degree of attention the viewers were giving to the various programmes, and, more important still, to the commercial breaks. To give some indication of the composition of the audience, each of the 1975 homes is asked to fill in a Tamlog for every quarter-hour of viewing. The Tamlog records the age and sex of the viewers and the number of guests who were looking in.

The Tammeter tapes are collected every week by field workers (T A M employs about 250 all over Britain) and immediately sent off to the firm's operations centre at Berkhamsted. Tapes from the first areas to arrive – London, Southern T V, Television for Wales and the West and Westward T V – get to Berkhamsted on Monday morning. When all the 1975 tapes are in, the results are then analysed (T A M have a staff of 300 at Berkhamsted). From the combined figures, an estimate of the I T V audience for each minute of air-time can be made, and a Tamrating affixed to each programme and each commercial break. The Tamrating simply represents a percentage of the total I T V audience who had their sets switched on. Some commercials shown in the early afternoon get ratings as low as 1, some of those shown during *Coronation Street* score 70 and above in the northern area.

Under the previous J I C T A R contract, the weekly T A M reports used to come out on the following Monday, but demands from agencies for a quicker service speeded things up. Some of the Berkhamsted staff used to work overtime on Thursday night, and about a score of copies of Part I, which covered the *nine* largest T V areas, were sent off to London by special car on Friday morning. The agencies then rushed special messengers to pick them up from the T A M headquarters in Eccleston Street, near Victoria Station. For this privilege they paid an extra £1 a week – but at least they got a chance to see what sort of ratings their spots had picked up before they went off for the weekend. Under the new contract, however, agencies will not be able to get the report on Friday.

T A M say they make 'only a normal commercial profit' out of the £475,000 J I C T A R contract – they do not say what they consider 'normal' – and add that the same is true of the colossal range of 'special studies' which they do – 90 per cent of them on the basis of information they already have but which they analyse more closely. These studies might be worth anything from £10 to £6000, and they might include work for Mars to find out how they were doing compared with Fry and Cadbury, an analysis to find out if the ABCs in the London area are biased towards the B B C, or a simple study of programme audience composition. (One such study showed the *This Week* audience to have a high working-class content, while *Panorama*'s was weighted towards the Establishment and the middle class.) The biggest type of special survey work might be a boundary study for Associated-Rediffusion or A T V, investigating the viewing habits of people living in the fringe areas which can receive programmes from two different I T V stations. T A M also do some analyses – a programme's average ratings over a period, for instance – which are designed to help the agencies in forward planning. Many of their studies are syndicated – thirty eight agencies, for example, used to take the alphabetical list of commercials which was prepared outside the J I C T A R contract. Now the list is included in the contract.

To meet the demand for more and more rapid information, T A M frequently experiment with new techniques. They now provide a novel kind of audience assessment known as a T V Q. The T V Q – originally an American idea – indicates how much the audience liked or disliked a particular programme. It should be particularly valuable for series where, although the opening show got a high T A M rating, many of the audience in fact disliked it and did not intend to watch the second instalment. A quick, accurate T V Q could enable agencies to move their spots before the ratings slump.

In the past, there was periodic criticism of T A M's research, the most common complaint being that the sample was far too small. In the old days, 150 Tammeters in the London area were used to deduce the behaviour of a potential I T V audience of over 3 millions. When the 150 were broken down by social class and size of household, the numbers were very small indeed; where the total sample for a region was only ninety, some agencies were reluctant to trust the evidence at all. However, since July 1964, T A M's contract with J I C T A R provides for more than double the old sample. There are now 400 Tammeters in London – and more detailed breakdowns will now be possible. Whether the sample is yet large enough to measure the behaviour of an audience of 3 millions remains to be seen.

Before the signing of the new contract, Adrian Sycamore of Thompson expressed a criticism of T A M which was common among media men. 'It's the best guide we've got,' he said, 'but the sample is very small and there could be a wide margin of error, particularly on low ratings.' T A M, he thought, was adequate for 'basic national ratings', but not so satisfactory when it came to estimating the behaviour of particular groups in one of the nine areas.

'Take Rowntree's chocolates, and their consumption by, say, upper-class adults or young housewives,' he said. 'If you tried to assess the viewing habits of those groups in the Anglia area, you'd run into real trouble. For one thing, T A M don't break down housewives by age further than into three groups – under 35, 35 to 49, and 50 and over. Elsewhere in marketing, 16-24 is the normal classification. Then again, they only split their sample into four social classes – A, B, C and D.

Everybody else have five – including E, so there must be some telescoping in the CD range.' Media men are now waiting to see how much the new contract will improve matters.

The other major criticism which agencies level at the T A M ratings is that they give no help in planning for the future. 'It's extremely difficult to use historical data in predicting future trends,' as Christopher Nuttall of L P E put it.

T A M's reply to this sort of criticism was a simple one. To the charge of having too small a sample, they pleaded the need to keep an overall cost in mind. 'We have produced an industry service with as small a sample as will produce satisfactory results,' said Michael Parkin, before the signing of the new contract. 'If the industry will pay more, we'll increase the sample.' The industry has paid more.

Nonetheless, most agencies use T A M as an invaluable baseline for want of anything better. Masius is typical. 'We use T A M in overall strategy,' said Michael Firman, 'finding out what sort of schedule to go for – peak or off-peak time, what months and so on. But when it comes to tactics, we never say that would be a good spot because of T A M.'

The cost of the weekly report to the agencies is calculated according to the size of their billings. Thompson, for example, say that their T A M bill for this year will be £17,500. They also pay out another £1500 a year for several of T A M's special studies.

The receipt of the T A M weekly ratings on Monday marks the end of what has invariably been a hectic week for the television media men. It begins with the arrival of early copies of the *Radio Times*. (The paper is normally published on Thursdays but the smart agencies manage to get it much more quickly.) At Masius, three go straight to the group buyers. They run quickly through them to check the possible danger spots – the ones that might coincide with very popular B B C programmes put on at short notice. 'You suddenly find you're opposite an American spectacular,' said Michael Firman, 'so you think, I must move that. We're on the telephone to the programme company within a quarter of an hour.'

This is when the negotiations and the wheedling begin. The first move is generally to recall some past favour or other, perhaps the time when the agency took some spot which the programme company couldn't otherwise fill. If that doesn't work, the final play is to offer to pay the extra charge needed to fix the spot in the place where it's wanted. 'If things get tough, then I rustle up the fixing charge,' said Firman, 'and some more complacent advertiser gets kicked out. It's the law of the commercial jungle.' Masius use more of their light-blue amendment forms than they do initial television time order sheets.

Their provisional schedules, of course, have been booked long before this – some stations require as much as two year's advance notice for their best peak-time spots – but anything can be cancelled up to eight weeks before transmission. After that, they can only be moved to another time. Firman picks his 'Banker' spots first, then adds others as time goes by. 'Bankers' can be I T V programmes like *Coronation Street*, or a series of Shakespearian plays on the B B C. 'You tell me when the next series is on,' said Firman, 'and I'll buy time blindly against it – or *Monitor*, *Gallery* and *Panorama* for that matter. If I T V put on anything cultural, we avoid it like the plague, simply because of the high capital cost maintained against a vastly reduced audience.'

For economy, he prefers to book spots in the period before peak viewing hours begin – 'early off-peak' is the media jargon – 'because we think we'll get a high ratio of housewives for a low cost at that time. But we don't like spots before six, preferably a little bit afterwards.'

Most media planners have preferences like this; but very few agencies change their spots with such urgency and intensity as Masius. They reckon to keep the programme companies sweet by the total amount of money they spend on television time, and by never booking speculatively. 'In return,' said Firman, 'if the companies move a single spot against our wishes, we are prepared to call a meeting at top level.'

In the middle of all this hectic spot-changing, Masius – like all the other agencies – have to maintain their social contacts with the men from the programme companies. This is the old-boy net which could be useful at times when favours are needed. 'Very rarely do I have a free lunch-time,' said Firman. 'After all, there are fourteen stations – with fourteen sales directors, fourteen number twos, fourteen senior group heads – that's almost fifty to start with; I could go to lunch with them – or take them to lunch – every day. Mind you, I think it's essential not to get too friendly – I've only been to purely social functions with contractors' people three times in six years.'

Masius is typical of the high-pressure T V agencies in London. Interestingly, the competitors Firman most admires are both American-owned, Young and Rubicam, and Foote, Cone and Belding. Thompson also move spots frequently. In 1963, for instance, the agency bought 32,000 spots altogether, but issued no less than 74,000 orders, corrections or alterations.

Thompson were one of the first agencies to do any work into the problem which had been worrying most people in the media game for some time. When the euphoria of the T V honeymoon was over, and one or two media men began to look up from the frantic scramble for the right peak-time spots, some of them began asking what notice the T V audience took of their advertisements anyway. T A M, after all, measured only sets switched on, not the degree of attention.

And Thompson's study on audience attention levels was one of the things which brought the honeymoon to an end. They interviewed 11,500 housewives in the summer and winter of 1961, and came up with some disturbing findings. The first was that between 20 and 25 per cent of women were actually out of the room while the T V set was switched on during peak hours, and another 40 per cent were either combining viewing with some other activity or considered themselves as 'not viewing' for some other reason. That left only 35 to 40 per cent paying "full attention".

Thompson related their findings to particular times. 'Let's take winter weekday evenings,' said Christopher Higham. 'Perhaps 30 per cent of homes are switched to the commercial channel, but our research showed that only 6 per cent are paying full attention, with 8 per cent knitting or doing something else as well as viewing. The other 16 per cent would either be out of the room, or in it and not watching T V. So, where others would say 30 per cent, we would say 14 per cent. And as for the peak, where according to T A M 52 per cent of the I T V audience might have their sets switched on, we would say only 37 per cent were giving undivided attention.'

The Thompson research, for instance, indicated that during 'early off-peak', 500,000 of the audience were paying full attention, while a million others had their sets on but were either out of the room or doing something else besides viewing. In peak-time 2.4 million were paying full attention, while 4½ million of the 'audience' were otherwise engaged. In 'late off-peak' – from, say, 10.30 to 11 p.m., the study showed that 1.8 million would be giving full attention, and 2.9 million either out of the room or else viewing and doing something else. Apart from the harsh realities which the research indicated, it also suggested to Thompson that 'late off-peak' was an economical buy compared with the 5.30 to 7 p.m. segment.

The 'housewives' medium had, in fact, taken a heavy knock, particularly in the same year that the Government had imposed the television advertising tax. Nor were its troubles over. That same year, the London Press Exchange published another study, which showed how wildly optimistic early estimates of the attention of T V audiences had been. It also demonstrated the extent to which a high level of 'viewer interest' in programmes led to better recall of advertisements appearing in them.

It showed that: on weekdays, 24 per cent of women, on average, were out of the room when the T V was on; that the absentee level varied – 34 per cent were out of the room between 6 and 7 p.m., only 19 per cent between 10 and 11 p.m.; and that of the total audience, a mere 30 per cent were viewing only.

It went on to compare the behaviour of the I T V audience during the different *advertising breaks*, and found more dispiriting statistics. In the breaks between 5.45 and 6.30 p.m., only 20 per cent of the audience were viewing and doing nothing else; between 6.30 and 7 p.m., only 24 per cent; and even between 8 and 8.30 p.m., only 37 per cent.

As for the ability to identify the advertisements which appeared *during* the breaks, only 45 per cent of those who were 'viewing only' could do so – and a mere 19 per cent of those who were out of the room when the set was switched on.

Even these studies were only a start on the long road of television research in depth. There was still a powerful unsatisfied demand in the agencies to know exactly what the audience to each of the fourteen stations was like. Very little detailed work had been done. For the first year and a half of commercial television, an organization known as The Pulse Limited, had provided information on the number and character-istics of viewers, but then folded; and in 1959 and 1960, three large-scale studies on the viewing of individuals were done by Research Ser-vices for Granada.

The only notable study elsewhere was a rather curious piece of mass psycho-analysis called *The Londoner* and published by Associated-Re-diffusion. With the aid of a high-powered advisory committee of statis-ticians, sociologists and psychologists, the survey set out to chart the nature of the Londoner and the characteristics of the London Market. It used a random sample of 10,000 and analysed them according to thir-teen psychological variables.

These were supposedly of most interest to media men when they were related to specific media. For instance, the survey suggested that *The People, News of the World* and *Sunday Mirror* readers were of below average intelligence, while readers of the *Sunday Express* were above average. *Sunday Express* readers were also, said *The Londoner*, more ambitious, more thoughtful, less radical.

The same technique was applied to eighteen different ITV pro-grammes, besides some from the BBC. The information yielded was curious to say the least. In a group classified as 'most extrovert males between 16 and 44', the most popular programmes were *Sunday Night at the London Palladium* with 63 per cent, and *No Hiding Place* with 60 per cent. Only 10 per cent watched *Biggles*. The most popular programmes for 'introverted women over 45' were *Emergency Ward 10, Double Your Money* and *Probation Officer*. Again only 11 per cent watched *Biggles*.

The Londoner was not well received in the agencies. One of Thomp-son's media men said that 'nobody in the agency could understand a word of the introductory survey' and Adrian Sycamore added that in any case they couldn't care less at this stage if people were neurotics or humanitarians. *The Londoner* was certainly comprehensive – it takes a separate trolley to wheel all the volumes round together – but it dealt in terms which were either too advanced or too obscure for the average media man.

By 1962, in any case, the commercial television boom was over. There was only a small increase in total bookings, while the newspapers and magazines – which had actually suffered from smaller total bookings than in 1961 – regained a bit of lost ground. Over the year as a whole, an average of 4.6 minutes of advertising per hour was transmitted from each of the fourteen stations – 1.4 minutes less than the permitted maximum, and although London, Midlands and the North were generally booked for 70 to 100 per cent of their available time, the other stations had to be satisfied with something between 50 and 75 per cent.

Nor does the future look a great deal brighter for the smaller stations. But, after the arrival of the B B C's second channel in April 1964, one agency – the London Press Exchange – made what turned out to be a somewhat reassuring assessment of the future of I T V audiences. Carried out between May 4th and 11th in the London area, it found that only between 7 and 8 per cent of homes had effective B B C-2 receivers – and that, of them, less than a quarter watched at all frequently. Only about 4 per cent intended to get a B B C-2 receiver in the near future. L P E concluded that it would take a radical change of policy by the B B C to affect I T V audiences appreciably. And L P E still believes that television will continue to increase its share of total advertising spending: the 'housewife's medium' may have sustained a series of shocks, but it still has the fascination of the great unknown.

15. Banks and Models

The arrival of commercial television had completely changed the media business. Now, a far more fundamental revolution looms ahead on the transatlantic horizon – the introduction of the computer to do the complex work of media planning.

British advertising agencies have as yet made very little use of computers. Until now the machines they have used (or hired) have been 'sophisticated punch-card sorters', as Dr Simon Broadbent, the mathematician who is Research Services' expert in computer development, calls them. The L P E, for example, has an I B M 101 of their own (Research Services have another), which can comfortably handle a quick analysis of L P E's television spot bookings and their cost or else follow a schedule through its life, keeping a check on how much is committed ahead to the different media.

Ownership of even a machine of this size is still a rare status symbol in British advertising. Thompson, for instance, pay £250 an hour for the use of the I B M 7090 which is hired by Associated Newspapers, but tend to use it sparingly – just a few minutes at a time, and again for comparatively simple jobs. It might, perhaps, tell the agency what would happen to the profile and coverage of a schedule if two or three papers were taken off it. Other agencies hire the same machine for much the same purpose. Only big American-owned agencies like B B D O can boast of having a sizeable computer of their own – and then it stays in New York.

In London, computers are usually still a sort of sophisticated flourish, which the media boffins occasionally turn to for a spot of quick calculation, though they are still used as a routine for exercises like the National Readership Survey. In America, for a variety of reasons, they have recently become one of the facts of agency life.

The first is that media planning on Madison Avenue is an infinitely more complex affair. The American media men have 12,000 newspapers, 9,000 periodicals, 500 T V stations and 3,600 radio stations to juggle with – and American marketing men commonly divide the country into no less than 3,000 different regions. By British standards, the volume of work is colossal. One agency alone, Leo Burnett – in the top dozen for size, but not one of the giants – books 27,000 T V spots every month. (Masius – which handles 2,400 – has roughly the same ranking as Burnett in this country.) As one computer expert said: 'In Britain, you can write down most media plans on one piece of paper. In America, you can't even do that for the daily newspapers – there are thousands of them.' A computer is a very handy way of cutting through the morass.

And, in any case, the top American agencies are big enough to be able to afford to buy and run a computer. Young and Rubicam, who have two – a Remrand Univac and an I B M 1620 – spent $1 million on their Univac, but they bill well over $200 million a year. It has been calculated that an agency needs billings of $50 million to make it economic for it to have its own computer – but on that reckoning there were twenty-three American agencies which were big enough in 1961 (there were just four in Britain).

So it is perhaps surprising that only six of the American giants – Y & R, B B D O, Thompson, Burnett, Benton and Bowles and Ted Bates – have so far acquired big computers. Many still prefer to put work out to the swarm of bureaux which either have computers or hire them, in preference even to renting a machine. Renting can, after all, cost £11,000 a month, not to mention the price of office space and air conditioning, and the salaries of the investigating and programming staff needed to man the machine.

In each of the six American agencies, the big computer has been given a lot of bread-and-butter work previously done by clerks or on punched-cards. They invariably record the agency's newspaper and television bookings and keep them up to date, their payments to media owners and bills to clients, the allocation of production costs, the payroll, and in addition process market research data.

But these jobs are off-loaded on to the computer only to help pay for some part of its total cost. Its real work is to help speed up the creation of accurate media schedules.

At its simplest, this might mean analysing the cost and cover of several media schedules at once. Or it might, to take a more concrete example, compare a product's sales with the advertising budget allocated to each of the 3000 different regions – and come up with the ones with below-average spending where extra local advertising might be needed. It might also take forecasts of competitors' likely schedules, see where they are likely to spend their money and then suggest the best counter-strategy. This sort of precision is impossible at the moment in Britain.

But, with a big computer, endless applications of this kind are perfectly possible. It can be used to store masses of data about particular media and then, when a schedule is being put together, it can be told when and where T V spots have already been booked – and come up with suggestions as to where more ought to be placed.

There are other, infinitely more sophisticated, ways of using it. One of the most complex involves building up in the computer an accurate model of the national market – using the profiles of thousands of typical individuals as the bricks. 'What you do in fact,' said a computer expert, 'is to construct an artificial population in the computer, with a vast amount of detail about all their habits and the media they use. You might put information on about 8000 people in.'

Such a model will reveal, among other things, exactly how each of these typical individuals is exposed to advertising – and hence be able to calculate what effect a particular schedule will have on specific groups in specially selected areas (or over the country as a whole) if it ran for a week, a month or a year. The computer can be made to produce just such information from this 'bank' as is felt to be relevant to the marketing of a particular product.

To take the simplest kind of example, the computer could assess how many times AB housewives between 24 and 35 with washing machines more than four years old, living in soft-water areas and having two or more children between the ages of two and eight, would see a half-page advertisement for 'Omo' if it were repeated on page four of the *Daily Telegraph* each alternative Friday for six months. In fact, it could make scores of these calculations at the same time.

Collecting and assimilating 'banks' of information like this is a very expensive business. It might cost easily $100,000 to programme such a model, but once all the preliminary building has been done, it might only cost $500 to analyse a single schedule.

A third application of the big computer in constructing more efficient media schedules is called 'linear programming'. The object, as in other techniques, is to get as many of the right sort of people to see as many of your advertisements as possible – or 'maximizing the number of impacts' in the prevailing jargon. This again involves storing a 'bank' of information in the computer – this time of information about the nature of hundreds of different media – or 'vehicles', as they are called. The method involves making several important value judgments about each of the media – what seems to amount to awarding them merit marks for the strength of their impact. From the enthusiasts' point of view, the most depressing shortcoming of this method is that basic information about media can be hard to come by.

But the most sophisticated application of all is the method which Young and Rubicam claim to have perfected. This is to tell the computer exactly how much of the market you want – say, 18 per cent of the total sales for Brand X detergent – and then ask it how much money you need to spend on advertising to get it, and what media you should spend it on. For this particular scheme, the computer must have a comprehensive bank of information about prospective buyers *and* the media they use, facts about the prices of competing brands and their likely advertising schedules, dealers' profit margins and so on. But to work effectively, it also needs what no agency in the world seems to have been able to divine so far – exactly how much effect on sales each advertisement has. Because of this, most of the other American agencies have reservations about claims made for the system.

For agencies which have not been able to perfect models of their own, there is the Simulmatics Corporation. Simulmatics had their first notable success on the political market. For Kennedy's Presidential campaign, they created a model which showed what issues voters were interested in and then told Kennedy what sort of topics he ought to talk about. Now they are using the same techniques to sell detergents.

To make up their model, they first gather information about thousands of typical, but imaginary, individuals who represent a cross-section of the entire population of the United States over the age of four and broken down by age, sex, region, rural-urban-suburban environment, race, employment, family size, consumer purchasing power and so on. All kinds of extra divisions can easily be thrown in – how many purchases the 'individuals' make at supermarkets, how many at groceries, how old the 'individual's' car is – *ad infinitum*. Then these imaginary, but representative, types are set down in hundreds of counties across America, counties which are also considered to be typical in one way or another. When they have been given 'homes', the model-makers can begin to deduce what media they are likely to use.

If the information is still not detailed enough, the bank can comfortably absorb any information which the client company may have about the specific groups they are trying to sell to.

Simulmatics have a second bank – information about media. For television, for instance, the Corporation keep track of local stations in the counties where their 'individuals' live – and also of 150 programme networks across America, classified by socio-economic groups and applied to the 'individuals'. From this they can work out the probability of the 'individual's' exposure to both certain advertising spots and to programmes.

To produce what is known as the Simulmatics Media-Mix, the two banks of information are brought together – and each of the 'individuals' is taken through the length of the proposed campaign, measuring at each stage the likely number of impacts the advertisements will make on him. The computer can take account of all kinds of likely deviations – in the case of T V, for instance, it allows for the probable effect of habit-forming in the 'individuals' viewing, the effect of satiation with certain sorts of shows, the impact of competition with other programmes and so on. It even simulates what effect a change in the time of programmes is likely to have.

The computer can also, of course, follow several different schedules at once – one of them, perhaps, the major competitor's – and come up with a picture of the people you are reaching, but your competitor is not. A typical report might have 3000 or 4000 sets of tables – of which the client might particularly want only 100.

There are obvious weaknesses in the method. In America, nothing like the amount of necessary information about media is available – and, as in the case of T A M, the sample could easily be too small to predict accurately the behaviour of small groups. Nonetheless, some experts like Broadbent think that some sort of simulation of this kind, may well be the technique ultimately adopted in the British media business.

Young and Rubicam employ a similar technique, though they claim that it is more efficient than Simulmatics. They use the normal demographic data – sex, age, region, income, etc – to define a maximum of 640 of what they call 'cells' – much the same thing as Simulmatics 'types'. For instance, one cell is 'males, 16-21, urban, in families of one child, with incomes of $5000-$9999'. Then the best available media data are spread across the 'cells' which the product needs to hit. Y & R have built up detailed profiles of 800 different media in their Univac – and, like B B D O, claim to have found a satisfactory way of assessing their respective 'auras', but they will not reveal exactly how they do it.

Young and Rubicam, of course, are the one agency which also claims to be able to get their computer to give them the exact advertising budget needed to capture a specific share of the market for a brand. If the advertising budget turns out to be too large, they simply cut down the market share they are chasing.

Whatever the shortcomings of computers and their banks as media planning tools – and there has already been a reaction in America against the easy optimism of the early days – they certainly promote speed of operation. At Young and Rubicam, for example, the media men can get a complete rundown on the reach and cover of a particular schedule of T V spots within three minutes – only fifty seconds of it spent on the computer. And any media buyer can 'phone the machine room and say what market areas he is interested in – and get back almost immediately on the teleprinter an up-to-date analysis of the T V spots which are available for those areas.

B B D O announced their method of linear programming with a great flourish. They simplify their bank of media information by putting T V spots and local newspapers into groups, and assessing them together. This generally reduces the choice for any schedule to between 50 and 100 'vehicles'. To give each of the 'vehicles' its right 'weighting', the agency's media men make all kinds of subjective assessments about its likely impact. Nor do they use the usual figures for the estimated reading and noting of advertisements in particular media – the most meaningful objective, they feel, is to get down to the reader's subconscious perception of the advertisements.

Having made their various 'weightings' for each vehicle, they value each one – by means of what they call a Rated Exposure Unit, which is obtained by multiplying its readership by its 'advertisement exposure rating' and then by its 'impact factor'. The Rated Exposure Unit per dollar of advertising represents the value of the 'vehicle'.

The critics say that there are too many subjective weightings at the beginning of the process to make it valuable, even though the method may then be capable of producing useful comparisons of the likely impact of hundreds of different schedules. They also think that the multiplication of all the successive weighting factors might easily produce far too large a difference in the R E U for different 'vehicles'.

This, then, is the small advance guard of computer men on Madison Avenue. But even some of them are cautious, not to say, defensive, about their use of the machine. Leo Burnett, for instance, are careful about the way they employ their I B M 1401. Only when buying decisions have been made, for instance, is the computer given the work of purchasing estimates, discounts and bills for T V bookings.

The speed of the computer's advance will be limited, in fact, until it can be fed with more reliable and comprehensive information. But as media statistics proliferate, there will be an increasing number of jobs which only big computers can do quickly enough. Experts think that no British agency is likely to want to put down the money needed for a big machine – anywhere between £50,000 and £200,000 – in the foreseeable future, and that what is much more likely to happen is that they will hire time on big machines belonging to other people. Perhaps they hesitate to pay so much for what seems to some people like mechanized guesswork.

PART 2.
PUBLIC RELATIONS

Introduction

So much for advertising which, whatever its faults, is a clearly observable effort to persuade. There are those, however, who believe their money is spent better by using subtler ways of influencing and informing the people they think matter. It may, indeed, be a job which the mere purchase of space and air-time cannot do. In that case they can, if they wish, turn to the public relations men, whose business it is to persuade as quietly and unobtrusively as possible. They buy no space; they are infinitely flexible in their method of operation; and they will do all kinds of jobs for all kinds of clients.

The client might, for instance, be a public company which has suddenly got a name for antiquated management – and whose standing on the Stock Exchange is suffering as a consequence. The P R man's job might be to see that the public gets to know that the company's management is, in fact, young and progressive.

The client might be a foreign government, whose policy – in their opinion – is not understood as it should be in the right quarters at Westminster. The P R men might undertake to see that it is so understood – and that men of influence are ready to speak up for his client.

The client might be a company which wants to try and make sure that it gets a contract or a company which is not getting any contacts at all, and which hopes that the P R man, with his contacts in the right places, might be able to put something in their way.

It might be a 'show-biz' personality, who wants the circumstances of his divorce properly explained to his fans; a noble institution short of funds; a debutante with no observable assets who wants to be launched as successfully as possible into society; and it might even be a famous man who wants as little publicity as he can get. Such is the raw material of P R.

But what of its influence, and success, compared with advertising?

16. Toby O'Brien

E. D. ('Toby') O'Brien is large, well-padded, bluff, charming and excellently connected. He has an Oxford drawl, wears a clove carnation and dispenses excellent dry martinis at the eighteenth-century house off Piccadilly which is the headquarters of the E. D. O'Brien Organization. Working at his Hepplewhite desk, he sits comfortably sandwiched between two noble Irish ancestors: the 4th Earl of Inchiquin gazes coolly over his shoulder, while the 2nd – dressed in the Royal scarlet (an honour bestowed on the family by Henry the Eighth) – stares him firmly in the eye.

O'Brien, too, is slightly larger than life. He bears more than a faint resemblance, both in appearance and manner, to Sir Donald Wolfit, and he might have been a good Shakespearean actor had his lights led him that way.

As it is, he is a public relations consultant and his job is to help a variety of clients to present as pleasant a face as possible to the world. It is not always an easy job. Hastily hired as consultant to the Portuguese Embassy shortly after the Angola trouble broke out, O'Brien had to explain Salazar's point of view to the British Press. Though he has now lost the Spanish tourist account, he still produces a fortnightly newsletter which is partly concerned with putting across the Franco régime. As P R to Tanganyika Concessions (the giant company with a £150 million stake in Katanga's *Union Minière*), O'Brien fought to organize support for Tshombe in the House of Commons. On behalf of Cunard, he set out to convince the doubtful M Ps that the Q3 was a national necessity.

All of which suggests that No. 2 Old Burlington Street is the centre of a highly political operation. O'Brien, however, claims that his political accounts (he also currently represents the Imam of Yemen) have come to him 'by accident' and that he is much happier 'on straightforward industrial accounts like Cunard'. He serves a good many non-political clients, among them Deinhard, the Hock and Moselle shippers; Gonzalez Byass, the Spanish sherry merchants; the Potato Marketing Board; British Nylon Spinners; and the Aynesley Trust, a group which includes such oddly assorted interests as the London Clinic and the Golf Society of Great Britain.

O'Brien has also, from time to time, turned his talents to the job of raising money for good causes like the Oxford Historic Buildings Appeal. This is a practice which is standard among top P Rs, to whom it is almost a *sine qua non* to have one worthy charity among their accounts.

Toby O'Brien's is one of about 300 such agencies which are scattered all over central London. The most ostentatious are to be found among the mansions of Mayfair (though even there the luxury is generally limited to the boss's office and the main reception room) but an address further east is not held to be a disadvantage for P R men who specialize in handling industrial public relations. Their staffs vary in size from one to fifty and they wield as much influence as their skill and the strength of their connections in the Press, television and Parliament permit them.[1]

Among the 300 are the controversial high-flyers of the P R business, the freelances who are tough and well-connected enough to survive without seeking the comparative safety of a company or Government department job. They are the professionals in a profession which is still notable for its high percentage of amateurs.[2]

A number are attached to advertising agencies – Thompson, Mather and Crowther, B B D O and a good many others have their own P R set-ups – and several of the big agencies have found the offer of free P R to be a useful carrot in landing big advertising accounts. Not surprisingly, the use of inducements of this kind has angered the firms who live off P R alone; they regard it as the importation of trading-stamp techniques into a highly specialized professional business beside which advertising is a comparatively crude affair.

Toby O'Brien is perhaps the most colourful of this small band which blossomed during the long years of Tory rule as an apparently almost inevitable by-product of the Conservative apparatus. But he was much more than that. He was also the pacemaker for the P R business, the man who showed what could be done by someone who came from the right stable. His career is in many ways a history of public relations in post-war Britain.

Before O'Brien's entry into the business, P R was not an industry so much as a game practised by a handful of skilful individuals.[3] There

[1] In 1963, there were thirty-four M Ps who had past or present connections with advertising or P R firms.

[2] Most of Britain's 5000 P Rs exist simply to explain the policy of Government departments or companies to the outside world. Many, far from being trained in publicity, are unwilling conscripts from other departments. A few companies, however, have ample P R sections, none more ample than the big car firms. British industry, indeed, has been estimated to spend something like £40 million a year on 1,800 P R house journals, which have a combined circulation of 17,000,000

[3] The use of the term 'public relations' to indicate a way of handling publicity was first made in 1924 by Ivy Lee, an American who advised the American Telephone and Telegraph Company and other leading U S companies.

were men like Sir Stephen Tallents[4] at the Empire Marketing Board and then in 1933 at the GPO – PR was known cynically as 'la carrière ouverte aux Tallents' – Sir John Elliot at the Southern Railway, Richmond Temple and Philip Gee. There were also a small number of PR firms: Sir Basil Clarke, who founded Editorial Services (now CS Services), helped Lloyd George with his PR problems during the Irish troubles – a formidable job. They were fragmentary beginnings.

Meanwhile O'Brien, like so many other top PR men of the post-war period, had begun life with strong political ambitions – which looked like being fulfilled. At Oxford he was one of the shining lights of that generation of young Tories (which included Alan Lennox-Boyd and Quintin Hogg) and duly became President of the Union. A brilliant career at Westminster might have been forecast for him, but O'Brien went into journalism instead and joined the *Daily Telegraph*, where he wrote the 'Peterborough' column for a time.

He still tinkered with politics, however, and as a 'High Tory with chromium-plated fittings' ('always prepared to defend our ancient principles by the most modern methods'), he moved smoothly and successfully among the various right-wing coteries. It was he in fact who engineered a meeting which led ultimately to the smuggling of Franco back to Spain from the Canaries and had a decisive effect on the Civil War. At that time, O'Brien was running a series of regular Sunday morning sherry parties in his flat in Chester Street, and at one of them he introduced Luis Bolin, the London correspondent of the Madrid Monarchist daily ABC, to the late Douglas Jerrold, then the chairman of Eyre and Spottiswoode (Publishers). Bolin wanted to meet Jerrold after reading his book *Storm over Europe*, which had been sympathetic to the Monarchist cause. O'Brien tells the tale with relish – as a supporter of Franco, it was an operation very much to his taste. It was also, indirectly, to bring him considerable benefit in later life.

As a result of their meeting in Chester Street, the two men hired a plane – a Dragon Rapide – from Croydon Airport. The Rapide set off for Casablanca with a bizarre crew which included Captain Bebb, the pilot, Hugh Pollard, a firearms expert and two blondes who, O'Brien explained, helped to lend credence to their story that they were eccentric British tourists. The blondes soon proved invaluable, because the Rapide had to put down suddenly at a Portuguese airport to refuel, and only the appearance of the blondes deterred the *commandante* from arresting the entire party.

Bolin himself could not go any further than Casablanca because of his known Monarchist sympathies, and Bebb flew on without him. Bolín

---

[4] Tallents wrote a booklet called *The Projection of England* at the Empire Marketing Board.

meanwhile waited anxiously for his return, sitting at the Casablanca airport having an evening drink with the *commandante*. Then the entire adventure came within an ace of foundering completely. 'Do you know,' said O'Brien with a smile, 'that Spain might have been Red in 1940 but for a small screwdriver? This is the story.

'Luis heard the plane approaching and said to the *commandante* – "here are my friends, switch on the landing lights". To Bolin's horror, the *commandante* discovered that the only electrician who could switch them on had gone home. Luis thought all was lost since there was no moon, but at that very moment the mechanic came back – he wanted to mend his radio, but had forgotten a small screwdriver and had returned to get it.'

This was Toby O'Brien's first taste of political adventure – a taste he has never quite lost. The happy sequel to the story, however, did not come until after the 1939–45 war. In 1949, Bolin came to London and dined with O'Brien. Over the meal, he asked if O'Brien could suggest someone to run a small publicity drive with the object of boosting the then virtually non-existent Spanish tourist trade. After various candidates had been discussed, Bolin said: 'I suppose you wouldn't take it on, Toby?' O'Brien said he would be delighted. Again he describes the acquisition as 'pure accident'. It did, nonetheless, start him on his career as an independent P R.

It was a similar piece of shrewdness on O'Brien's part in 1938 which had first led him towards public relations. In that year the *Daily Telegraph* had sent him to Libya to follow Mussolini from one end of the country to the other, and when he came back he put in a report to Lord Lloyd at the Foreign Office. Lord Lloyd, then starting from scratch all our overseas propaganda, as a result suggested that O'Brien might come and help. Thus O'Brien found himself a founder-member of what is now the Central Office of Information.

The war, curiously enough, was the seed-time of the modern P R business. While O'Brien, under Lloyd, helped to pioneer the techniques of mass propaganda which kept the national morale high, hundreds of other men were practising the same arts in other ministries. After the war, like Army drivers who had never had cars before, they did not lose their taste for their war-time work, and drifted into P R. For O'Brien, the art of mass persuasion was to come in particularly useful when he was given the job of creating a new and brighter image for the Tory Party. His boss was to be the late Lord Woolton, the war-time Minister of Food.

Immediately after the war, however, O'Brien went to the Rootes Group. The British car magnates were notoriously reticent but O'Brien let journalists know that Lord Rootes was always accessible and could always be relied on for a quote. It was an immensely successful operation. Lord Rootes got a great deal of publicity which cost nothing apart from O'Brien's salary and entertainment expenses.

O'Brien still hankered after something more overtly political – perhaps he was still hoping to find his way to Westminster. So, when in 1946, Lord Woolton (then chairman of the Conservative Party) asked him to go to the Tory Central Office, he accepted even though it meant halving his salary. His arrival – as public relations consultant to His Majesty's Opposition – made history. It was the first time that a professional publicist had been employed to change the image of a political party. The appointment marked, if anything did, the opening of the P R era in Britain.

When he arrived at Central Office, the publicity department consisted of two girls – 'one of whom nearly did shorthand. If I hadn't brought my own girl with me, there'd have been nobody to take a letter.' Press releases were sent by post only to *The Times, Daily Telegraph, Financial Times* and Press Association and there was no such thing as a newspaper cutting service. When O'Brien asked for cuttings on Socialist Party finances, he discovered that there was only one Labour Party file, which covered everything from the time of Keir Hardie.

He ordered regular cutting of both national and provincial papers. Three weeks later, he asked for the first two paragraphs of an *Evening Standard* story about (the first) Lord Hailsham and drew a blank. After checking under Hogg, he inquired what happened to the cuttings. 'Oh,' replied a secretary, 'when everybody has seen them, we throw them away.'

Slowly O'Brien built up a smooth and efficient publicity machine. The staff were reinforced, salaries went up and twelve regional information officers were appointed. Nor did O'Brien himself become a faceless P R: the phrase 'Toby O'Brien commented . . .' became commonplace in Press stories.[5] He also specialized in cheerful little pranks to show that the Tory Party was still alive and kicking. One Christmas, he had all Central Office letters franked with the greeting 'A Happy Xmas and a Tory New Year'. 'When the Labour Party didn't rise to the bait,' he said with a chuckle, 'I sent a Young Tory masquerading as a Young Socialist to complain to the chief postmaster of the district. He rose to it like a trout to a fly and had the second part of the slogan blacked out. There were questions in Parliament, and of course we said we'd withdraw.' The incident gave O'Brien the opportunity of writing a funny letter to *The Times*.

But perhaps his toughest job was to attract the national and international Press to the annual conference. He had taken over at Central

[5] There was soon a revulsion against this personal type of P R. 'A Central Office spokesman' is now standard practice.

Office on the eve of the Blackpool conference in 1946, and one of his first moves was to find out what facilities the Press were given. Had they a room of their own?: good heavens, no. And telephones?; there were, O'Brien was told, plenty of coin-boxes in the Winter Gardens.

The following year, he again clashed with officials about arrangements for the Brighton conference. By that time, interest in the annual gathering had increased and there was a huge demand for seats. O'Brien wanted 200 places for the Press, but was told that the number allotted was thirty-five. He inquired how this figure was arrived at, and was told that it had been laid down in 1934. O'Brien insisted on 200, but only the threat of an immediate telephone call to Lord Woolton did the trick. Not everybody in the Party seemed to want a bright new image.

O'Brien also thought up the idea of raising £1 million for Party funds. 'Before the Brighton conference,' he recalled, 'I was lying in my bath thinking. "God, I thought, we're so broke, we must raise a million." ' Immediately afterwards he sent a note off to Woolton suggesting the idea of a £1 million Fighting Fund.

Woolton – whom O'Brien had worked hard to project as the paternal Uncle Fred – launched the appeal on the last day of the Brighton conference. He also – on O'Brien's suggestion – made records of his speech beforehand so that they were on sale as the delegates came out of the meeting. 'Uncle Fred, the great perfectionist and old trouper that he was, rehearsed for two days to get it exactly right, with his collar and tie off,' said Toby, 'but it was worth it, copies of the record went out to all the constituencies and the contributions poured in.' The 'Fighting Fund' idea became part of Tory mythology, and is still a splendid fund-raiser even for the safest by-election.

By the time he left Central Office, O'Brien had laid the foundations of the Tory P R machine. He had also become closely acquainted with both the leadership and the rank-and-file of the Party. Not only did he know most of the Cabinet intimately, he also got to know the younger Tories who were on their way to the top. He worked with both Reginald Maudling and Iain Macleod. Selwyn Lloyd, whom he had first met in 1945 at a Burke Club dinner (the Burke is a club for right-wing peers, M Ps and writers), became his close friend. His broadcasting officer was John Profumo – 'brilliant, one of the best chaps I had.'

O'Brien, instead of being merely well connected, became eminently well connected, a most valuable asset for any P R. (Just how well connected, he was to prove in later years, when Cecil B. de Mille hired him to help push his film *The Ten Commandments*. Among other things, he was able to arrange for Winston Churchill to see the film in a special showing at his home.) He belonged to the right clubs – White's and the Coningsby and the 1900 among others – and he knew the right people. Nobody could accuse him of forcing his way into the House of

Commons to lobby on behalf of clients, particularly in the early years after he left Central Office; O'Brien met the people he wanted to see in the normal course of events, and there were all kinds of ways in which – having declared his interest – he could set before them, quite naturally, his client's point of view.

He operated from outside Parliament, but he had splendid contacts inside and great freedom of movement. He now describes himself as 'a failed politician', but in the early years after Central Office at least, it is arguable that he exercised far more political power as an outsider than he would have done as a Member of Parliament.

When he left Central Office, his first big account was Spanish tourism and he quickly began to let top people know that the Costa Brava was *the* place for a holiday. 'I always say I have thirty whisperers in London,' he explained, 'so I got on to them and set them whispering that Spain was a splendid place for a holiday. In less than no time, the most unexpected people were coming up to me and suggesting that I ought to go to Spain for a holiday.'

And, as a loyal P R man should, O'Brien did holiday in Spain, taking Selwyn Lloyd and his wife to make up a foursome. Since then they have gone to Spain together every year – usually to S'Agara on the Costa Brava – except the year in which Lloyd was Foreign Secretary. O'Brien has also taken Iain Macleod with him to Spain. Had it helped the Spanish Tourist account? 'Well, of course that wasn't the object of the exercise, but naturally it helped.' The trade certainly boomed; the numbers of British holiday-makers going to Spain soared in the fourteen years that O'Brien handled the account from 13,000 to a million.

O'Brien also had a hand in the early battle for commercial television. Here he does not deny that he was a hidden persuader. Like a lot of other Tories, he felt that 'left-wing influence at the B B C' had played a considerable part in the Tory defeats in 1945 and 1950 and he wanted to break what he called their 'left-wing monopoly'.

So, years before the Popular Television Association was formed to lobby for commercial television, O'Brien was advising its keenest supporters. One of them was Norman Collins, ex-B B C himself, and very strongly in favour of a commercial channel; another was David Gammans, then assistant Postmaster-General. 'For several years before the P T A was formed,' said O'Brien, 'I used to meet first Collins and then Gammans – they couldn't meet because Gammans was a member of the Government. Then groups of us used to get together at the Reform Club – an unexceptional venue – there'd be six or seven of us. Ian Orr-Ewing used to come, I remember. Christopher Mayhew claimed that he had the bishops and the heads of colleges at Oxford and Cambridge (very few of whom had seen a T V programme incidentally) behind him, so that at this late stage we had to get the canons and archdeacons and the one remaining uncommitted bishop – Chichester – on our side.'

These were the early days of the commercial television lobby. As it grew in strength, O'Brien continued to help with the strategy. He claims credit for inventing the title of the Independent Television Authority – ' "Independent", I said, "but not Corporation, that smacks too much of the B B C. Let's say Authority".' He also gave some important advice when the Popular Television Association came to be launched in July 1954.

Just before the launching, Anthony Fell (the Tory M P) and Ronald Simms, who was to be secretary of the P T A (and later went as P R O to the Tory Central Office), invited O'Brien to lunch. They told him that they were going to launch the P T A with letters to *The Times* and twenty provincial papers. Toby disagreed. 'I said, "you might just as well not launch it at all. *The Times* is our bitter enemy, it's a stamping-ground for Mayhew and the bishops. The *Telegraph* is our only friend, but if you just send it to *The Times*, you'll offend the *Telegraph*." '

Simms and Fell agreed that they should ring Lord Derby, the P T A's Chairman, to ask him whether he would be willing to sign any letter they produced. Derby was willing and O'Brien phoned the letter to the paper. It appeared at the top of the letters column. 'Now that,' said O'Brien with satisfaction, 'was a real example of public relations.'

His favourite campaign, however, was the one he fought for Tanganyika Concessions. O'Brien was hired to do the job by a former Backbench Tory M P, Captain Charles Waterhouse, who was also chairman of 'Tanks'. When the Congo exploded in 1960, the company's £150 million holding in *Union Minière* was clearly at stake. Toby O'Brien's job was to put Katanga's case in Britain, and to M Ps in particular although, as he said, 'the company didn't give a damn who ran the Congo. They simply couldn't see why the one part where there was law and order and a multi-racial society should be disturbed.' He flew out to Elisabethville, liked Tshombe – who called him 'O'Brien le bon' to distinguish him from Conor Cruise O'Brien – and fought enthusiastically for him when he came back to Britain.

He began to turn out a fortnightly news sheet, *Congo-Africa*, which went to all the M Ps who said they would like to receive it (about 120 did so). The magazine still has a circulation of about 600. O'Brien also sought such allies as he could in the House of Commons, though he is chary of calling them a lobby. 'There were some people who joined in on some aspects of the Congo business,' he said, 'but not on others. A lobby is not a tight, cohesive organization. In any case,' he added, 'there have always been lobbies, and I see nothing wrong with them, they simply put a point of view across.'

Nor does he think the campaign was a complete failure. 'Katanga,' he said, 'would have collapsed much earlier if there had not been people well informed through us.'

Another more recent job which O'Brien got through a back-bench MP was that of PR consultant to the Imam of Yemen. In this case, the MP was Colonel Neil (Billy) McLean – 'He'd been out there,' said O'Brien, 'and asked me if we could help.' The Imam, at that time (December 1962), had been deposed by a Nassar-backed candidate, and was hiding among his faithful supporters in the Yemeni desert. The same machinery was set in motion, though this time on a smaller scale. This time O'Brien did not go out to the Yemen himself – he appointed a man in Jeddah to represent him – but he did send out propaganda for the Imam to thirty or forty MPs and journalists (the *Express* and the *Telegraph* were particularly sympathetic) and organized lunches so that the Imam's *chargé d'affaires* in London could meet MPs who were likely to be sympathetic. The agency also helped several writers – one from the *Yorkshire Post* – to go out to the Yemen.

Toby O'Brien in fact, has become recognized as a man who has the most useful contacts with the Establishment, both political and religious. Occasionally, the reputation lands him in bizarre situations, like when he invited bishops and church leaders to see *The Ten Commandments*, and to make quotable comments. 'I got twenty Church of England bishops along,' he recalled, 'so I had to see the damn thing a score of times myself. Then there was the Chief Rabbi, who brought eighteen people, but nobody else was allowed into the viewing theatre that time.'

The exercise proved very successful – 'they all made suitable noises and said they were sure it would be a strong moral influence' – and the culmination was a Foyle's Literary Luncheon. He sat next to the Jesuit, Father D'Arcy, and told the distinguished priest that he (D'Arcy) should treat him with some respect in future. 'You see in me one who was described at the top of the list of the people Mr de Mille was to meet in London, England, as "Mr E. D. O'Brien, public relations consultant to *The Ten Commandments*" – though possibly you might take the view that the Holy Father could more reasonably claim such an appointment.'

O'Brien still claims 'twelve friends and five thousand acquaintances' in the Tory hierarchy – and he still mixes in the right circles, though as his period of power at Central Office has slipped into the past, he has probably lost something of his influence. But O'Brien has never been a man to limit his friendships. 'George Brown dines with me Monday week,' he said. 'That's the charm of British politics, you can disagree and still remain friends.'

17. The Tory Succession

Ronald Simms's offices are strategically placed for a PR man with political inclinations. His firm, Industrial Aids Limited, is to be found in a rather dull block off Great Peter Street, just behind Westminster Abbey and equidistant from the House of Commons and the Tory Central Office in Smith Square.

Simms himself might, at first sight, be either a middle-aged Anglican priest or a Back-bench MP for one of the safer Tory seats in Dorset or Norfolk. He is florid-faced and bulky with a deliberate and confidential manner, hospitable (though he keeps his refreshments in a steel filing-cabinet) and perfectly frank. Much less ebullient than Toby O'Brien, there are a surprising number of similarities as well as the fact that the two men are godfather to each other's children.

Simms, like O'Brien, was PR man to the Tory Party – from 1957 to 1961; he too played a leading part in the commercial television lobby; and Simms, like O'Brien, nourished strong political ambitions, strong enough to fight three elections – all unsuccessfully. Simms then came to the opinion that over-forties had 'no chance of getting a safe seat these days', dropped out of the political stakes and concentrated all his energies on public relations. PR was for him a perfectly natural and satisfying substitute for politics: and it has already yielded him a CBE.

Simms was born in Balham – 'of all places' – went to a minor public school (Emanuel) and then started work as an advertising copywriter at 25s a week. He had time to do some university extension lecture courses before the war, joined the Army, and afterwards sank all the £5000 his father had left him into an advertising agency which flopped. He then joined another advertising agency as general manager.

He also tried to make his way in politics; and stood for Bristol South-east in the 1950 election; his opponent was Sir Stafford Cripps. Simms lost comfortably, but got to know Cripps well enough to be invited to Downing Street frequently while Cripps was Chancellor. He also acted as usher at Peggy's wedding to the Ghanaian politician, Joe Appiah. When Simms turned to public relations, one of his earliest accounts was to represent the Ghanaian Opposition.

In 1952 (he had lost East Willesden in 1951), Simms joined Gollings, the advertising agency, to start their PR department. While he was there, he did several jobs in local government elections for Mark Chapman-Walker, then the Tory Central Office P R man. And it was Mark Chapman-Walker who recommended him to Lord Derby as just the man to hold together the administration of the Popular Television Association.

Simms was secretary from July 1953 until the end of 1956 (he lost East Willesden again in 1955), by which time the P T A had become simply 'a watchdog organization'. At the same time, he had also begun to develop an independent P R operation. He had got the Ghanaian Opposition account from Dr K. A. Busia after Toby O'Brien had turned it down. Busia was afraid that Nkrumah intended to create a one-Party State, and wanted to get safeguards put into the Constitution.

Simms was able to put him in touch with a good many M Ps and, with the help of Isobel Cripps, got introductions to Labour leaders such as Lord Attlee and Arthur Creech-Jones. Joe Appiah had by that time already joined the Opposition to Nkrumah. Simms also held press conferences on Busia's behalf, and circulated a good many documents to M Ps about the Ghanaian Constitution. The result was that certain safeguards were written into it, but in the long run Nkrumah was able to do much as he liked.

In the same period, Simms fought a highly successful campaign on behalf of a group of radio manufacturers and users of mobile radios – such as big car-hire firms. They were incensed at the Postmaster-General's decision to clear them off Band Three. Simms, as he explained later, realized that this was 'a highly specialized business, and not something either the public or the average M P would get hot under the collar about. I realized we had to find a gimmick to get us some publicity, so I got a barrister to go through the mass of Post Office Acts with a toothcomb. He unearthed the astonishing fact that the Postmaster-General had, in fact, because of a gap in the legislation, been levying money from licences quite illegally since 1904.' Simms then briefed Lord Gardiner to fight the case, and his clients ended up with more frequencies than they had originally.

With the passing of the Television Act, Simms became the natural successor to Chapman-Walker in the seat of supreme P R power at Central Office. He went at the beginning of 1957 and stayed for over four years. It was Simms, working with Colman, Prentis and Varley and top people inside the Party like Lord Poole and (the then) Lord Hailsham, who helped conceive the massive advertising campaign which cost them £500,000 in the two years before the 1959 election. The idea of the campaign was to identify the Tories with an image of prosperity and opportunity.

It was Lord Poole and Simms who suggested to C P V that they might start with eye-catching pictures of little children – and captions like: 'Will she be fenced in when she grows up?' 'Then,' said Simms, 'we decided we must personalize it, and do it in a way which would startle people and also project us as a party for all classes. So we brought out posters showing all kinds of unusual people, and the caption "You're looking at a Conservative"; for instance, we had a tough-looking chap in a cloth cap eating an apple.'

Simms also turned up the slogan: 'Life is Good with the Conservatives, Don't let the Socialists spoil it', and although Hailsham improved on it – he wanted 'better' – and C P V altered 'spoil' to 'ruin', the slogan stood as the basic theme of the campaign.

When he left Central Office at the end of March 1961, Simms, like O'Brien before him – was set for a career as a top P R man. As he mildly put it: 'It may cut a bit of ice that the Central Office is the biggest publicity job in the country.' He agreed that it gave him a large number of contacts. The contacts included almost the entire Cabinet, but more than that, Simms had learnt at first hand exactly how Conservative, and to a lesser degree, Labour, M Ps ticked.

He took trouble, in fact, to get to know people on both sides of the House. He claims acquaintance with a number of Labour M Ps like Woodrow Wyatt – not to mention trade union men like Sir William Carron and Harry Nicholas. He describes Canon Collins as 'a very great friend – of course, for obvious reasons I've not helped him with C N D, and he would never have thought of asking me to do so, but I have done some publicity for his Defence and Aid Fund which is non-political.'

When he left Central Office, Simms soon built himself up into a very prosperous public relations consultant. He now has five rooms in Great Peter Street, all of them furnished sparely; 'in this business,' he said, 'you don't want a vast show of wealth.' Nonetheless, he is able to employ an assistant, a personal assistant (whom he brought with him from Central Office) and four others and to make a handsome income for himself after taking care of rent and rates of £1600 a year and a wages bill of about £8000.

One account which he picked up immediately he left Smith Square was the successor to the Popular Television Association – the National Broadcasting Development Corporation. The P T A was by then more or less in abeyance, but its backers wanted to try to make sure that the Pilkington Committee, then sitting, recommended a second channel for I T V as well as one for the B B C, that it approved of the idea of Pay-T V, and they were even hopeful that it might recommend an experiment in local commercial broadcasting.

The N B D C – which, incidentally inherited just £276 from the P T A – again had powerful backers. Its president, Lord Lloyd, had been Minister of State at the Colonial Office; the chairman, Sir Harmer Nicholls, M P for Peterborough, had also been Parliamentary Secretary to the Minister of Works. Then there were powerful Tory peers like

Lords Woolton, Mancroft and Grantchester; Tory Back-benchers like Sir Herbert Butcher (a director of Beecham), Captain L. P. S. Orr (chairman of the Mobile Radio Users Association, and a director of one of the Pye group of companies) and Sir Tufton Beamish (director and shareholder of a company formed to exploit commercial sound radio in the South of England); top advertising men like Dan Ingman, managing director of Young and Rubicam, and Leonard Garland, chairman of Garland-Compton; not to mention distinguished academics like A. J. P. Taylor.

Simms estimates that they spent roughly £5000 on promoting their views. Nor does this include the large sums which were spent by the commercial programme companies who backed the idea of a second I T V channel; their entertaining was far more lavish than anything the N B D C laid on.

Simms denies that they ever tried to create a pressure group in the House of Commons, but there was obviously a great deal of informal lobbying, 'We did talk to a lot of M Ps,' he said, 'but we've never deliberately lobbied it, though if conversation has come round to the subject, naturally we've spoken about it. I also talked to members of the Cabinet, but only very informally. I've never invited a Minister to lunch or dinner to talk about commercial television. If I've met them socially, I've asked them what they thought, but everybody does that kind of thing.'

Simms also organized lunches for journalists, held three Press conferences in London and one in every provincial centre, and supplied speakers for about a hundred Rotary Clubs and Chambers of Commerce.

The result was that, long before Pilkington came out, Simms had a shrewd idea exactly where every member of the Cabinet stood, and how many could be relied to back the N B D C's point of view, and he also had a very shrewd idea of what support they could hope for in the body of the House: 'about two-thirds of the Tories were with us, and a good many of the Labour men'. This, if nothing else, provided a considerable assurance that, even if Pilkington went against them – and Simms's own visit to the Committee to give evidence convinced him that it would – all was not lost.

Simms also had a secondary role in the same battle. Not only was he secretary of the N B D C, he also acted as public relations consultant to British Telemeter Home Viewing, one of the companies formed to develop Pay-T V. He did the same thorough job for them, organizing trips for between seventy and eighty M Ps to see over the Telemeter system – more Tory than Labour, as was to be expected – besides encouraging important local officials like town clerks to pay them a visit. About 150 came. From July 1961 onwards – when he was appointed – Simms calculates that B T H V spent £5000 on public relations between the middle of 1961 and the middle of 1963.[6]

Simms acquired a number of interesting political accounts as a direct result of his work at Central Office. One was the job of representing the Kenya Opposition Party, the Kenya African Democratic Union (K A D U). Sir Michael Blundell and Sir Wilfred Havelock, the former Minister of Agriculture in Kenya, recommended him for the job after Opposition leaders like Ronald Ngala and Muliro had said that they thought the K A D U case was going by default in Britain.

As Simms explained: 'The only people known in this country were Kenyatta and Mboya, and Ngala and the others felt they were being sold down the river.' Simms went out to Nairobi for a week to find out what the K A D U policies were and then came back to help them fight for what they wanted, a regional constitution. He arranged meetings and interviews with the British Press, and sent K A D U propaganda to a large number of M Ps. During the Kenya constitutional conference in London (April-May 1962) he advised the K A D U leaders what they ought to say to the Press.

He did not take any M Ps to Kenya, but many went and Simms talked to them when they came back. The campaign was successful, though Simms's estimate of his own part was modest. 'I don't say it's a result of what I did,' he remarked, 'but they did get their regional constitution.' It is one of the most bizarre facts about the dissolution of the British Empire that the former imperial power could even provide public relations men to fight the case of the subject peoples. Whether the P R men were right to take such a heavy responsibility on the basis of a brief visit is more doubtful.

K A D U was not a particularly profitable account for Simms; he made £2500 in fees in two years from it. Much more profitable was his contract to handle publicity for the Shah of Iran. He got the job through a merchant banker friend who does a good deal of trade in Teheran and was asked by the Shah to suggest someone who could help improve his image in Britain. The Shah, said Simms, was worried about 'the peacock-throne image he had got, and wanted more attention paid to his land reforms and the generosity of his gifts to the Iranian peasantry.'

As a result of the offer, Simms went to see the Shah in February 1962. The Shah impressed him – he knew the result of every British by-election since 1945' – did not give him any particular brief but asked only if he would help. Simms worked to get favourable publicity for the Shah in the British newspapers until the end of 1963 (when he lost the account); he also arranged meetings between the Iranian Ambassador and leading

[6] Pay-TV, in fact, had considerable P R backing. British Home Entertainment employed Baron Henry de Westenholz to represent them, and the Rank P R empire was behind Choiceview.

editors. In October 1962 he went to America for the Shah's State visit. Altogether, he was very pleased with his efforts. 'We got very full coverage for the Shah's land reforms,' he said.

Simms is also retained as a consultant by a number of large firms. One is British United Airways, who called him in during their battle for routes with B E A and B O A C. His job, working closely with their own public relations department, was to help build up B U A as 'big-time operators' – it was an amalgamation of a lot of companies – and to create in the staff a sense of working for B U A and not for one of the smaller components. In June 1962, B U A were granted eleven new routes by the Air Transport Licensing Authority. He was also called in by Courtaulds during the take-over battle with I C I, partly because of his Parliamentary contacts.

Part of Simms's usefulness has undoubtedly been his intimate knowledge of the political game. He also had the advantage of being virtually indistinguishable from the average back-bench M P and was thus able to evolve a soft-shoe philosophy of how to influence opinions without treading on anyone's corns.

As he explained: 'It's a case of being tactful and knowing the ropes. There are some things you can get away with and some you can't. You learn from experience which is which.'

But he claimed: 'I've never lobbied in my life. It just embarrasses people who might otherwise help you.'

Simms denies that he has ever asked anybody to speak in a debate in either House. His technique is 'to bring things to the notice of people one knows are interested. Everybody knows that there are twenty or thirty M Ps on both sides of the House who're interested in, say, T V or aviation. If you send them something before a debate – and I do certainly prepare documents for selected M Ps – then it's highly likely that two or three will use the information. Some people may use it in a hostile way, but that's a risk you take. Sensible M Ps search about for information anyway, and that's where you as a P R come in.'

Simms, like many another P R man who seeks to wield influence in Parliament, justifies the effort by pointing to the lack of information from which many M Ps suffer. 'Most M Ps are honestly grateful for the sort of information I give them. After all, if you're an M P, you're a busy man. How many subjects can you be expert on? On the whole, and as long as you don't feel lobbied or got at, you'll feel grateful for the sort of assistance a good P R can give.' Simms of course, speaks as one who might easily have been a M P, but the existence of people like himself seems another testimony to the age-old weakness of democracies run by amateur politicians in the face of well-informed and determined professionals like himself.

He looks upon journalists in much the same way. 'Recently,' he said,

'I was handling an industry under the threat from the Monopolies Commission. It had been having a lot of bad publicity, but I knew the Commission's report was going to exonerate them. Normally this would have been missed by the papers, but I knew the report was coming, so I took out a number of City editors, just before publication and made sure that they knew our side of the tale – and where to turn in this great thick document for a good story.'

Simms also believes in helping journalists on subjects utterly unconnected with his clients' business. 'Then later on, when you want them to do something for you . . . well, he's just more likely to do something for you.' This is the old-boy net, P R-style.

Unlike most P R men, Simms is not a lavish entertainer, and only reckons to give six or seven parties a year. If they happen to be parties of M P's, he generally takes them to the St Stephen's Tavern, which is close to the Commons and has a Division bell, so that they know immediately they are needed in the House. 'Then,' Simms added, 'they generally come back for another drink afterwards.' If he wants to give a dinner for half a dozen he frequently uses the Stafford Hotel, and occasionally the Junior Carlton for still smaller groups. But he is firmly of the opinion that 'no M P can be bought with a good dinner'.

Simms gains a good deal from his modest, quiet approach to P R. In his view, the most dangerous part of the business are 'the little chaps who think they can influence Cabinet Ministers.' He is much more cautious. 'I always say, I can't do anything for six months. After that it's a matter of chance.'

Michael Rice has his offices in one of the plushier parts of Mayfair. On the mantelpiece of his large and elegant room is an Egyptian twelfth Dynasty statue of a scribe, an appropriate ornament for the public relations consultant to the United Arab Republic in Britain. Rice himself, a young man in his middle-thirties, was wearing a gigantic signet-ring and dark glasses when we saw him. He is single, lives in a flat in Hyde Park Place, drives an Alvis and is probably the youngest P R man in London to be able to boast a turnover of £100,000 a year. (In January 1965, his firm acquired control of another P R outfit – Brunskill, Little and Partners.)

He explains his entry into the profession characteristically. 'I was very dogmatic in my middle twenties, and it became obvious that I would be hopeless as an employee. I always felt I knew far better than my bosses how to do the job. This did not prove to be a universally popular point of view, so I decided the reasonable thing to do was to start on my own.' It was 1955, and Rice was 27.

He had previously worked as assistant advertising manager for a chain of shops, and wanted to do something concerned with publicity. He was also a prominent Young Tory – on the national committee, a speaker on Mr Maudling's election platform – and had what he described as 'an obsessional interest in politics'. To Rice, the public relations business combined the two perfectly. 'It has always been difficult for me to disentangle P R from politics,' he said, 'which seems to rather frighten people. To me, the two are almost identical.' Later on, when asked if he would rather be in politics, Rice replied with a smile: 'In politics? I am in politics.'

Of all London's leading public relations men, Rice is the frankest in admitting that – so far as he is concerned – P R is not merely a poor substitute for politics, but even a far more satisfying way of practising the art of political influence.

He set up shop in a fourth-floor office in St James's Street 'with a lease which said I wasn't allowed to slaughter cattle there'. He had plenty of useful friends, particularly among the rising generation of young Tories, and in 1957 he landed his first big fish with a short, six-month contract to work for Carreras-Rothman, the cigarette firm. He still works for them. Rice has not looked back since.

His first big political account was to represent the Government of Ghana. The contract, signed in April 1960 was worth £20,000 a year for three years. He got the job through a friend working for a construction company in Ghana; the friend talked to a Ghanaian Minister and an approach to Rice followed. It seems that Ghana – then moving towards Republican status – wanted to be sure that 'people in Britain were made aware of Ghana's contribution to the stability of Africa.' 'The Ghanaian Government,' said Rice, 'wanted themselves recognized as moderate, reasonable people.' On one of his early visits to Ghana, Rice met Nkrumah – 'who seemed a bit puzzled by the whole affair' – but the contract was signed by the then Foreign Minister, Kojo Botsio.

One of Rice's first moves was to take a party of M Ps out to Accra for a tour of the country. Humphrey Berkeley, the Tory M P, had joined him as a director of the agency, and it was Berkeley who helped him pick out a suitable group. 'You see,' Rice explained, 'there had been an election in 1959 and there were a tremendous number of relatively inexperienced people who made up the Government's majority. Many of these younger members were less swayed by tradition and prejudice, and this was therefore the group to go for.'

But he was careful not to incur the charge, levelled at other P R agencies, of making the invitations for the trip himself. Berkeley took soundings and informed the Ghana Government which M Ps were likely to accept, and the Ghanaians then sent out the letters themselves. As Rice said, 'If it's a P R firm that does the inviting, there's a reservation in the public mind and that doesn't help the client.'

Six M Ps ultimately made the trip in June 1960: among them were

Christopher Chataway, Peter Emery and Peter Tapsell. Rice and Berkeley had reconnoitred the ground together – 'it was like a State progress', Rice recalled. 'One found oneself waving to villagers like the Queen Mother' – but it was Berkeley who led the party himself. The trip lasted twelve days.

So far as Rice was concerned, it paid off enormously. Just after the party had returned, the Congo flared up and Ghana was immediately involved. Ghanaian troops were among the first to enter the country. Nkrumah was known to favour Lumumba, and Rice spent his time commuting between London and Accra, explaining Ghanaian policy to Press and television, to Parliament through his political contacts 'even occasionally – with great respect – to our own Ministers'. When Lumumba came to Britain, one of Rice's executives helped run his Press conference. He was in his element, exercising a powerful influence on opinion from behind the scenes.

He was particularly pleased that they had at least six MPs who had been taken to Ghana. He provided briefs for a good many Members who were seeking information, and scores of people rang up his offices.

Unfortunately for him, the tide of Africanization arrived somewhat rapidly in Ghana. Africans, said the Nkrumah Government, must be seen to be responsible for the top jobs and Rice was sacked in October 1960. He got a generous compensation payment, and is still 'very pro-Ghanaian, although I would make strong reservations about the present (1965) policies of the government'.

Ghana launched him into the field of foreign politics. He acts for the tourist administration of the United Arab Republic – and claims that they have been able to overcome 'the traumatic effect of Suez'; he worked briefly for Cyprus; and has even handled occasional jobs 'with the approval of the Foreign Office', when visiting dignitaries (like Felix Houphouet-Boigny, premier of the Ivory Coast) needed to be introduced to the British Press. Rice would not, however, act for an Iron Curtain country. 'Our criterion,' he says, 'is that we must be satisfied that the interests of Britain are not likely to be prejudiced.'

His firm already had a connection with Jamaica: Lady Huggins, who was married to an ex-Governor, is a director. Rice's main job is to boost Jamaica's tourist industry, but he also acts as adviser to the High Commissioner's Office on a variety of problems including integrating the Jamaican community into Britain. 'We want to show that Jamaicans are a highly intelligent and sophisticated people,' he said. 'They are doctors as well as bus conductors.' His latest overseas account is the Government of Bahrein.

Humphrey Berkeley ceased to be a director of the agency in 1961, though he is still retained as a consultant. Rice now has – like at least one other agency, Voice and Vision – a full-time political specialist who knows the workings of Parliament and the Tory Party intimately. This is Maurice Chandler, for twelve years education officer for the Party in the Midlands, for nine their Press and publicity man in that area.

Chandler, a short, squat man, said that his job was to 'give clients an idea of the channels of communication in the House – the back-bench organizations and the Ministers themselves. I can also give an indication on which M Ps are likely to be interested in a particular subject.'

'It is,' he said, 'much more than just knowing the House. You've got to know if it's the chairman of the committee who influences the policy, or the vice-chairman, or the influential back-bencher whose advice is valued from the Prime Minister downwards. You've got to hand-pick people.' It is Chandler's job to do the picking, to make sure that exactly the right people get to know his client's point of view. 'If you go about it the right way,' he remarked, 'they're jolly glad to be informed. We have a small axe to grind, but provided the information is factual, then you're rendering a service.'

For foreign clients, Chandler hopes to keep the appropriate Minister informed, particularly if the client is trying to get British industry to emigrate. At home, on the industrial front, he keeps clients advised as to what the House is thinking about their particular interests, and what sort of legislation is projected. He continually informs 'M Ps who are interested – not those who're willing to represent us, but those who will represent our client's point of view.'

He gave one or two varied examples. 'Charringtons, the coal merchants, were very interested in the Weights and Measures Bill,' he recalled. 'We didn't get anybody to lobby for them, but we did find half a dozen M Ps who were interested in the Bill, and brought two or three M Ps and a Peer to see their mechanical bagger when it was exhibited at Earls Court.' This sort of activity can easily be explained as the informing of Members, but the line between information and lobbying is obviously only as strong as the particular Member's independence of mind.

When the Royal College of Physicians published their report on cigarette smoking and lung cancer, Rice advised Carreras that the Government was likely to take its strongest action against children smoking – which it did. He also saw to it that the Conservative Party Health Committee had an opportunity of hearing Carreras's views, 'particularly on the value of filter-tips'. They were able to arrange a lunch between the Carreras managing director and Lord Balniel, the committee's chairman.

Chandler himself takes care not to be seen around the Commons too often – 'if I have a meal there socially once a month when they're in session, that's it'. Public relations men have, in any case, found it much harder to hold lunches and dinners in the House than it used to be. (Rice says *his* agency regards this sort of affair as a completely improper use of the Commons – and that they have never done it.) In the past, the Refreshment Department – short of cash because it is not subsidized – used to make money by letting off its five dining-rooms (the biggest will take sixty or more people) to outside bodies who wanted the prestige of a feed in the House. All that was needed was one M P to dine and in effect officiate as host. As one Labour M P said: 'On a Saturday night, the place used to be crowded out with cars.' Then it was rumoured that a washing-machine manufacturer had asked if he could launch his new machine at a dinner there – and the Refreshment Committee tightened the rules quite considerably. 'They're even stricter than they were at the Lords,' Chandler added. 'A political dinner there is a real headache to fix.' Hence the P R retreat to the pubs and hotels close to Parliament.

Chandler himself still lives in the Midlands (where he edits his parish magazine in his spare time), and remains active in Tory Party circles. He is chairman of the Conservative Commonwealth Council in the Midlands and does some work for the North Kensington Tory Association.

Rice is one of London's more obviously prosperous public relations men. He also has a profitable associate company which specializes in selling air-time for Commonwealth and foreign commercial radio and T V stations in Britain and Europe. On his P R accounts alone, he expects to make a profit of between 20 and 25 per cent (small firms, he says, can make 30). All costs are extra – standard P R practice – and are as much as 200 per cent of the basic fee in the case of some overseas clients. It is perhaps not altogether surprising that Michael Rice now has no ambition to enter the House of Commons.

18. PR at Take-over Time

Company public relations men are, with one or two notable exceptions a somewhat retiring breed. They prefer to stay out of the public eye except when they have some triumph to announce (sometimes they have a full-time job helping to keep their own employees happy); and much of their work is defensive and concerned with anticipating or replying to such criticisms as the outside world inflicts upon them.

Occasionally, however, situations arise which drive them and their masters out of this happy obscurity. Very few people, for instance, had heard of the Oil Appliance Manufacturers Association before the heater scandal in 1959, and indeed not too much has been heard about them since it died down. But the classic case of a company's P Rs being dragged into the public arena came during the I C I-Courtaulds take-over battle which raged between mid-December of 1961 and March of the following year. With the continued independence of the entire organization in the balance, public relations became – quite suddenly – enormously important to Courtaulds, not to mention I C I.

Before the battle ended, several of Courtaulds' top executives had been gently pushed aside; the company's entire financial policies had been changed to capture the confidence of shareholders; under the pressure of events, the directors even went so far as to issue profit forecasts for several years ahead. And this from a company which had, as the *Financial Times* put it, 'made something of a tradition out of reticence'. It is surprising what can happen to a firm's attitude to P R when a take-over bidder comes along.

Before December 18th, 1961, when the I C I bid for Courtaulds first leaked out, Courtaulds simply did not believe in public relations. They possessed a P R man, Miles Pitts-Tucker, in appearance a slimmer version of Lord Boothby, and a Press officer in Ken Hibbs, but their functions were strictly limited.

To many of the directors, in fact, the Press was anathema, Sir John Hanbury-Williams – who had been chairman since 1946, though he was due to retire in July 1962 – did not like talking to the Press, and as a result became so inaccessible that Ronald Simms, called in to act as Courtaulds' outside P R adviser, said later: 'It was harder to see the Courtaulds chairman than to get an audience of the Queen.' Nor was the chairman-designate, Sir Alan Wilson, a scientist by training and temperament, a great deal more forthcoming.

The result was that, on the company's financial affairs, both comment and explanation were thin. There was the directors' report and accounts – and Pitts-Tucker had managed to introduce the innovation of a Press conference to go along with it – and there were announcements when factories opened or closed. That was the extent of the light shed on the Courtaulds operation for the benefit of the outside world. (It should be added that the company gave plenty of information about their products to fashion writers and the textile Press.)

In 1956, when Courtaulds closed their oldest rayon factory, the managing director said that the affair wasn't the business of the Press or the outside world and that was all he wanted to say about it. Even when, in the same year, Courtaulds acquired British Celanese, T V cameramen were not allowed to take pictures of the Courtaulds board.

The financial Press, not surprisingly perhaps, felt that the company did not talk because they had something to hide. The facts revealed in the take-over battle were to prove that they were by no means altogether wrong. A company with £18 millions lying idle in reserves could be excused for not emphasizing the point in public.

So, when the battle began, most City journalists were somewhat hostile. The *Evening News* said the company's image in the City had been that of 'a lethargic giant'. A leader in *The Times* said that the 'initial impression' of Courtaulds had been of 'a somnolent family textile concern', and Harold Wincott, writing in the *Investors Chronicle* half-way through the struggle, was even more trenchant. Courtaulds, he said, were largely to blame for the predicament in which they found themselves. 'Its public relations,' he went on, 'have been really pretty dreadful. We are now hearing, and will continue to hear, the Courtaulds side of the case. But undeniably the ICI Board got a head start simply because Courtaulds has neglected its shareholder relationships for many years past.' Had it needed a take-over bid, he asked, before the company was willing to reveal important information?

Courtaulds, then, got off to a bad start. It had the image of a heavily-veiled Victorian dowager, and the Press was tired of its deliberate policy of obscurantism. The Board's final disastrous act had been to cut the interim dividend for the half-year April-September 1961, and to offer a gloomy profit forecast to the shareholders. In fact, there were miti-gating circumstances. The company had just closed its oldest factory in Coventry, and with the Rootes Group plants on strike the men could not find work. The Board felt that the shareholders must bear some of the burden but this was, of course, not explained to them. Nor had the directors seen the results for October, which showed an unexpectedly sudden upturn.

It never seemed to have occurred to them that this was just the kind of move which would encourage ICI to put in a bid. Such a thing seemed inconceivable. Yet within a fortnight, the ICI chairman, Paul Chambers, had begun to drop hints at private dinner parties.

ICI began with all the trump-cards. Their large PR department had worked hard over the years, and the company's image was that of a large, progressive concern with good labour and staff relations. When their financial record came to be more closely examined, the picture darkened somewhat, and the Press noted that the first news of the take-over came through what seemed like a leak to the *Daily Mail*.

The Chambers announcement, in fact, also came as a complete sur-prise to the Courtaulds PR men. During the previous week, Hibbs had been in Coventry and Pitts-Tucker visiting the group's factories in Flint-shire. But Hibbs had a hunch to return, and as soon as he arrived back, the *Sunday Express* were on the telephone, asking him just what was going on. Hibbs immediately got on to H. R. Mathys, one of the Courtaulds directors, but he let nothing out of the bag, and the inquiry passed off. Then, on the Monday, came the *Daily Mail* story.

The bid set off a whirl of urgent activity at Courtaulds. The board had to move quickly if they intended to save the company, and talks with I C I began to try to reach an agreed compromise, which provided a valuable breathing-space. On the P R front, two things seemed absolutely essential. First, the company had to eat its dismal words of October, and offer a brighter financial future to the shareholders; second, there had to be a Press conference, to present an image of a bright, go-ahead management – men who could match the drive and personality of Chambers, in fact.

Hanbury-Williams had been away while the talks with I C I were going on, and when he came back said that – since others had handled the business so far – he would let them carry on. The talks had been conducted largely by Sir Alan Wilson, but he had gone rather further towards I C I than some of his colleagues wished, and the way was therefore open for a younger group of men with a taste for a fight, men like Frank Kearton, Mathys, Koppel and Knight.

These younger men were well aware that the company had to spruce up its image, and they immediately brought the P R men much closer into touch with the Board. Indeed, instead of the traditional Courtaulds' practice of the P R being called to the chairman's room, the Board — or some of them – began to go to him. His room was on the ground floor of the Courtaulds' headquarters in St Martins-le-Grand, and the younger directors made it a practice to drop in on him on their way into the office, to go through the morning papers and decide what steps needed to be taken. There were, in fact, informal P R meetings every morning, before the evening papers began to get on the telephone about nine o'clock.

Then, in the evening, after the telephones had finished ringing, the talks began again. Seldom did they break up before ten, and often they adjourned to the directors' board-room.

After Ronald Simms had been hired, on the suggestion of one of the Courtaulds financial advisers he also used to drop in on these evening conferences.

There was a lot to talk about, apart from the rush of day-to-day events. The entire P R strategy had to be decided, and they could not afford to make any further mistakes. The group very soon came to the view that they were not going to rush into a Press conference – despite the brilliant performances Chambers was putting up – just because that was the accepted way of doing things. Instead, Pitts-Tucker would fix times with either Kearton and/or Mathys and Knight for individual meetings with financial journalists. These men made themselves easily accessible and there was a deliberate effort made from the very beginning to give an impression of a team-effort, rather than emulate the one-man band of Chambers.

The younger Courtaulds men also decided that they would keep off TV, even though they were continually being pressed to appear. They decided that if they had nobody who could do the job really well, they had better avoid it. Wilson was not a good performer and Kearton had had no TV training.

By this time, Courtaulds had called in their financial advisers, Baring Brothers and Binder Hamlyn, and over Christmas and into the New Year they worked hard to produce a blueprint for a policy which would capture the shareholders' imagination. The ammunition had to be ready for the time when the talks with ICI folded up. Courtaulds had so far merely conducted a holding operation.

Finally, on January 17th, 1962, Courtaulds announced that they had *not* been able to reach any agreement with ICI. Pitts-Tucker worked all that evening to produce seven pages of background notes for the Press – a statement of unprecedented length for Courtaulds. Neither he nor Hibbs left the office until midnight, and Pitts-Tucker got up again at four in the morning to draft the rest of the material.

Now Courtaulds had to move fast. Plans for their Press conference were already well laid by the time the ICI talks collapsed, and agreement about a New Deal for the shareholders had been reached with the financial advisers. The conference was called for January 24th in St Martins-le-Grand, and – by a deliberate PR decision – the young Courtaulds men were to be given the stage at it as soon as possible. Their performance would either create the new image which the company needed, or merely confirm the old one.

Even the logistics of the occasion were not simple. Courtaulds unlike ICI, who had a cinema handy – were not set up for receiving 100 journalists. After looking over the games room – green walls and too much echo, they thought – the PR men decided that they would have to convert the basement. They had it carpeted, installed a temporary platform, put in six roving microphones and roped in some pretty girls to show the guests in.

The Press, however, were still dubious of the Courtaulds case. Indeed, a few days before the conference, Fred Ellis of the *Daily Express*, had said sarcastically that it made a change to get information by telephone instead of by carrier pigeon. Kearton, who was determined to give the occasion a touch of humour, thereupon sent out a man to get hold of a basketful of pigeons, which he hoped to let loose for Ellis's benefit at some convenient point in the conference. Such a moment never in fact arrived, but the gesture was typical of the new spirit in Courtaulds.

All through the morning, and again after lunch, the key directors were trying each other out with mock questions. This was, after all, a unique occasion. Hanbury-Williams, who was to be in the chair, came down and tested the microphones. Then, the journalists began to arrive. By the time they left, the new Courtaulds image had been launched.

To begin with, the Press were astonished to be given, several hours before they arrived, a financial statement which not only promised steadily increasing dividends, but also calculated precisely the profits Courtaulds expected as far ahead as 1964–5. This was revolutionary indeed, but they still had a good many questions to ask.

Wilson answered the first queries, perhaps with too much detail. He got involved in a complicated explanation of dates that seemed irrelevant to many of the Press. Then Knight answered a question quickly and clearly. Then Kearton spoke. He demonstrated convincingly that Courtaulds were in a phase of expansion. On the other hand, he said, there was over-capacity in almost every chemical I C I made. Their profits had been down 24 per cent on the first half of 1960 – and he would stake his reputation that they were 25 per cent down in the second half of the year. Courtaulds, by comparison, were only 5 per cent down. Kearton was backed up ably by Mathys, and a notable victory had been won. The Courtaulds' Cavaliers, as they came to be known, had been successfully launched.

This was a major advance, but Courtaulds had other guns still to fire. They had previously done little institutional advertising – largely because they spent £2 million a year on product advertisements. They did possess a house-mark but it was fussy and out-of-date. I C I, on the other hand, had spent a great deal of money projecting their corporate image through advertising.

On January 23rd, Courtaulds got in touch with G. S. Royds, the advertising agency, and asked them about the possibility of mounting, at top speed, a company prestige campaign of the traditional type. Royds got together a special team, which worked continuously for the next forty-eight hours in a private suite in the Mandeville Hotel to work out practical proposals to put before the Courtaulds Board.

Royds advised the company against the standard type of prestige campaign, because they said it would take a lot longer than six weeks to create a corporate image. They suggested instead that the campaign should stick to the main points Courtaulds wanted to get over to their shareholders. The advertising, they said, should take the form of guidance to the public.

Courtaulds agreed, and asked Royds to get down to the creative planning. The agency worked right through the next weekend and came up with the 'guiding hand' symbol and the base-line 'Courtaulds alone can make the most of man-made fibres' as the themes for the campaign. Then they booked four-column spaces in the daily and Sunday Press and full-pages in the financial magazines. The first advertisements were launched on February 4th, and continued for five weeks. The campaign probably played an important part in influencing the small Courtaulds shareholders to remain loyal to the company.

At the same time as the Press conference, and just after the call to Royds, letters from the Courtaulds Staff Association – representing 90 per cent of the employees – appeared in the *Financial Times*, the *Guardian* and the *Daily Telegraph*. The letters expressed the loyalty of the staff to the Courtaulds board, and their dislike of the prospect of a take-over. They were independent, and quite unauthorized, but all the more effective. Nor could they have been better timed. Shareholders were hardly encouraged to get rid of their holdings by the thought that almost the entire company personnel were unhappy at the prospect of take-over.

Things were now going badly for I C I, and by February 14th they had to raise their first offer. That same day there was a debate on monopoly in the House of Commons, and *The Times* weighed in with a long leader which raised very serious doubts about I C I's own financial performance.

Courtaulds replied the following day with an effective counter, which promised a dividend of 12½ per cent for that financial year, and not less than 13 per cent for the following year. They also had the notion of sending out postcards with the statement, asking shareholders to send them back as quickly as possible. The Press quickly caught on and began to telephone daily for the totals.

At the same time, to rebut I C I's charge that they had poor research facilities, Courtaulds brought forward an announcement that they had discovered a new flame-proof fibre, which was still known by its code-name, B H S. They had not intended to make this known until the summer.

Finally, to show how confident they were, they replied to an invitation for their directors to speak to the Society of Investment Analysts by saying that they would be delighted, *if* the Press were also present. The meeting took place in the library of the Institute of Bankers and the financial journalists were there in force. A similar meeting was held – again with the Press present – at the request of the National Association of Investment Clubs.

By March 9th, Courtaulds knew that they had survived and the champagne flowed in St Martins-le-Grand. The *Statist* described the victory as the 'triumph of sentiment over £.s.d.' But the campaign had cost Courtaulds 37½ per cent of its Ordinary stock and, in cash, £361,695 – £112,000 of it the price of the Royds advertisements, £60,000 for financial advertising, the rest made up of fees for financial advisers, brokers and chartered accountants, and printing and postage costs. It was a high price to pay for a new image, and the cost to the company of neglecting its public relations over the years. They had only made one lapse into their old style – when one of the directors tried to carpet Richard Fry, the financial editor of the *Guardian*, for making what he thought was unfair comment.

The repercussions of the battle did not end on March 9th. Sir Alan Wilson resigned with Sir John Hanbury-Williams in July and a new chairman, Sir Dallas Barnard, took over with Kearton and Mathys as his deputies, Kearton being chairman of the operations executive, the Cabinet below the Board. Kearton himself was appointed chairman in October 1964. The public relations department is now much freer to speak to the Press; the attitude at Courtaulds is no longer 'why should we speak?' but rather 'why should we not speak?' The company even had a new house-mark designed – with as its symbol an arrow which points backwards. Perhaps it was intended as a reminder of past folly.

19. Persuasion in Smith Square

The Labour Party first caught on to the importance of a thorough-going and professional system of public relations after their defeat in the 1959 election. Up to that point, P R had been both a dirty word and a field in which the Party's conscience-keepers preferred to remain studiously amateur. When the Tories – with the aid of massive P R and advertising backing – had beaten them for the third time in a row, some of the less conservative Party leaders began to wonder if the time had not come to relinquish their amateur status.

A number – the late Hugh Gaitskell among them – decided that they would not risk losing another election because they presented a blurred or unattractive image to the voters. So it was that, for the first time in Labour history, the 1964 campaign was fought (and, as it turned out, fought successfully) with the backing of highly-skilled P R men.

The crucial change-over came early in 1962, when the old-style press relations men at Transport House moved out, and the new publicity bosses – John Harris and Percy Clark – moved in. The power of the new arrivals was not particularly relished by the traditionalists at Labour headquarters, who saw it as an admission that Tory P R techniques were needed to convert people to Socialism.

Both Harris and Clark had been rebels under the old régime, chafing under the negative, defensive tactics often adopted towards the Press. Harris, a brisk, confident man of 34, typical of the professionalism of the new generation of Labour, had come by way of provincial journalism in Bournemouth and Leicester to be deputy editor of *Forward*, under Francis Williams. He made his mark during the 1959 election when he toured the hustings with Gaitskell and became the leader's personal friend. He was given the newly-created job of Press officer to the Parliamentary Labour Party, and then became the first Director of Publicity in 1962.

When Harold Wilson succeeded Gaitskell, Harris travelled everywhere with him during the first few weeks and took on the task of moulding the Wilson image with almost academic precision.

Clark, too, was a professional journalist. A pleasant Northerner with a ginger goatee, he started his newspaper career in Bolton, then founded a Manchester news agency and finally came to London to edit the Labour Party pages in *Tribune*. He particularly had grim memories of the old amateur era at Transport House. 'I was never allowed to have anything to do with Press relations before 1959,' he said, 'because that's what I knew about. They seemed terrified of anybody who knew anything about the job.'

Their salaries did not begin to compare with the fairly lavish emoluments available at Tory Central Office (Harris was reputedly hired at £1750), but they had the backing of the Party leadership.

Harris and Clark had their offices decorated in bright colours, bought smart executive-style desks, installed strip-lighting and decked out the walls with impressive charts. Harris had a huge guide to the placings of all the Labour Party advertisements, with different-coloured markers for each newspaper. *Daily Mirror* advertisements, and their dates, were marked in white, *Daily Herald* insertions in red. The *Daily Express*'s colour was purple. The *décor* was very different from the dull cream dens of many of the inhabitants of Transport House.

Then Harris began looking for new men, all specialists in their own fields. He recommended the appointment of Clive Bradley from the North American service of the B B C to look after the T V and radio side of the operation, and of Michael Pentreath, formerly the sketch writer of the *Yorkshire Post*, who came in from L P E to handle public relations for London and the Home Counties. Gerald Corr, head of the Accrington office of the *Blackburn Evening Telegraph*, was set up in Birmingham to look after the East and West Midlands.

Harris's department in fact, suddenly seemed to swarm with bright young men in pyjama-stripe shirts and smart suits, until it began to have the air of one of the busier advertising agencies.

Harris made a point of interviewing and choosing all the new men personally, soon increased the staff by 50 per cent and was spending £20,000 a year in salaries.

To make sure that the North was adequately covered, he recommended to the National Executive Committee of the Party (who make all appointments) a PR firm in Newcastle, run by Dan Smith, also a a master-decorator and leader of the Council. Smith in turn arranged for ten journalists in the key Northern marginal seats to give advice on public relations to the candidates and agents.

But the New Look did not stop with the hiring of bright young men. In addition, Harris took advice from top PRs outside, such as Alan Eden-Green, a former President of the Institute of Public Relations. To give advice on advertising, he enlisted the aid of David Kingsley, a director of Benton and Bowles, Brian Murphy from Erwin Masey, Michael Barnes of Crawford's and a number of other executives, including one from CPV. Mark Abrams did a lot of the research which lay behind the various advertising campaigns; the Party, in fact, could lay its hands on a thoroughly professional team.

The new professionalism soon became obvious in a number of ways. Harris and his men took the initiative in putting out stories to the Press, and they began to provide an efficient service to the newspapers. When Aneurin Bevan died in 1960, a good many journalists had complained at the lack of up-to-date information; two years later, when Hugh Gaitskell lay dying, Clark stayed at the hospital day and night, sleeping in the physiotherapy department for six days and only going home twice for a change of clothes. Clark admits that he made himself a nuisance to the specialists, but this time there were several bulletins a day, instead of one.

In the months before the election, Harris's men also gave intensive training in PR to as many of the Party's political agents as they could get to Transport House. When there were local feuds – there was, for instance, a row between the Reading agent and one of the local editors – a trouble-shooter from headquarters was sent out to clear the way for good publicity.

Short courses in television technique were set up for the benefit of candidates, and before every broadcast which Party leaders gave (George Brown's appearance after President Kennedy's assassination was exceptional), the likely course of the programme was thrashed out with the PR men.

For over a year before polling day the panel of PR and advertising consultants met fortnightly, sometimes even weekly, either in Harris's office or at the Reform Club. Over lager and sandwiches, they would talk over future policy.

The work which lay behind the first major advertising campaign ever run by the Labour Party was particularly significant. To begin with,

Research Services had been hired to do frequent surveys to find out what voters – and particularly floating voters – were interested in. Mark Abrams had been impressed by the work which the Simulmatics Corporation had done in America, to find out for Kennedy what topics most concerned the electorate.

Abrams adapted the same technique for British use. He started with a large sample, then separated off the hard-core Labour and Tory supporters, until he was left with the floating voters. Then he asked them what issues they were concerned with. The information was passed on to the men who were planning the advertising campaign – and duly incorporated as the leading themes of the campaign.

The surveys, which could be done frequently both before and after particular advertisements were printed, resulted in significant changes of emphasis in the image which Labour projected for itself. 'This is one of the reasons why we're appealing to people who want their own houses,' said Clark, 'and not just to the council-house owners.'

Clark claimed that the Party's National Executive did not intend market research to influence the formation of policy – but added that the Publicity Committee had allowed it to influence them in deciding to which items of already established policy they should give 'propaganda precedence'.

The planning for this first campaign, which ran until November 1963 and cost approximately £160,000 was done by an *ad hoc* group, mostly Harris's own friends. They changed the original slogan from 'Let's Go Labour', to 'Let's Go *with* Labour' and chose Housing, Education and Economic Expansion as their themes, on the results of Abram's work. Once the advertisements had been drafted, they used the *Daily Herald* to place them – 'of course, they didn't get the 15 per cent commission,' said Harris.

These ran weekly in the *Express, Mirror* and *Herald*, and in sixty provincial papers up and down the country, picked out because they covered marginal seats.

This was followed in the spring of 1964 with a second major campaign (cost, roughly £90,000). Then, as Percy Clark said 'we did nothing during the holiday months, and restricted ourselves to a few last bangs in the last few weeks before the election'. The 'few last bangs' consisted of more full pages in the *Express, Mirror* and *Herald*.

So far as the Wilson image was concerned, the Labour PR men – though they were anxious not to 'Americanize the campaign' – did want to portray their leader as a Kennedy-type figure. The other members of the socialist 'New Frontier' were not, however, always very prominent – partly because nobody wanted to diffuse the image, partly because Wilson was clearly the Party's strongest asset in a campaign where economic issues seemed to be the only ones which really counted.

Wilson also was prevented from falling into the 'whistle-stop trap'. At the previous election, Gaitskell had decided that he must go wherever Macmillan went. Wilson and the new campaign planners asked George Brown to do the whistle-stopping, leaving Wilson free to stick to a handful of major mass-meetings. As a result, he appeared to stroll through the campaign.

And to make sure that the campaign was staying on the rails, there were two key meetings of the P R men every day at 8.30 a.m. At one, Harris met with people like David Kingsley and Michael Barnes from the agencies, and Mark Abrams was there on most days. At the second, Labour's T V team – which now included Christopher Mayhew, Anthony Wedgwood-Benn and Shirley Williams – gathered to discuss strategy. Then, at 10 a.m. Wilson would call Transport House from the field, and co-ordinate the day's programme. George Brown also came on the air on some occasions.

But Harris studiously played down the impact of the P R and advertising experts. 'We exploit opportunities now, whereas in the past we didn't,' he said.

It is an interesting side-light on the different psychology of our two main political parties that the uneasy conscience which some Labour supporters still have over the introduction of public relations techniques to Transport House, never seems to have troubled the Conservatives at all. Even as recently as the 1963 Labour Party Conference one elderly Labour M P remarked that the arrival of Harris at Transport House had been a terrible event for the Party and that Labour had no need to resort to 'hidden persuaders' of their own to win their elections. 'Besides,' he added, 'the man smokes cigars *and* belongs to the Reform Club!'

The Conservative Party has always been more realistic (or less idealistic, depending on your point of view) over these matters. Whereas the Labour Party began as a popular movement, the Conservative Party always has been first and foremost a machine to ensure the election of the greatest possible number of Conservative M Ps to Westminster. It has no inborn suspicion of public relations men if they can help in this one great cause. Because of this the Conservative Central Office, behind its red-brick, insurance-company-Georgian façade on the opposite side of Smith Square to Transport House, has been able to build up the most adroit political propaganda machine in the country.

As George Hutchinson, who was head of the party's publicity during the 1964 general election, put it 'the Conservative Party, being made up of practical men of affairs, is usually ready to employ practical men to attain political ends. If the techniques of business can be applied to politics, we never hesitate to apply them.'

It was, of course, Lord Woolton, who realized the importance of the publicity department when he was given the job of reorganizing the

Party machine after the 1945 defeat. It was largely thanks to his backing that men like Toby O'Brien and Mark Chapman-Walker achieved the position of influence which they held within the party, and it is thanks to him that, in over three years at Smith Square before the election, George Hutchinson had a staff of over fifty people, plus twelve full-time publicity officers working in the constituencies. He had separate departments dealing with posters, publications, press and broadcasting and was responsible for a large warehouse in Southwark where the party stores its publicity material. At the beginning of 1964 he hired Jeremy Murray-Brown, a one-time director for B B C's *Panorama*, to coach and produce Conservative politicians for their appearances on television. Because Conservatives are noticeably modest about such details it is not known exactly how large his budget was, but as he himself put it, 'we have a great deal more money to spend than the other side and we believe in spending it where it will do us the most good.' At the same time Roger Pemberton was loaned to the Conservative Central Office (who paid his salary) by Colman, Prentis and Varley in order to take on special responsibilities on the advertising side.

One of their advantages, indeed, is that the Conservatives have always been able to make a point of employing their outside advisers and helpers on a purely professional basis, and paying top business prices for them. By contrast, Labour's policy of relying on the unpaid or underpaid support of its actual sympathizers places the party in a far less satisfactory position. In something as down-to-earth and potentially controversial as party publicity it is always dangerous to have to rely too much on the unsupported enthusiasm of volunteers.

But while Central Office has the advantage of money, of size and of experience over Transport House in these matters of propaganda, it too has been undergoing a subtle 'readjustment of attitude' to the whole function of publicity and public relations men in politics. Because Central Office is a far more discreet organization than Transport House will ever know how to be, it has not caused anything like the stir the arrival of the P R men did in the Labour Party. But it has been there just the same, and in its way it has been just as important. For at almost the same time that Labour has been discovering about public relations, a number of influential Conservatives seemed to be having their doubts about them.

One of the reasons for this was nothing much more than a simple concern for appearances, and the feeling that the P R men were getting the party a bad name. This feeling began during the fuss following the disclosures, in Professor H. H. Wilson's book, *Pressure Group*, of the connections between various members and past members of the Central Office publicity department (among them Mark Chapman-Walker, Ronald Simms and Toby O'Brien) and the setting up of the Independent

Television Authority. It was bad politics to allow the idea to get around that the Conservative Party was a sort of puppet of the image builders. The Labour Party, hard at work though it was building up its own cadre of P R advisers, began attacking the Conservatives on this extremely vulnerable point, and inside Central Office it became accepted that something would have to be done about the influence the publicity department had acquired during the immediate post-Woolton heyday.

But it did not end there. It is interesting that the most telling attack on the influence of advertising on politics about this time came not from Harold Wilson, but from a Conservative and former chairman of the Bow Group, David Hennessey (the present Lord Windlesham) in an article he wrote for the *Political Quarterly*. And it is also interesting that when, in 1961, the party needed a new publicity officer, Mr R. A. Butler should have offered the job, not to a professional P R, as had been the invariable practice in the past, but to a working journalist, George Hutchinson, the former political editor of the *Evening Standard*. Significantly Hutchinson had had no connection with commercial broadcasting. And with the exception of Guy Schofield, who had held the post briefly in 1956, he was the first journalist to have the job since the war.

This was important, for as a newspaperman he came into the job with distinct reservations about the myth-making and image-building pretensions of many professional public relations men. A retiring, quiet, grey-suited figure, Hutchinson always made a great point of never attempting to enter the limelight himself. He had no ambitions as a politician and when the general election was over he left Central Office, as he had previously said he would – 'one general election is probably enough for one man in this game' – and became managing director of *The Spectator*, with an office next door to that of the editor, Iain Macleod, his one-time boss at Smith Square.

But all the time he was at Central Office, Hutchinson made no bones about his function and the function of publicity within the party.

'I am,' he used to state in his rather easy-going way, 'a propagandist. But,' he would continue, 'I happen to believe that, in political propaganda, you get much further if you remember what time the Sunday newspapers go to press than if you spend your time thinking up a new image for a particular minister. You see, I believe that people *are* interested in policy and that it's my job to get as much of my own party's policies into the papers as I can. The only way this can be done is through finding genuine news. Political journalists are really too smart to be taken in by professional myth-builders. Because of this, the most useful service I can render my party is when I can give them a bloody good story.'

None of this means that Central Office has given up its elaborate machinery of publicity and information. Colman, Prentis & Varley is still employed to manage its advertising (Roger Pemberton, Hutchinson's successor, came, incidentally, from C P V), Ronald Simms's organization, Industrial Aids, had a hand in the publicity campaign for Greater London during the municipal elections, and as much money goes into all this as before.

Nor does it mean that Hutchinson himself was a mere pipeline for information without any wider influence during his years at Smith Square. It is possible that in practical terms he had as much influence as the P R men preceding him. But it was a different type of influence. The timing of the celebrated occasion, for instance, during the 1962 Stockton by-election, when Harold Macmillan came out for the first time wholly in favour of the European Common Market was the result of Hutchinson's own last-minute intervention. Travelling up to Stockton on the train he had written the declaration about the Common Market and then passed it to the Prime Minister as a suggested addition to the speech.

Similarly, the way that Macmillan's pamphlet on the Common Market, *Britain, the Commonwealth and Europe*, suddenly appeared and dominated the weekend press, actually being printed verbatim in several papers, was not a matter of chance. From start to finish, Hutchinson was very much behind it, in the writing, the timing, the tipping-off of editors that it was on its way.

During the general election of 1964 Hutchinson's role continued as very much that of the technical expert helping the politicians get their policies across instead of the image-builder who sees politics as primarily a matter of inducing a certain mood among the greatest possible number of impressionable voters. He was very much in favour of using advertising in the newspapers as a means of putting the Conservative policy statement before the public, and he made little secret of his dislike of happy families and beaming pensioners produced by C P V over the slogan, 'Don't chuck it away,' an echo of 1959's winning campaign on the slogan 'Don't let Labour Ruin it.'

'The truth is,' he says, 'that advertising is useful as a means of getting over a policy, but not as a substitute for one. And in the last election Labour didn't win because of their advertising any more than we lost because of ours.'

Now that he has left Central Office the arguments for and against political image building will presumably continue, but what Hutchinson's spell in Smith Square does mark is the end of the old comforting Conservative belief in the saving magic of advertising and public relations in politics. The turmoil and the inner strife of the party during the time he directed its publicity would have required the greatest public relations medicine man in the world to gloss over. And Hutchinson is no medicine man. While he was at Central Office he was a party propagandist with a life-time's knowledge of how journalists operate. This was his function during these uneasy years.

But old beliefs die hard, especially for Conservative politicians.

'Not long before the election,' he said, 'I was rung up by the wife of Blank (a certain member of the cabinet). "Why is Blank so unpopular these days?" she said. "Surely it's your job to do something about it?" '

20. PR–to the Left and Right

Several PR agencies in London handle accounts for Right-wing clients; only one has so far taken on the job of representing Communist Government Departments. The agency in question, Lex Hornsby and Partners, has so far done work both for East Germany and for Hungary. (Up till the end of 1963, these accounts were handled by Notley Advertising, of which Lex Hornsby was a director in charge of the PR operation.)

When Notley's took on the East German trade account, in October 1960, there was a considerable outcry, some of it from moralists in the business whose own affairs would not have withstood careful inspection. Lex Hornsby, the agency's PR director and a grey-haired, dead-pan Glaswegian who operates from an office in Hay Hill (just off the south side of Berkeley Square) – blamed a good deal of it on the West Germans. He was, he added, sorry for the East Germans, 'who are a lonely lot' and, as a 'middle-of-the-road Liberal' himself, regarded them as 'much the same as any other Socialist country – they have a bureaucratic control, but they are very easy to get on with'. Easy to get on with, that is to say, if you happen to be a British PR man helping them boost their trade.

Hornsby, who learnt his public relations during and after the war at the Ministry of Information and when he was director of publicity at the Ministry of Labour and National Service, regards the East German account as 'completely non-political' and adds that he never went to political meetings with the Minister of Labour, and if he could remain divorced from politics then, why not in this new situation?

Why not indeed? But Hornsby, after mentioning that Notley's insisted on a clause in their contract absolving them from doing any ideological work for the East Germans, admitted that the account was affected by politics in so far as the British Government does not yet recognize the Democratic Republic.

One of the minor curiosities about the way in which Notley's got the account was that it was first of all offered to Brigadier Terence Clarke, a Tory M P and a Director of Voice and Vision. Voice and Vision were then representing the Federation of Rhodesia and Nyasaland, but that by itself would not have deterred them from taking on East Germany as well. The thing which made the offer too embarrassing to accept was that the advertising agency linked with Voice and Vision – Colman, Prentis and Varley – were then handling the Tory Party's advertising business. Clarke therefore suggested Notley's as a possibility to the East Germans.

For the first year after Notley's took the job, Clarke was retained as a consultant, at a substantial fee – and so was another Tory M P, G. B. Drayson. Both men were in the habit of visiting East Germany to encourage trade and both spoke in public advocating closer relations. Lex Hornsby no longer retains either – 'I can positively say that we do not have a single M P on the payroll.'

His present advice to the East Germans is to be 'just good trading partners' and not to try to influence M Ps because political propaganda is 'not acceptable in Britain'.

The acceptance of the East German account caused something of a rumpus in the agency. At least two of their executives resigned as a matter of conscience. But Notley were prepared to stand a few knocks, because the East German account soon became their biggest – large enough to have four executives working on it. Hornsby himself now visits East Germany four or five times a year.

Hornsby's brief is to publicise East German trade and commerce – and recently there has been some tourist propaganda to handle in addition. The main event of the year is, of course, the Leipzig Fair, and Hornsby generally takes about fifteen journalists and between fifty and sixty commercial people over there. Some M Ps who go – from both parties – are paid for by the firms for whom they act as 'advisers', Hornsby says. He offers the rise of East German export figures to Britain as proof of the effectiveness of their efforts.

Hornsby hopes to get a further account from Hungary. He did his first piece of work for the Hungarian Communists in 1963, when he handled the first big display of Hungarian consumer goods – particularly food and wine – in Britain since the end of the war. The display, entitled 'A Window on Hungary', was laid on at Lewis's store in Manchester in July 1963.

Notley executives went to Budapest three times to fix the general strategy. Advertising space was taken in the Manchester evening papers, and 300 specially designed posters were displayed, many of them on the main-line Manchester railway stations. The P R operation was much more important. The Hungarians brought a Gypsy Band with them – and arrangements were made for them to give concerts in the Piccadilly Gardens. A party of mannequins were brought across to give twice-daily parades and Notley's saturated the area with publicity.

Altogether, twenty-seven Press releases were sent out (one of them began: 'Unofficial ambassadors of Hungary in many lands are her dolls', while another started: 'Above all, Budapest is a city of spas . . .') and 10,000 copies of an eight-page leaflet were distributed. Not everybody, however, showed enthusiasm for Hungarian dishes. Approaches to local Young Farmers Clubs with offers of lectures on Hungarian food and wine met with interest, but as the Notley report said: 'No request for talks of this kind were forthcoming.'

Nor did the local worthies turn out in force to greet the Hungarians. The Lord Mayor had a previous engagement (he visited the exhibition after it had opened), and so had a number of other 'leading figures'. Notley's tried to stir up public interest by starting a competition – the public were asked to list six items which had led to the success of the exhibition – and succeeded in getting the President of the Hungarian Chamber of Commerce on Granada T V and the Gypsy Band on B B C television.

When the entries for the competition came in, the mannequin parade was an easy winner, with the Gypsy Band second, and Hungarian food a poor third. Summing up the results of the exhibition, Notley's said that it might be thought too much attention had been paid to the mannequins, but added (no doubt by way of explaining to their Communist bosses the odd tastes of capitalist countries) that this was 'inevitable' and that the girls had drawn attention to the fact that there was a Hungarian exhibition in progress. The end, in fact, justified the means.

They also reported that 6000 Hungarian meals had been sold in Lewis's restaurant, that 40,000 people had attended the exhibition and bought 942 bottles of Hungarian wine between them. During the exhibition, the Ghanaians also placed an order for £10,000 worth of Hungarian tomato puree in 2½-ounce tins. There were ninety-seven Press cuttings to show for their efforts – forty-five were in the trade press, another forty in provincial papers and only nine in the nationals (including, of course, the *Daily Worker*) for what was strictly a local affair. A reasonable result, Hornsby thought.

Notley's have fought a number of other interesting campaigns. Some years ago, they were approached by the broiler industry, who had only £10,000 to spend and who did not think this would make much impact through advertising. They therefore hired Notley to try to boost the sale of chickens with a public relations campaign. Notley's first of all did a survey of 3000 housewives and came up with some interesting findings.

They discovered that most housewives at that time thought of chicken as an unattainable luxury meat; and that they also believed that broilers were a cruel way of raising chickens and caused their taste to suffer by comparison with farm-bred birds. Notley's advised their clients to change their name to the British Chicken Association (which it now is), though they did not alter their method of raising birds. They also organized sample tastings of broilers and farm birds all over the country (on the lines of the margarine-butter competitions) and poured forth a stream of chicken recipes through the various publicity channels.

The campaign, allied with a fall in the price of chickens, has helped increase the popularity of chicken in Britain.

Hornsby is convinced of the force of public relations. 'The power of P R, make no mistake, is terrific,' he said. 'If you have enough money, there is little you could not do in this country. With something like £2 million, you could even put the Liberals in at the next election.'

In the same year as Notley's took on East Germany, Voice and Vision got the job of helping to rescue the Federation of Rhodesia and Nyasaland of which Sir Roy Welensky was Premier, from dissolution. They failed to save it, but the way they handled the account gave them a certain reputation.

Voice and Vision's boss is Sydney Wynne, a balding man with a smooth, urbane manner and a prominent nose, to whom superlatives come naturally when he is talking about Voice and Vision. He was once an ardent left-winger, working for the *Daily Herald* as a crime reporter and leader-writer and making hot-blooded speeches for the Labour Party. His wife is Ernest Bevin's daughter, and he has what he calls 'a pleasant but not sumptuous' office just off Park Lane. As the years have gone by, he has drifted further and further to the Right.

Wynne has, however, some reason for self-congratulation. When he joined Voice and Vision just after the war, things were not going well and he began by making some drastic changes of staff. Since then business has certainly looked up. The turnover has gone up seven times, there is a staff of fifty ('the best team in London') and an impressive list of sixty clients. Nor is Voice and Vision anything like so dependent on its advertising associate Colman, Prentis and Varley. When Wynne arrived, about 80 per cent of the accounts were held jointly with C P V; now 80 per cent are held independently of them. Voice and Vision also has gone international, with affiliated companies in ten countries. The agency has a number of celebrities working for it, including Brigadier Terence Clarke and Major-General A. C. Shortt. Voice and Vision also employs a number of eminent advisers, among them Sir William Emrys Williams, a former Secretary-General of the Arts Council.

According to Wynne, the agency got the Federation account after Welensky had talked to both Harold Macmillan and Iain Macleod about them. He himself first heard of the offer when he had just arrived back from a trip to Geneva. At that time, he confesses, 'I hardly knew where the Federation was. I'd admired Welensky on T V, but I went to see him with quite an open mind. In my first meeting with him, I was completely captivated.' Wynne thought Welensky was rather like Ernest Bevin – 'both had tough backgrounds, both had union life behind them, both were big men'.

He added that now, even though the Federation had flopped, he would still work for Welensky 'for free'. He still has three maps of Africa and a handsome carved tribal head as office decorations.

The story of Voice and Vision's handling of the Federation account was taken up by Miss Paddy Brown, a slim, attractive, Rhodesian whom Wynne brought over to Britain in 1960 as a useful liaison with the Federal High Commissioner's Office in London. Miss Brown had been in P R in Rhodesia for five years before she came to London. She knew most of the politicians, and her presence here was a reassurance that the agency were not simply Englishmen sticking their noses into Rhodesian affairs.

The first job, she said, was to reorganize the Press and P R set-up at the High Commission. They were then, she thought, 'quite good for a Government machine, but there was sometimes a lack of imagination, a failure to see yourselves as others see you. The whole thing needed trimming and the re-allocation of personalities. And,' she added, 'some of the P R people did tend to go home at 4.30.' She herself was working an 8 to 6.30 day, with Saturday mornings and most evenings thrown in.

Voice and Vision had two main targets – the Press, radio and T V, and Parliament. They made a particular effort to convert moderate Labour M Ps to their cause.

Wynne had decided that the best way to gain support was to send M Ps of both parties out to the Federation. They had, first of all, to recommend which M Ps would be suitable candidates for a trip – 'we were looking for honest men whom we thought hard-working, uncommitted chaps,' explained Miss Brown. To help do the job, the agency hired Alec McWhinnie. Like Wynne, McWhinnie was an ex-*Daily Herald* man – he had been news editor – and he was in a particularly good position to win friends and influence Labour Members, since he came to Voice and Vision from Transport House, where he had been Director of Public Relations before the 1959 Election. But the majority of Labour M Ps were, and remained, irreconcilably opposed to the Federation.

'Alec's job,' said Miss Brown, 'was on the Parliamentary side.' The Government Whip's Office, also proved helpful – and 'gave us advice about who they thought were both open-minded and interested in Central Africa.'

The result of all this sifting out was that between September 1960 and

August 1961, seven parties of M Ps went out to the Federation. There were usually six in each party (three Conservative, three Labour) and Mc-Whinnie went as guide with each of them. Voice and Vision also took out well-known journalists like Arthur Christiansen and John Connell, and a number of writers from important provincial papers like the *Glasgow Herald* and the *Yorkshire Post*. Both sent leader writers. Then there were two Church of Scotland men – a particularly significant interest to the Federal cause because, Miss Brown said, 'as a church they had the reputation of being committed to the view that every black man is right and every white man wrong.'

The trip cost between £500 and £600 per man (which came out of the £40,000 annual budget Voice and Vision were given to spend) and the results were satisfactory so far as the agency was concerned. Of the forty M Ps who went, only one (Dr. J. D. Mabon, Labour M P for Greenock) came out against the Federation. And, as Miss Brown pointed out, 'this kind of thing does not end with the visit. Broadcasts on radio and T V, articles in the Press followed and there were talks in the House. Thirty-eight people made firm statements for the Federation.' They made a point of keeping in touch with their supporters – 'never forcing ourselves on them, but keeping them informed with facts and advice. Thirty out of the forty kept in close touch with us and some were very active in tabling motions critical of the Government.'

Another triumph, she claimed, was that they had been able to drive a wedge into the ranks of Labour. At first, the corporate view in the Party had been similar to that held by the Church of Scotland, but there were very few Labour M Ps who had visited Africa. 'We succeeded in setting up a different point of view,' she said, 'and two Labour M Ps put their view in the Party. Of course, the leadership were furious.'

Voice and Vision's job also involved them both in the internal politics of the Federation and in the Katanga issue. 'We sailed pretty close to the wind so far as the line between Government and Party politics was concerned,' said Miss Brown. 'We didn't directly help Sir Roy's party, though, but acted in the interests of the Federal Government.' As for Katanga (she had a thick file labelled Katanga on her table): 'We had no direct contact but there are no borders in Africa, and we felt great concern because a multi-racial system was working there.'

Nor did Voice and Vision fight only on the political front. They also obtained a good deal of Press coverage for the Federation's economic case, and even managed to get Sir Roy Welensky on to the Institute of Directors' platform in Britain. They already had a contact with the Institute in Rhodesia, where they handle their account.

Wynne felt they had done everything they could to save the Federation. 'We did build up an effective lobby of M Ps – there were at times more than one hundred Conservatives against the Government and perhaps a third of the Labour Party in the House were unhappy about the official line.' The Voice and Vision campaign is probably the most thorough political exercise yet conducted by British public relations men.

The agency have also handled a number of other jobs in Africa. They prepared a booklet for the Somalis stating their case against Kenya – 'I asked Welensky about it,' said Wynne, 'and he told me, "If they have a case, do it for them" ' – and still handle the P R for two gold companies, Consolidated Goldfields in South Africa and Ashanti Goldfields in Ghana. Their brief in these instances is 'to get the local people to understand what the company means to them'.

One of Wynne's most interesting co-directors is Major-General Shortt, the former head of P R at the War Office. He has clearly not forgotten his time in the Army. 'Well,' he said briskly when we went to see him, 'what's the object of the exercise?'

The first account he had to handle was a teenage wind orchestra from Pittsburgh. They happened to have fifty-seven players, were sponsored by H. J. Heinz and played on a converted barge all the way down the Thames from Greenwich to Oxford. General Shortt came through the ordeal triumphantly. 'I ran the whole thing like a military operation,' he said, 'billeting and feeding them, and getting in fireworks from Belgium.'

He brought a wealth of experience and contacts with him from the War Office. He illustrated their value by talking about the case of a small firm which manufactures precision instruments. 'They were badly hit by the way in which large firms were getting all the big contracts,' he said, 'and what they wanted from us was to exploit our contacts in Fleet Street and Whitehall. I was able to go through my friends to get people at least to go and see this firm. I always found somebody I knew.'

It was an interesting illustration of the way the battle for defence contracts can be fought, but this time it failed. 'I got a lot of people interested,' said General Shortt, 'but unfortunately the Managing Director of the Company fell ill and it was very much a one-man show.'

Since then, he has been involved in a number of major campaigns. He has tried to help change Gibraltar's old image – 'apes and sieges' – into one more attractive to holiday-makers; negotiated for what would have been an interesting account, the job of educating the citizens of a large Midland city to conserve their water – Voice and Vision suggested that the Council might put up a production and consumption barometer in the centre of the town; and also took part in the *cause célèbre* of the oil heaters in 1959.

During the latter part of that year, a whole series of domestic fires broke out – for which the blame was laid at the door of the design of some oil heaters. The panic spread and in a very short time, a number of smaller firms were facing disaster. The Oil Appliance Manufacturers

Association then came to Voice and Vision and asked them to help. At that time v & v felt o a m a were not adopting the kind of attitude likely to win public sympathy. The managing director of one firm called the publicity given to the stories of disaster 'this wicked outcry'. Voice and Vision's job was to re-establish public confidence in oil heaters.

They first of all persuaded o a m a to show that they did want to co-operate with the public in curing the defects in heaters. Production was halted, and some inefficient stock withdrawn and adapted. Then they persuaded the Association to give the Government departments who were preparing new standards for oil heaters their full assistance. Finally, they began to approach m ps. Sir Gerald Nabarro, who had tabled a Private Member's Bill with the object of prohibiting all sale, import or letting of oil heaters not conforming to specified standards, opened an exhibition for the Association – and eighty m ps, according to the Voice and Vision report, 'came to regard themselves as friends of o a m a'. Mr Butler, who had previously been critical of the industry, spoke in the House approving their 'prompt action' and Lord Thomson also spoke in public approving their new attitude. The sale of oil heaters stopped falling.

'We are not hidden persuaders,' said Mr Wynne modestly. 'We are just a bit more expert than the chap next door in the field of communication.'

21. The Anatomy of Non-Involvement

One of the most frequently heard claims made by p rs acting on behalf of a politically controversial client is that after all, politics apart, there is always a straightforward, non-political tale to be told and that it is this that he, the p r, is out to tell.

'Nothing else to it, my dear chap. We're not interested in the politics of the thing. We just want to let people know some of the other facts that all this political nonsense tends to obscure.'

This is the sort of argument every journalist hears from time to time, and the question always crops up of just how political is 'non-political'.

What is in the minds of the people who pay P R firms good fees to have this non-political information disseminated about themselves? And how do the P Rs go about their task in these controversial situations?

Usually these are questions it is difficult to get answered honestly, but one such case was over the brief but not entirely ineffectual campaign the P R firm of Sidney-Barton Ltd ran in 1961 for the South Africa Foundation.

In those days the most important and impressive man in Sidney-Barton was the firm's founder and chairman, Mike Williams-Thompson. A large, florid man in a business remarkable for its large, florid men, Williams-Thompson was the togetherness man to beat them all. Not for nothing had his chauffeur-driven Humber Super-Snipe the registration number PRO 1. Williams-Thompson had spent several years trying to trace the number before he found it on a greengrocer's van in North London. He bought the van at a price considerably above its market value for the privilege of changing the registration to his own car.

Williams-Thompson[7], who claimed amongst his friends people as diverse as Gamal Nasser and Ernest Marples, was the supreme public relations exponent of what might be called saturation hospitality. Several times a week he would have a lunch in his own room at Brown's Hotel for any of the politicians or journalists or business men he had met and wanted to meet again. In addition to these most excellent lunches there were also the parties he gave and the dinners he held. His firm used to do P R for the Short s c 1 vertical take-off plane, and every year at the time of the Farnborough Show, Williams-Thompson would take a house in Farnborough for the week. During the day he would drive PRO 1 over to the show, the boot filled with cold chicken and champagne.

For a professional public relations man the advantages of intimacy on this scale were considerable. He took immense pains to keep his friendships in good repair, and there was no cause or campaign so obscure that he could not write one of his letters beginning, 'My Dear So-and-So' to somebody about it. Because of this he was remarkably useful to firms who for prestige purposes wanted a Minister to open a new factory for them or a particular personality to be present at a press visit.

'Often you know,' said Williams-Thompson, 'I'm truly embarrassed to have to keep on asking favours from people I know as close personal friends. But then, I'm usually the sort of person who likes people and who people generally like back in their turn. And business is business.'

All this was quite harmless, and Sidney-Barton Ltd had made quite a name for itself handling a certain type of industrial account, when

[7] Williams-Thompson also learned the P R business partly in Government Service; he became Chief Information Officer at the Ministry of Supply in 1946.

a number of News Editors of the main London newspapers received an invitation from Williams-Thompson which seemed strangely out of character. 'I would be delighted,' it ran, 'if you could meet me at the Savoy Hotel (Manhattan Room) at 12 noon this Thursday (May 4th) as I am most anxious to tell you something about the part my firm is playing in the activities of the South Africa Foundation. I feel,' the letter went on, 'that too little is known about this organization and my firm's part in it. Too many wrong guesses are obviously being made. This is NOT a press conference in the ordinary way. That is why I am sending this invitation to you personally. However if you are too busy (and I hope you will not be), I shall be delighted to meet and to entertain anybody you would like to send to represent you.'

Twelve noon is always an enticing hour to offer entertainment to thirsty journalists, especially in the Manhattan Room of the Savoy Hotel, and the meeting was a fairly crowded one. But once the smoked salmon and the champagne cocktails had begun to circulate it became obvious that the words of the invitation had been only too true. This was not a press conference in the ordinary way. Everyone was given a large and expensively printed brochure with the words *South African Foundation 1961* in red on the front, and a message inside, headed 'The Objective'. This explained that the Foundation was 'an association of leaders in every sphere of national activity who have come together with a single objective – to present to the world a true picture of South Africa, the human and material riches with which she is endowed, the historical and natural forces which have shaped the destinies of her peoples. . . . The Foundation,' it continued, 'is independent of political parties and political policies. Individually its members may hold or express whatever political views they wish.' Further, the brochure informed everyone that the Foundation's President was Major-General Sir Frances de Guingand, former Chief of Staff to the 8th Army and Chairman of Tube Investments (SA) (Pty) Ltd and that it was being supported by a large number of wealthy and influential South African business, educational and religious interests.

But the strange thing was that although the brochure proclaimed the Foundation's objectives so proudly, there was no one from it quite proud enough to meet the press at its own press conference. Instead the unfortunate and clearly embarrassed Williams-Thompson was left to face a barrage of good-humoured but distinctly hostile questions (the Sharpeville shooting was still quite recent) and to explain that although he personally was firmly against the principle of Apartheid, he had taken the account on, because he honestly believed that there was a public relations job to be done for the non-controversial side of South African life, notably South Africa's industrial potential.

Journalists, not unnaturally, are fairly cynical about remarks like these. There were one or two more questions about why South Africa House could not do its own publicity and whether this was one more white-washing operation for Apartheid. Williams-Thompson appeared to be sweating profusely – the room was very warm – and there this press conference which was not a press conference ended.

But the curious sequel to all this was that despite the lack of sympathy for the South Africa Foundation, and despite the extremely fair warning Williams-Thompson had given of where his own interests lay, a considerable amount of pro-South African news appeared in the press, emanating directly from the agency.

Part of the interest of the campaign lies in the pains the agency took over the slightest and most apparently trifling detail about South Africa. For the Foundation apparently had a tendency to judge the agency's work by the number of column inches they could get into the cuttings book. Typical of this was the story about a South African dentist who had perfected a technique for extracting teeth to music instead of using an anaesthetic. 'It all helps give the Union a good press over here,' one Sidney-Barton man explained hopefully the morning after it appeared. 'Facts like these could finally convince people that there is more to be said for the place than Sharpeville and Apartheid.'

Before long, however, the agency was doing a good deal better for South Africa than musical dentists. Most of the hard work in the campaign fell on Don Ogilvy, who has now set up his own Public Relations company in Johannesburg, and Peter Cattle, an ex-*Empire News* staff writer. An experienced newspaperman – Cattle had been twenty-seven years with the paper before it was closed down after Roy Thomson took over the old Kemsley empire – he set about his new task with quite remarkable enthusiasm for a man who like Williams-Thompson himself, was at heart against Apartheid.

He had to work hard. One of his first successes was to find a Portsmouth toolmaker with six children who actually wanted to emigrate and settle in South Africa. This came at the end of an unsuccessful attempt on the part of the agency to persuade a newspaper or television company to sponsor an 'Export a Family to South Africa' competition, with the winning family being chosen, as Cattle cheerfully outlined the scheme, before several million viewers. (The Foundation would pay for the costs of the competition and of settling the family in South Africa).

But nobody had seemed particularly interested in the idea. When Cattle spoke to the deputy editor of the *Daily Mail* about it, he had replied, 'excellent idea. Where did you say it was to, Australia?'

Because of all this the discovery of his Portsmouth toolmaker came as a godsend to the agency, and Cattle was off straight-away to meet the man before he changed his mind. Both he and Ogilvy grilled him fairly hard to make sure that his story was genuine, and when they had convinced themselves that he was 'a reliable fellow' they told him that his passage would be taken care of by the Foundation, and persuaded him to come to London to meet the press. After Cattle had also carefully checked his story, he was brought to London, put up in a good hotel, and a press conference was held in his honour.

This could have misfired badly, but Cattle had done his job thoroughly. 'It all went swimmingly,' he says. 'There was a woman reporter, of course, who tried to shake him but he stuck to his guns about wanting to go to South Africa because he thought he would get a better job and his kids would have a better start in life than anywhere else in the Commonwealth. And it worked. Next day all the papers picked it up, and the quotes were there, good and strong. A lovely job.' The family, indeed, marked the beginning of a Government-sponsored immigration scheme to South Africa.

Some of Ogilvy's and Cattle's work was fairly humdrum, like arranging what Cattle called 'my second-eleven lecturers' to take on the Rotary Clubs and the Women's Institute circuit to talk about South Africa. 'You can't ignore any opportunity when you're doing this kind of job.' But when they asked the Foundation to send over a coloured or an African lecturer 'largely for the sake of the story', the Foundation was not able to oblige.

Nor was the Foundation particularly anxious to spend money in addition to the 'fairly whacking' fee (as one employee put it) it was already paying the agency, in order to take a number of British editors for a tour of South Africa as Cattle suggested. When the campaign had been going for two months he was reminding the Foundation sadly that a statement had just been made in Parliament at Salisbury, Rhodesia, to the effect that £184,000 had been spent to bring British M Ps to visit the Federation: (Voice and Vision point out that £30,000 was spent by them.) 'At this stage,' said Cattle, 'we might have had £5000 to spend on the same sort of work. Certainly no more.'

Still, with the money that was available, he had not done too badly. Fox Photos, one of the big London press picture agencies, for instance, had agreed to let him pay for one of their cameramen to visit the Union at the Foundation's expense.

On the face of it, this was a surprisingly generous deal to offer a prosperous commercial picture agency like Fox. The Foundation would pay everything and arrange for the photographer to see anything he wanted. Better than this, since the Foundation really knew their own country, they would prepare a list of suggestions that might make good subjects for the agency. The photographer would not have to follow them, of course (nor was any itinerary prepared for him), but he would probably find them useful.

Then, in addition to all this, it was specifically stated that the agency would have all the profits from marketing the pictures and that they would be offered to the newspapers in the normal way without any mention of the Foundation.

Cattle explained that this was not just modesty, 'but we know perfectly well that the pictures stand a far higher chance of being considered for a paper if they come from a reputable agency than if they are issued under the name of the Foundation.'

'So there would be nothing on the pictures to identify them as originating from you or the South African Foundation?'

'No nothing.'

This particular effort cost the South Africa Foundation around £700 in fares and expenses for the photographer. In return for this they got a large number of photographs on the files of a leading London picture agency and also several pictures of humane, non-controversial South Africa into the newspapers at a time when such ideas were surprisingly hard to get across.

The *Daily Mail*, for instance, published one picture showing the son-in-law of the South African prime minister, Dr Verwoerd, teaching black children in a mission station, along with a caption about the young man's deep religious sense. Another picture showed Lady Oppenheimer, the wife of the South African diamond king, teaching in a school for jewellery for poor whites. 'Unfortunately,' said Cattle, 'there were no Africans in these pictures, but they were still very useful.'

As well as arranging for the visits of photographers to the Union, the South Africa Foundation also gave assistance and advice to visiting British journalists. These included Anthony Smith, the science correspondent of the *Daily Telegraph*, who wished to see something of the mining, and hydro-electric projects being planned in South Africa. Lord Birdwood was another visitor the Foundation helped, and when he came back Cattle had the task of trying to place an article which insisted on mentioning in the first paragraph the fact that the author had been invited to South Africa by the South Africa Foundation.

Certainly in the case of Lord Birdwood, who was a member of the United Nations Committee on South-West Africa, the Foundation went out of its way to try showing both sides of the picture in South Africa, and at his request they arranged a meeting with the opposition leader Chief Luthuli. (The Chief was already under restriction by the South African Government, and at least one well-known British journalist visiting South Africa at the time on behalf of a leading Sunday newspaper was not given a chance of getting near him.)

'As an ex-journalist myself,' said Cattle, 'I would say that the principle we work on is that the facts that get into the press over here are not wrong but unfairly represented. We say to our visitors, "if you want to see the slums of Cato Manor or Sophiatown – which are being cleared very rapidly – we will take you there," but if you go on to suggest that all natives in the Union live like this we insist on the right in return to show you that you are wrong. We'll say to you "what about the Bantu schools? There are some Bantu schools that are really wonderful. All we ask is that you let us take you there as well".'

Put like this the talk of a P R about 'correcting the picture' sounds perfectly fair. After all, if a foreign government feels it is suffering from bad propaganda abroad, it is quite at liberty to create its own propaganda in return. What is more debatable is when well-paid P R firms are engaged to do it for them, and if these firms in their turn claim that they are being non-political about it all. What is worse is if the P R firm pretends that it is somehow above the whole controversy.

Just how far from the propaganda business Sidney-Barton Ltd really was in its work for the South African Foundation emerges in the action it took when it heard that I T V was planning to screen the anti-Apartheid film *Let My People Go* in an off-peak period in place of a religious programme that had been previously planned.

Cattle immediately wrote to the producer of the programme, pointing out that this was 'a strongly biased film', suggesting that I T V should have a speaker in the studio to put the case for South Africa and pointing out that Sidney-Barton could put I T V in touch with a great deal of excellent film material showing a better side of life in South Africa.

This, however, was an occasion when the agency drew a blank. So, strangely enough, was its effort to extract the maximum of favourable publicity from the visit of the then Prime Minister, Harold Macmillan, to South Africa. The agency had outlined its plans for this in a letter it had written to the Foundation when the visit was first announced. 'It had,' it was suggested, 'the utmost importance for the work they were doing to present South Africa as a country of industrial expansion, tolerance and agreeable living. If the Prime Minister,' it went on, 'through his personality and actions contributes to this picture, we shall be in a strong position to put across other pictures of comparison.'

Alas for such hopes. As it turned out, this was to be the visit which ended in the 'Wind of Change' speech, and after this there was little enough that even the smartest of P R men could do to establish parallels between Mr Macmillan's actions in South Africa and a picture of tolerance and agreeable living.

And by Christmas 1961, Sidney-Barton had resigned the Foundation account after a final inclusive argument about expenses.

'Frankly we decided,' said Williams-Thompson, 'that the account just was not us. You see, most of us were strongly against Apartheid deep down.'

22. The Old Boy Net

1

'There is no mystique to personal P R, old boy. It is simply that, human nature being what it is, there are certain people who will take a lot of trouble to get into the public eye. I manage to chalk up £6000 a year after tax by helping them get there.'

These were the words of one of the most adroit of the freelance personal publicity men, a middle-aged, hard-working, former newspaper columnist who, in a mood of self-revelation not uncommon with such men, was attempting to explain how he operated.

'It is,' he added, 'purely a matter of knowing the ropes and never forgetting who your friends really are. Mind you, it's never difficult in this business getting to *know* people. The knack comes in being able to put the people you know to good use. That's where my six thousand comes from.'

It is also where an important part of the persuasion industry earns its fees and spends its expense accounts. For the creation of fame is one of the most publicized and least understood activities of the public relations man. Here, more than ever, one is up against the difficulty of separating sales talk from success and deciding exactly what part public relations can play in building up a celebrity. What can a public relations man actually *do* for anyone in search of success? Can P R make a personality? Can fame be bought? Does the personal public relations man get results or is the entire battalion of advisers, consultants and press men part of an elaborate confidence trick?

2

One area where personal P R has a fairly obvious function is in the film business. For here, the star system being what it is, becoming known is an important part of becoming successful, and in the States the public relations man is as accepted a member of the big star's entourage as his agent, his accountant and his lawyer. But in Britain the position of the personal film P R is nothing like so clear. One of the few men who have managed to stake a claim for himself as an established professional specializing almost entirely in the film business is Theo Cowan of Theo Cowan Ltd. He has dealt with Peter Sellers, Dirk Bogarde, Stanley Baker, Sir Michael Balcon and Judy Garland as well as many others. He also undertakes publicity for individual films, usually those produced by independents who are outside the publicity organizations of the big studios. He has a second floor office in a rather ancient house in Clarges Street just off Piccadilly. True, it is Mayfair. Anatole de Grunwald Productions have an office in the same block and there is a blue plaque on the house next door saying that it was once lived in by Charles James Fox. But this is not plushy Mayfair and the first impression you get of Cowan himself is of a solid, baggy-suited, pipe-smoking man with a gold watch and a Gunner's tie sitting in a leather arm-chair by an elderly gas fire. His manner is more like that of an accountant or an engineer than of the stock picture of the image-maker. A faint mid-Atlantic accent is the one noticeable relic of the twenty-five years he spent in the film business doing personal publicity for the stars employed by the Rank Organization.

He has been working as an independent for rather less than two years but is already capable of an agreeably cynical aside about his calling. 'Let's face it,' he said when he got his pipe well and truly alight. 'When anyone comes to me and says "I want some PR", what he really means to say is "I want to appear to be a little more important" and by the time his name is known by everyone, he is more important than he appears.'

He explained that one of the chief reasons why he thought that the time had come to set up on his own was that during the last few years there has been a fundamental change going on within the star system itself. In the old days, almost all the biggest stars were under contract to one studio or another, often for several years at a time. But recently this has been changing. Hollywood has been cutting down on its big contract artists. Stars are engaged separately for each film, and although most film actors have welcomed the greater freedom this gives them to work abroad or on television or in the theatre, their publicity has suddenly become something of a problem. In the old days, the studio would reckon to take care of all the necessary publicity in building up the stars it had on contract. The whole publicity personality of the star was an important piece of the studio's property, and the studios would take great trouble to project it for all it was worth.

'Today,' claimed Cowan, 'all this has changed. Say a star signs up to do a six-month stint on a picture in Spain. Okay. The studio will do the publicity while the film is being made, but these days you tend to find the publicity slanted towards the film rather than towards the star. Then suppose the star has a three-month spell on Broadway. Same thing happens. You see the danger,' he said in his dry accountant's voice, 'the star's image can all too easily get chopped in pieces, so there's only one thing the star can do. He must have someone who can look after the long-term state of his image. And that,' he added, 'is where I may come in.'

He went on to explain how he had set up his business, with a secretary and a room in Wardour Street. How he had a call on some thousands of pounds but did not need to use a fraction of that amount, and how his business simply grew out of the people he had got to know during his twenty-five years with Rank.

'When I started my business,' he said, 'my three most important pieces of equipment were my memory, my address book and twenty-five years of friendship in and around the film industry. For, you see, *benevolent* contact is the most important thing of all in public relations. My theory is that no contact you make with another human being is ever wholly unimportant, so it's up to you to see that it is a benevolent one.'

'As a matter of fact,' he continued modestly, 'I'm lucky to be able to remember not just a name and a face for everyone I meet, but also an association and a circumstance. Most people have an aspect and a label. Remember it. Note it down. Remember everything you can about them. You probably won't believe it but I've been able to make a contact with someone I met ten years before simply because I had a note of where he bought his groceries and had his shoes repaired.'

If one thing is clear from all this it is that Cowan is undoubtedly a professional who takes his business with a high, almost pedantic seriousness. But what exactly did he do? What sort of advice did he give 'to keep' as he puts it, 'my client's image in good, long-term health'? And was it ever possible for someone like him to build up a star out of next to nothing purely by public relations techniques?

It was in reply to these questions that Cowan finally explained his own private philosophy of the star system and the part public relations played in it. 'It's my own theory,' he said with a diffidence rare in his profession. 'I call it the theory of the three-legged stool.'

'First,' he said, 'think of your actor as a rocket which has to go as high as possible into the sky. And think of this rocket being launched from a milk bottle that is placed on the top of a three-legged stool. Are you with me so far?' he asked anxiously as he finished filling his pipe.

'Well, it's obvious that if this rocket is to go as high as it can, the top of the three-legged stool must be as level as possible. And for the sake of my theory you must think of the three legs of the stool being made up by the three qualities which together provide an actor's potential for stardom. The first leg is ability-cum-talent. Whether it's natural ability or the ability to be directed hardly matters. But without it you can't begin. The second leg is visual attraction. Again it needn't be obvious good looks, but there must be something there to make the public want to look. And the third leg is even more difficult to define. I call it the P factor – P for penetration. It's what makes the star memorable in the public mind – newsworthiness, publicity-awareness, personality, P factor.'

'Now don't forget,' he continued, 'the object is to keep the top of that stool as level as possible, and as a P R consultant it's my belief that there is nothing at all I can do about the first and the second legs of the stool. Either your actor's got the looks and the ability or he hasn't. But this third leg, the P factor. Often you find that this can be adjusted. And this,' he said puffing happily at his pipe at last, 'is where I come in.'

'Whenever I take on anyone new, my first job is to sum up the length of these three legs. This is where experience counts. If I make a mistake here, the whole campaign will go wrong. But I have to try to decide whether it is possible to make the top of the stool a little more level by raising or lowering this third leg.

'Often you can't and that's that. There are many extremely successful people in the entertainment business who are not stars and who never will be stars. This can even apply to very eminent actors. One can't mention names, of course, but certain great actors will never be complete stars because their third leg, their P factor, will always be so much lower than their ability. And sometimes you find people whose P factor is too great. These are the people who are talked about more than they are actually seen. A very famous shapely lady is a good example of this.

'But usually, thank God, some adjustment of this third leg is possible. Often with a youngish personality who is in a hurry to get to the top, I find that the P factor is too great and I have to advise them against overexposure. Well, that's easy. I tell them to back themselves less frequently into the press, not to arrive at London Airport wearing dark glasses, and to go to the second night of a play, rather than the first night. For you'd be surprised,' he said, 'how easy it is for a celebrity to live anonymously if he really wants to. It's usually just a question of avoiding the obvious places where you know beforehand that the Press will be attending.

'Then, of course, I sometimes get the exact opposite – someone who has tended to drop out of public knowledge. This in fact is usually easier to do something about than the reverse. I'm against gimmicks. Gimmicks are unnecessary in this game. All that's needed is to be seen around in the right places and above all, to play it carefully. For the way people make up their minds about a star is often quite illogical and I always tell my clients that it's bad if the public know so much about you that they don't want to know any more. So be intelligent about the things you say in public. If you decide that your style is to dress casually, make sure that you dress casually smart. And above all, never forget that the only place you can afford to be entirely natural is in your own home.'

3

By no means all the personal publicity men take Cowan's long-term professional view of their clients. Some of the smartest men in the business make a point of mounting the short, *ad hoc* publicity campaign and actually enjoy the challenge of working for quick results. A good example is 35-year-old Kenneth Pitt of Kenneth Pitt Ltd. A tall, fair-haired, rather withdrawn man who once worked as a junior reporter on the *Evening Standard*, he specializes in winning the maximum publicity for visiting show business personalities, calculates his success very largely in column-inches and works in the obscure show-business world where publicity and management merge. He has a staff of six, a turnover of around £20,000 a year, and for the sort of short-term, personal appearance work he likes best, he expects to charge clients two hundred guineas a week plus expenses.

For this they get, in the person of Pitt himself, a guide, philosopher and friend who will guard their every interest in the dangerous, treasure-laden jungle of show business publicity. For like some wily old *shikari*, Pitt knows. He knows the picture editors and can size up as skilfully as they can, whether the celebrity who has just arrived at London Airport will make a two-column picture on page seven of the *Evening Standard*, or a larger spread on the entertainments page of one of the quality Sundays.

He knows the columnists and which are likely to be enthusiastic for his client and which will make mincemeat out of him. He knows whether to have a press conference and whether it is sensible to have an interview with an individual critic.

And above all, he knows when it is necessary for his client to remain *incommunicado*. When he was working for Frank Sinatra on one of the singer's visits to London which happened to coincide with a great deal of press speculation about the possibility of marriage, Pitt acted as his watch-dog, staying with him permanently at his hotel, warding off any journalist he recognized in the lobby and constantly reiterating his one piece of advice 'keep your mouth shut, Frank.'

Mel Tormé, the singer, has been another of Pitt's clients in England. 'In his case,' says Pitt, 'I always take a lot of trouble about the appearance he is making for his fans and the cameramen. If I ever saw him frowning at the airport or coming out of the theatre, I would pull his coat and just say, "Smile Mel".'

Pitt makes one trip a year to America where he contacts, through their managers, celebrities who are planning a visit to London. And, while he is looking after his clients in London, the incidental services his organization takes care of can range from answering fan letters to shipping an E-type Jaguar back to the States.

Also the Pitt organization has never despised the carefully-timed gimmick. 'There was a young singer I took on one summer,' says Pitt. 'She was not in the big money by any means. There might have been twenty a week in it for me – certainly nothing more. But she was coming over from the borscht circuit round New York for a short season at the Astor Club, and it was a big break for her. She was great and I was determined to get her into all the papers. She'd been appearing in Paris so I phoned her up to ask her what she could do for the photographers when she got off the aircraft at London Airport. She said she'd stand on her head if it was necessary. But then I remembered she had told me once that she kept her head shaved and always wore a wig. So I asked her if she'd mind taking her wig off for the photographers. "Sure," she said. From then on it was a natural. I tipped off all the photographers, and there were pictures in all the evenings of her waving her wig as she came down off the plane.'

Not all the Pitt organization gimmicks involve show people and they are not all quite as simple as this. There was the case of the managing director of a firm specializing in luxury goods who came to them in search of advice. He had a meeting arranged with his shareholders in a few weeks and knew from the state of the balance sheet that it was likely to be a stormy one.

'This,' says Pitt, 'was a tricky one. It needed thinking about. Now as it happened, Princess Margaret had just got engaged and a few days later I was at a party where I happened to meet a very eminent person whom I had worked for once or twice in the past. I chatted with him for a while and a few days later all the gossip columns in London published a story that this very eminent person had given Princess Margaret an extremely expensive wedding present. It cost £300, although the very eminent person never had to pay for it. You see, it was made by my client's firm, and after publicity like that my client had no more trouble with his shareholders.'

4

In London the old boy net is inclined to run through the strangest places, and the PR who knows where the threads lie, and where the knots occur, has gold in his hands. Sometimes it is merely a case of a client who wants to be talked about and who thinks that a few guineas paid to an agent to see that he is mentioned in the right columns and pictured in the right society magazines is money well spent. And sometimes the client is hoping for something more tangible.

This part of personal public relations is one of the fringe areas of the trade. Some of the so-called PRs who operate here are con-men pure and simple.

Others, rather frighteningly, do get results. One of the most efficient of them is a retired Commander R.N. He specializes in public figures who want honours. This, he hurries to explain, is not the whole of his business. After the war he worked for a while for several charities and appeals – 'always for a fee this. Not ethical to accept payment by results,' – and he has staged one or two successful campaigns for society painters in search of sitters. 'The secret here is to make sure of *one* titled subject in the first place. This may mean dropping the fee a bit, but in pushing a painter there's still nothing to beat a duchess in the Summer Show at the Academy.'

But the Commander insists that his first and last love is really politics. 'It always cheers me up,' he said, 'when I meet someone with some money who wants nothing more out of life than a peerage.'

One of the advantages of the way he works is that his overheads are minimal. He has to dress well, of course, and there are the fees at his two West End clubs. But apart from the rent of his office and the salary for his secretary who also answers his telephone, the entire turnover of his flourishing little organization can be considered his own personal profit.

'I won't say that good public relations is the only thing that counts if you are after an honour,' he said, 'but it is quite remarkably important. The sort of chap you *seem* to be really matters, so that you have to make sure that every public appearance you make counts for all it's worth. You'd be surprised,' he added, with a chuckle, 'just how much I can do about that.'

Part of the secret of his success seems to be nothing more than sheer hard work. 'It is most important to show that your client is really alive,' he said and he goes to great lengths to make sure that his client attends every possible event that might get him a mention in the press or even, with luck, on television. 'Any reception involving royalty is particularly important. Apart from the fact that you are more likely to get a picture in the Press then, it also gives the right impression of your client being in the swim and being thoroughly acceptable. Royalty still counts for a lot.' And so as to leave as little as possible to chance, the Commander always takes great pains to coach his client on how to make sure that he is in the picture as close as possible to royalty when the photographers are around.

'Then for the columnists,' he added, 'you have to make every little detail count. It is surprising what the press boys will take for news in a bad week. There was one client of mine who had gone abroad for a week and happened to get his bags mixed up with those of a well-known film star. Nothing to it, but I made sure that all the columnists had the details and it got into three of the nationals. One even printed a photograph I sent.'

But his efforts would hardly be likely to work if he confined his activities to these purely superficial parts of the business. He is anxious to point out that he never does. 'I believe in planning a campaign in depth. Diversifying. Showing the world that my chap is a thorough all-rounder.'

As an example of this he cited the case of a peer of quite recent creation whom he claims was one of his clients. 'Luckily,' he said, 'there was something to build on in his case. He was rich. He was spending quite a bit on various charities and he was something of an expert in his own line of country. The whole trouble was that none of this was getting over. It was a straightforward failure of public relations.

'Now if you are working this thing through the charity angle, the whole point is to give where it shows. You must use your brains over this. Pick the sort of medical research project that is likely to make news rather than an obscure cottage hospital in the middle of the country. It's the same with endowing scholarships. They can be a dead loss, but on the other hand, properly chosen and exploited from a publicity angle they can be extremely valuable. But these days it's not enough to show that a man is thoroughly generous if he wants an honour. He has to be a bit of an expert on something as well. He has to have views. Well, that can be managed, of course. I wrote most of the letters he sent to *The Times* myself and took a lot of trouble arranging for articles to be written in his name for various newspapers and a number of influential technical journals. There are always quite clever young journalists around who will do this sort of work for you if you know where to look for them.

'No, from a public relations point of view, it's surprising how easy it is to mount an operation like this. All you need is time and patience to get your man established as a name and an authority. Of course it is always advisable to back this up with some sort of political activity as well, but I always try to make it clear from the start that this isn't my department. I just refuse to give any advice over contributions to party funds and so forth.

'With this chap it took me three years to get him where he wanted. Perhaps that was a bit on the slow side, but between you and me, it saves a lot of time if you can get good material to work on in the first place.'

5

It is interesting to speculate how large a part organized personal public relations play in keeping the wheels of social snobbery and class consciousness turning today.

On the face of it, it is extremely odd that in the middle of the twentieth century our newspapers, our magazines and even occasionally our television programmes should give so much time and space to reporting so-called 'society news'. At a time when incomes are theoretically being levelled out and the idea of an Edwardian-style social world would seem to be more and more of an anachronism it has become quite hard to dodge the latest news of society weddings, titled divorces, débutante parties and the antics of eligible young Old Etonians about town.

Several theories have been put forward to account for this. One is that the newspapers are catering for the dreams of vicarious happiness of their socially deprived female readers in a drab modern society. Another is that there really is an aristocratic reaction going on against the welfare state and that the really rich have never had it so good. A third theory is that perhaps much of this 'society' news is simply the work of conscientious publicity men and that since public relations has moved into society, it has helped to change it almost out of all recognition. Nowhere is this seen better than in the débutante business.

The idea of the débutante was originally a simple one. It grew up in the eighteenth century when well-to-do families living in the country came into London in the spring with the idea of seeing a little of society and finding eligible young men as husbands for their marriageable daughters. The girls were given the stamp of at least minimal respectability by being presented at court and the marital introductions on which so much depended were made in a series of balls and formal parties throughout the season given by the aristocratic families concerned.

Of course, the *nouveaux riches* families tried to push their way into what was theoretically a preserve of the aristocracy and, almost from the beginning, there were people willing to help them get there – at a price: elderly dowagers who would take on the daughters of a few outsiders and steer them through the London season, supervising their behaviour and getting them the necessary introductions and invitations.

But despite this, the deb world was a fairly closed one ruled by certain families, dominated by the need of being presented to the monarch, and lasting from the beginning of May until Goodwood Week in July. And when the Queen announced in 1958 that she was abolishing the presentation parties on the grounds that they had outlived their usefulness, it was generally thought that this would mark the death of the deb.

The exact opposite was the case. The need for being presented at Court was shown to have been a restraining influence on the system. It had kept the numbers down and confined the whole business to the daughters of aristocrats, near aristocrats and the very rich.

Now it became a free-for-all, a high-pressure, highly competitive world in which for the first time publicity really counted. The number of debs actually increased. The season began to expand. The gossip columnists exploited its news-worthiness more than ever and it was soon clear that for any young girl on the make it was even better to be a celebrity than to be a somebody.

It was an obvious situation for the P R men. Before long they were making the most of it, and many of the leading debs were employing press agents.

At the moment there are probably 1500 girls in London calling themselves débutantes, whereas before the war there could never be more than 300 girls presented at court in a single year. And catering for the publicity needs of this year-long industry there is now a small corps of society photographers, etiquette advisers, publicity agents and P R men.

Not all of them are as successful as they would like and probably few of them can equal the skill and knowledge of Mrs B., an ex-regular army colonel's wife who for some years has been taking on a few girls each year and seeing them through the London season.

A kindly, humorous woman with a habit of referring to the middle classes as distinct from 'us', she is acutely aware of the need for good publicity for her girls if they are to get anywhere.

'Good looks,' she said, 'certainly help a girl these days. She also needs to be moderately intelligent and should at least look clean. But unless a girl is terribly gorgeous or the father is extremely well liked, if she is not from an accepted family, it is rare for the class thing to be broken down without a great deal of careful publicity.'

'In the old days the season was short and the whole thing was a relatively small affair. You really did tend to know all the girls in those days. But since H.M. has stopped the presentation parties the whole deb business has been flourishing as never before. Frankly, it has become dominated by LSD, and this has led to two quite distinct groups among the girls – those who count and those with money.'

Adroit publicity is now the most obvious way a member of the second group can become a member of the first. For the no-man's-land between the two appears to be larger than ever.

'Normally,' Mrs B. went on, 'I tell parents from the start, "there is a certain amount I can do for your girl. With luck we might even get her invited to a garden party at the Palace, but you mustn't set your heart on it, and you mustn't be disappointed if such-and-such a duchess doesn't invite her to her party." And of course,' she continued, 'all too often the poor girls just don't fit in anyhow. They're just plain miserable most of the time. They've never hunted. They've never seen a cock pheasant, and as the six months or so the season lasts are the time the girls make their friends for life, not to mention picking up a husband, all this is pretty fundamental.'

Also now that the restraining influence of the Queen has gone, the deb business seems to have turned into a remarkably high-powered industry in which the snobbery and the status scrambling have become more marked than ever before. 'The mums are getting tougher and having their lunches in September. The girls are tending to be launched at the first parties in January. They rush off for a quick freshening-up holiday abroad for a fortnight and then they're back for the start of the Scottish season before the London season opens in May.'

Clearly this is a situation in which the ambitious girl and even more the ambitious parent, needs the right publicity for all she is worth. Some of the agents swamp the gossip columns and society magazines with news items and photographs of their clients. But Mrs B. is inclined to think that this is overdoing things. 'Good publicity can certainly help any girl these days, but I find it difficult to know how far to go with it. Too much can put people's backs up. I've always found that a gentle puff at a good moment with a flattering photograph can work wonders for a girl. Just one really good picture in the papers at the right time. That's all you need.'

<h2 style="text-align:center">6</h2>

Finally, in this strange world of personal public relations, there is the case of the public relations man who acts for a client who does *not* want publicity. This type of client is the antithesis of the actress who judges her success by the number of times her picture gets on to the front pages of the newspapers. This client wants to be left alone to get on with his business and to have a sporting chance of knowing that if anyone does write about him the facts at least will be accurate.

This was very much the case with Aristotle Onassis, the Greek shipping magnate, when, in 1955, he took the advice of several influential friends in England and decided that the time had come to employ a personal consultant. It was through two of these friends, Sir Lionel Heald and the late Lord Bracken, that he was put in touch with a man named Nigel Neilson.

In some ways Neilson must have seemed the very last person to suggest to a Greek millionaire in search of anonymity. He is round-faced and exuberant. He originally came to London from New Zealand on a R A D A scholarship and has sung in cabaret at the Savoy and toured in *Hellzapoppin'*. It is in character that the one event he is proudest of in a distinguished war record is to have taken part in what he claims to have been the last genuine cavalry charge in history when he rode with the Transjordanian Frontier Force in Syria against the Spahis of Vichy France.

Even today he is still quite unlike any other public relations man in the business. He is as purposefully relaxed as only an ex-actor could be, and his office with its grey fitted carpet, its flowers on the table and the photograph of Onassis framed like some minor Central European royalty on the desk, could be a sitting-room in quietest Kensington. On the bookshelf *Mme de Staël and her Lovers* is next to the *Oil and Petroleum Yearbook* and Wordsworth's *Greece*.

In 1955 he was working in the P R department of J. Walter Thompson, where his accounts included Whitbread, the Cheese Bureau and the London Stock Exchange. It was from this position that he was invited to go to Monte Carlo and see Aristotle Onassis.

At this time, Onassis's concern over his personal publicity was not an example of another rich man with one skin too few. In the past he had tended to work on the policy that people could say what they liked about him provided they did not interfere with him making money and he had tried to operate by simply ignoring the press. He never gave an interview unless he absolutely had to and did his best to dodge the reporters whenever they were within the vicinity.

But by now he had found that his unattainability was producing exactly the contrary effect to what he wanted. With his dark glasses, his impassive face and his unyielding reticence he was turning into precisely the sort of mystery man the newspapers love. Since he said nothing, anything could be and was being said about him. One story got around that he was intending to sail his tankers under the Vatican flag, another that he was going to build a mammoth casino in London, another that he intended to restore the Colosseum in Rome, and yet another that he was going to build refineries in India.

Worse still, as Neilson himself said, the sad fact is that the public likes to read about cads, and the newspapers are not interested in writing about the normal or polite or well-behaved. They aren't news. And since Onassis wouldn't see journalists, they couldn't give the true picture of the man.

By 1955, Aristotle Onassis was beginning to find that being cast in the role of a villain by a few popular newspapers could actually be bad for business. For once a reputation has been formed, even by the wildest of gossip columnists, it has a habit of growing. And rich though Onassis was, the one thing he could not afford was to be universally distrusted.

This was the situation when Nigel Neilson called on Onassis early in 1955.

By this time Onassis was understandably pessimistic over the whole business of his personal publicity. He and Neilson talked generalities about publicity for a while. Then, according to Neilson, he went over to a desk, said rather gloomily, 'I don't suppose anything can be done', and opened a drawer with presentations from P R firms in London who were clamouring for the job of handling his public relations.

'Each one said how many men they would need to handle a client of his importance, how many social secretaries and so on. Onassis asked me what I would need to do the job. I replied, "just myself and my confidential secretary." I don't know if my reply had anything to do with it, but I was informed shortly afterwards that he wanted me to represent him in Britain.'

'The relations between a P R and his principal,' Neilson remarked, 'should be like those between a doctor and his patient. If you take on a doctor you must not keep anything from him, and you must expect to act on his advice.'

In this case the advice Doctor Neilson gave his million-dollar patient was quite simple. 'I knew perfectly well,' he said, 'that if anyone does not know the facts he will make up a story. And as a P R man I knew that it's never any use denying a story. At the point where you have to say "it's not true", the damage has been done. The story's still there. It's in the cuttings libraries of all the newspapers and it will go on being cooked up in articles for years to come. So, as far as the Press went, the first thing we had to do was to make sure that there was one decent, accurate series on Onassis in the cuttings library of every newspaper in the country. So when Graham Stanford, one of the staff-writers on the *News of the World*, told me of his difficulties in writing a series on Onassis I was pleased to co-operate. He worked hard and produced first-class articles – true yet interesting. The fact is that Onassis is dramatic enough in his own right. Nobody needs to invent.'

For Neilson this was a start in giving his client's image a professional face-lift. His next concern was with Onassis's yacht – *Christina*. 'Rumours were getting around,' he said, 'that it was a sort of floating gin-palace with all sorts of things going on aboard. In fact, this was nonsense. It's simply lovely, so I took some reputable journalists down to see for themselves.'

Once again, this seemed to work, and encouraged by the more agreeable publicity he was getting, Onassis began to be more amenable to the idea of meeting the press. Within a fairly short time of taking over the business of Onassis's P R, Nigel Neilson had achieved his first objective. 'My theory in public relations is perfectly simple,' he said with considerable candour. 'Unless you're doing something perfectly ghastly, tell the facts. Someone will still twist them, of course, but not so badly as if you tell them nothing at all.'

Acting on this particular theory, he had given a flawless example of how a P R man can use the press to create a favourable impression of a client to counter an existing unfavourable one. To do this he had used the invaluable P R technique of giving minor scoops to a limited number of reputable journalists, who were presumably grateful for what they had received. Not that gratitude carries a P R very far in his dealings with the Press. What was more to the point was that he had established the fact among the journalists he had dealt with that he was the best, in point of fact, the only source of genuine news on his client.

This is an enviable position for any personal P R to be in and certainly it takes an adroit man to get there. It also requires a considerable amount of trust between the P R and his client if it is to last, for as soon as there is any hint that the client is not taking his adviser's advice, the PR's authority as the main source of news immediately collapses. But throughout the period Neilson has worked for Onassis, the confidence the shipping magnate has placed in him has been such as most PRS would envy. Whenever Onassis is in London, they meet daily, and at other times Neilson is usually on the move, in Monte Carlo, in Greece, aboard *Christina*, or anywhere that his presence is needed. He gets on well with Onassis himself, often acting as his *de facto* representative in London and advising him on business matters usually well outside the scope of the normal PR man.

He had hardly ever been known to produce a press handout. 'The old theory of public relations has been superseded,' he said. 'There's a great deal more to PR these days than being a not very good writer.

'By now I know the people in the Press that I can trust and they know me. Because of this I can tell them the whole background to a situation and they ask, "how much of this do you want to publish?" Obviously, business transactions must be secret. I have never been let down by a journalist – and I've never tried to deceive one. It's all a matter of mutual trust.'

Throughout the persuasion industry the most difficult thing of all is to assess success. Invariably, publicity is only one factor among many which go to produce the success or failure of a campaign, so that it is usually as unjustifiable for a publicist to claim the whole of a success as for a client to blame him for the whole of a failure. You can never sell a flop.

This is so in advertising. It is even more so in public relations and it would clearly be wrong to see too much of Nigel Neilson's handiwork behind the quite remarkable change there has been in the way the Press has been handling Aristotle Onassis recently. All that one can do is to notice the difference between the sort of publicity Onassis was receiving when Neilson took over his publicity, and the sedate way in which the Press treated the news of his divorce and the later stages of his friendship with Maria Callas.

For Neilson the Onassis account was the beginning of greater things. When he was confident that his policy was continuing steadily he approached Onassis and asked if he might widen his practice. When the *Star* and the *News Chronicle* closed down, Ralph McCarthy, the editor of the *Star*, decided not to seek another editorial chair but go into the fast-growing business of public relations. He and Neilson went into partnership. The firm grew swiftly. They now have two more directors, a controlling interest in a publicity company, and accounts which include some of the most important organizations in London.

PART 3. 'LEGAL, CLEAN, HONEST AND TRUTHFUL'

23. 'Legal, Clean, Honest and Truthful'

There is something euphoric about Eastbourne and there is something still more euphoric about the closing sessions of advertising conferences, but neither fact quite explains the almost apocalyptic words of the then Parliamentary Secretary to the Board of Trade, Mr Niall MacPherson (now the Rt Hon the Lord Drumalbyn) when he spoke at the closing session of the 1962 Advertising Association conference.

'I believe,' he said, 'that in time to come economists and historians will point to 1962 as a year of great significance in the development of advertising in the twentieth century, because it was then that the conference was held at which the Advertising Standards Authority was finally brought into the world. In creating the Advertising Standards Authority,' he told his audience, 'you are once again demonstrating to the public your determination to exercise self-discipline, individually and collectively, and steadily to improve the quality and integrity of the service that you give.'[1]

As he spoke these words the sense of relief within the hall was almost

---

[1] The public relations business has its own 'watchdog' – The Institute of Public Relations, founded in 1948 (first president, Sir Stephen Tallents). Only half the members of the profession, however, are in membership which still has to reach 2000. This limits the I P R's disciplinary powers, but it has been tightening up its entry qualifications and, from July 1965, new members will have to pass an examination which will include a study of the ethics of the business. The I P R laid down a new code of ethics in 1964 which the president of the Institute, Colin Mann, was quoted as saying would 'make it impossible for any public relations man in future to sail under false colours'.

tangible. When he concluded, the applause was heartfelt. For top advertising men tend to feel, rightly or wrongly, that society has a habit of picking on them as scapegoats for the sort of ills society is too lazy to do anything more positive about, and at these annual advertising junkets, this sense of anxiety has a habit of showing itself in a round of sincere and somewhat emotional self-justification.

But before this particular conference they had been becoming more *angst*-ridden than usual. For months past the more sensitive of them had been sniffing real trouble in the wind. The Board of Trade had set up a committee under J. T. Molony to inquire into consumer protection and although its report had just been signed and was to give advertising in general a far cleaner bill of health than many had expected, it was felt that official inquiries into advertising set a dangerous precedent.

The Royal College of Physicians' report on the relation between cigarette smoking and lung cancer had also recently appeared and sections of the Labour Party were already making threatening noises about tobacco advertising.[2] General criticism of advertising as a whole was clearly increasing. When Francis Noel-Baker, M P, formed his Advertising Inquiry Council to scrutinize the work of the advertisers he had even secured Lord Fisher of Lambeth, the former Archbishop of Canterbury, among his list of sponsors in place of the usual and more easily discountable crop of social cranks and critics who had tended to criticize advertising in the past. And as everyone in the hall knew, across the Atlantic, where there was now an administration notably out of sympathy with Madison Avenue, the agency business was suffering the attentions of an organization known as the Federal Trade Commission. This was a government-sponsored board which scrutinized all advertising as it appeared, had power to call for proof of any advertising claim, and frequently clamped down with brutal decisiveness on anything it thought anti-social or misleading.

But at Eastbourne that fine summer morning anxiety at last seemed unnecessary. Mr MacPherson was a member of Her Majesty's Government. He had used those words like 'quality', 'integrity', and 'self-discipline' which are so dear to the persuasion industry itself. He had given his official blessing to the new organization the Advertising Association had just voted into being to make sure that the quality, integrity and self-discipline continued. And he had made it clear that for the time being at any rate, the danger of outside interference was over. If advertising needed to set its house in order, the industry was to be given a chance to do the job itself.

But how exactly had British advertising disciplined itself in the past?

[2] The noises have now produced a result. From August, 1965, television advertising of cigarettes will cease.

What was this new organization which had just been set up? And if the industry as a whole was already as disciplined as it claimed, why was it necessary?

These are deep questions, the complete answers to which lie tangled within the obscure undergrowth of committees and *ad hoc* organizations which have grown as advertising has grown, and which together, in their erratic and Burkeian way, formed a sort of collective conscience for the industry. To even the most clear-headed of outsiders it must all seem the most baffling arrangement of overlapping powers and jurisdictions, although for anyone who is determined to master the subject the Advertising Association has issued a small orange-coloured booklet, priced 1s 6d, on *How Advertising Disciplines Itself*, with the optimistic subtitle, 'A Guide to the Voluntary Controls set up by Advertising to ensure that all advertising is legal, clean, honest and truthful'.

In the past these unexceptionable ideals have been striven for on the general principle that each part of the industry should interpret them for its own members largely according to its own lights. Far from there being a single censoring or direction-giving body for advertising as a whole, there were several quite distinct organizations, each with its own prerogative and each quite capable of advancing its own interpretation of 'legal, clean, honest and truthful'.

The strongest and most influential of these individual organizations was traditionally the Newspaper Proprietors' Association. It was strong for the simple reason that it represented the people who collectively owned the most important advertising media in the country – the London, but not the provincial, press. As such it held the power to withdraw its recognition from any advertising agency it disapproved of. At the same time it ran a joint advertising committee with the Newspaper Society, who in their turn operated a special advertisement Investigation Department to make sure that readers were not 'defrauded or misled' by anything the newspapers printed. This Advertising Investigation Department also had the task of collecting information about the status of advertisers, the worth of their products if any doubt existed, and to warn advertising managers of member newspapers about any dubious cases in their confidential 'Advertising Newsletter'.

The periodical proprietors had a separate committee to vet advertisements for their publications. So did the poster industry, the Kinematograph Renters, British Transport Advertising Ltd (who published their own leaflet on 'Policy on acceptance of Advertisements'), the screen advertisers, and the manufacturers of proprietary medicines (who issued their first code of advertising standards in 1937).

To make the situation still more complex, the Advertising Association – described by its publicity officer as 'the authoritative organization in advertising, the umbrella organization of agencies, advertisers and media owners' – had its separate advertising investigation department. This had the task of investigating any cases of 'supposed fraudulent and undesirable advertising', and as the Advertising Association itself puts it, 'to promote confidence in advertising by the correction or suppression of abuses which tend to undermine such confidence'. It had no direct power to enforce its findings, but as the secretary of the Advertising Association, Mr Leslie Room said, 'because of the standing of the A A and because our inquiry department has been going a long time, media owners usually accept any advice it gives them over types of advertising they should not accept.'

Finally, there was one more organization with its finger in the advertising standards establishing pie – the Institute of Practitioners in Advertising. The I P A is the organization of the agencies and agency men, combining the functions of a trade organization for the major agencies (whilst its membership does not include anything like all the agencies in the country, those it has got as members gross about 85 per cent of total national agency billings) with that of a professional organization for agency men. As such it runs its own examinations in all branches of advertising, and membership of the I P A is the nearest to a professional qualification advertising possesses. Currently there are 1500 members and 2500 students.

The I P A has never had the power over the agencies or its individual members that, say the B M A has achieved over individual doctors, but it has always tried to be very much that sort of body and prides itself on possessing what its director, James O'Connor, calls 'the top strata of agency society, the strata of the professionally qualified. If a man's not in it, people would begin to wonder why.'

In its capacity as a professional organization, the I P A, particularly since O'Connor has been its director, has been concerned with the professional standards side of advertising and with ruling out any behaviour which a profession would naturally try to ban among its members.

Such, very briefly, was the advertising industry's apparatus of control as it existed until the Eastbourne meeting of the Advertising Association. It would be wrong as well as churlish to deny that it had operated over the years to raise the whole standard of honesty and accuracy of our advertising. This was particularly so within clearly defined areas. In the patent medicine field, for instance, the Code of Standards of the Proprietary Association had been slowly clearing up a whole mass of misleading and semi-magical advertising carried over from a less scrupulous age. There are, of course, illnesses for which any mention in an advertisement is forbidden by Act of Parliament. These range from whooping cough to venereal diseases, from goitre and impetigo to gallstones and sleeplessness. But in addition to all this the Proprietary Association has ruled out a number of wider abuses in patent medicine advertisements. It forbids the use of the word 'cure' in an advertisement. It bans the diagnosis of treatment by correspondence. It rules out claims to cure baldness or to treat illnesses by hypnosis and it bans advertising for any product claiming to increase or overcome sexual weakness.

In much the same way the joint copy committee of the Newspaper Proprietors' Association and the Newspaper Society and the Advertising Inquiry Department of the Advertising Association, has managed to prevent the appearance of large numbers of purely fraudulent advertisements appearing in the press. This has been particularly the case in the less reputable area of fringe advertising, classified advertisements and 'money back' offers. The Advertising Association, for instance, advised its members against accepting advertising for royal bee jelly. Each year media owners have been asking it to investigate large numbers of suspect mail order and investment advertisements, and as Leslie Room said, 'if we found the firm was unreliable we would advise against it. Our advice didn't have to be accepted of course, but I do not remember a case where it was not'.

Finally, the I P A had its own area of concern. It waged a long and successful war against 'knocking copy' – 'not,' as O'Connor explained, 'because we feared one advertisement criticizing another, but because the total effect would have been misleading to the public and have got advertising a bad name'. It played a part in helping to suppress advertisements for a practice known as 'switch selling'.[3] It issued a report roundly condemning subliminal advertising, and it has always acted to raise what is nebulously but quite legitimately described as 'the standard of taste' expected of its members.

So much for the apparatus of control as it used to exist. The description could go much further, but it is sufficient to establish the most important points. The first was that there was no attempt at a total scrutiny of British advertising. The sort of advertising the apparatus concerned itself with was with isolated cases in sensitive areas. The second was that there were few real teeth in the operation – rulings were usually given in the form of advice rather than orders, and although they were usually accepted, this was by no means always the case.

The third point was that there was considerable and quite alarming variation across advertising as a whole. Where there was no single code, it was hardly surprising that what was banned in one medium would frequently appear quite openly in another.

The fourth was that these rules and organizations operated over the 'respectable' side of advertising. In less reputable areas, advertisers and

[3] The advertising of one product at bargain rates, and the attempt, when anyone inquires about it, to switch the offer to something else. Another word for this practice is 'bait advertising'.

media owners could still behave much as they liked provided they did not actually break the law. The rules of the I P A for instance, naturally had no effect on the great number of smaller agencies who were outside its membership. Nor did the patent medicine rules necessarily influence firms outside the Proprietary Association or media owners outside those (of course the large majority) who had accepted its code.

And lastly and, in a way, most important of all, in all these codes and committees, what the advertisers chose to call 'self-discipline' was what lawyers call being a judge in your own case. In any questions where the interests of advertising might clash with the interests of the public at large, advertising itself settled the issue. This is not to say that the self-discipliners would not act honestly and impartially. But the fact was that all these bodies had developed as buffers between the advertisers and the public. They were there to clamp down on flagrant abuse which might, in the last resort, have earned advertising a bad name. Their job was to avoid trouble. They could hardly be expected to court it by leading opinion and imposing the much tighter standards over taste and innuendo which outside critics had begun to demand.

When Leslie Room was asked, for instance, what he thought about the habit of cigarette advertisers of showing glamorous young people smoking cigarettes in romantic situations (at the time when the controversy was first coming up), he replied 'these things are simply not for us to comment on'. Another official of the Advertising Association told us that 'in general our attitude is that if people are free to manufacture something they should be equally free to advertise it'.

In fact, of course, the real test of the industry's ability to discipline itself came with the setting up of the Independent Television Authority. If the principle of self-discipline had really worked as effectively as its exponents claimed it would presumably have been adopted for this new medium just as it had for all the others. But it was not. Instead, for the first time in British advertising, a set of fairly clear, and all-embracing, rules were imposed as the result of an Act of Parliament on a group of media owners.

Under the 1954 Television Act the Independent Television Authority was given the task of making sure that the recomendations of the Advertising Advisory Committee set up under the Act were complied with.

As the more far-sighted advertising men must have realized this was a dangerous precedent. If a code could be successfully imposed on one medium by Parliament, there was not a great deal to stop it being imposed on all the rest, and it was to forestall such an event, as well as to repair what were admitted to be the loopholes in the old system, that the new proposals of self-discipline which had been so rapturously received at Eastbourne, were finally worked out.

In essence there were three parts to these proposals, all of which have now been carried into operation. The first was that Advertising, with a large A, should agree to its own minimum code of practice, and that all the independent advertising bodies, from the Newspaper Proprietors to the Master Sign Makers Association and the British Direct Mail Advertising Association should subscribe to it. The second was that this code should be administered, interpreted, publicized and generally kept up-to-date by yet another committee called C A P (the British Code of Advertising Practice). And the third was that, to give that touch of disinterested and authoritative external control over the industry as a whole (which it was fairly clear that if the industry itself did not arrange for, a government one day would), a further body should be set up with the impressive title of the Advertising Standards Authority. This was to have the last word on any question of advertising standards. It would deal with any serious complaints. It would have the power to enforce its decisions. It would possess an independent and generally acceptable chairman appointed from outside the industry.

So much for the organizations. All the copy committees and individual disciplinary bodies which had existed before were to continue, subject only to the minimum requirements which the code, the Authority and the C A P committee adumbrated. With such a wealth of machinery for 'self-discipline' the only question was how the industry was to use it.

So far, the answer seems to be – gently. So gently in fact that the cynical outsider might wonder what all the fuss was about at Eastbourne, and whether the addition of two more committees and codes really justified all those heroic words by the Parliamentary Secretary to the Board of Trade.

The Advertising Standards Authority had a quiet first year. Professor Sir Arnold Plant, the economist, was appointed its chairman (by the Advertising Association), along with five 'advertising members' and five 'independent members', and up to December 1963 it had secured the withdrawal of two advertisements for horror films ('which in its view fell in the first case below the minimum standards of decency and in the second case exposed children to frightening influences'). It had also tightened up conditions over advertisements presented in the style of editorial or news matter, initiated an inquiry into the slimming business, and confined advertising for clinics attempting to cure baldness to the simple details of name, address, telephone number and hours of attendance.

Otherwise the authority had little to show for its first year's activities and in its annual report remarks somewhat sadly on 'the surprisingly few representations . . . from persons and organizations with a first-hand knowledge of the advertising business'. But it consoles itself with the thought that 'for this the main reason is undoubtedly to be found in the effectiveness of the existing system of self-discipline and voluntary controls inaugurated by the advertising world itself'.

But is the existing system now really as effective as all that? In the first place there is the straightforward question of enforcing the British Code of Advertising Practice, which the seventeen key organizations in British advertising have agreed to observe as their minimum standard. It might be thought that an elementary step in making sure that a code is observed would be to watch methodically and check up on infringements. Not so the advertisers.

The CAP committee which is responsible for enforcing the code has a full-time secretary, an amiable barrister called John Crockett, and relies on the Advertising Association for its premises and its secretarial staff. It costs the Association possibly £5000 a year to run and, as Crockett himself quite openly admits, with its present budget and facilities, the committee has not the faintest chance of performing a regular scrutiny of all advertising as it appears.

Instead, the committee relies on 'self-discipline' which in this case boils down to persuading the different parts of the industry to send their representatives to the CAP committee's meetings, where the enforcement and any infringements of the code can be talked over and action be secured on, as John Crockett puts it, 'an informal basis'.

As a description of how advertising has tended to control itself in the past this is unexceptionable, but as a way of enforcing a code it is rather the same as if the police agreed to withdraw all traffic police on condition that representatives of motoring organizations attended a monthly meeting to discuss the highway code and then gave their word that their members would never break it.

This may sound a little far-fetched, were it not for the actual experience of the CAP committee itself. Realizing the need to carry out some form of scrutiny on advertisements it was particularly concerned about, it commissioned the Legion Publishing cuttings agency to collect all advertisements in the British press on a number of topics including slimming, hair clinics and sewing machine advertising. According to a report in the *Advertisers' Weekly* for March 20th, 1964, the result was to show that 43 per cent of the slimming advertisements contained contraventions of the code.

Encouraged or disturbed by these discoveries, the CAP committee says that it is now intending to continue its experiments into other fields of advertising. But until the CAP committee or the Advertising Association has proper facilities to scrutinize every individual advertisement as it appears, it is impossible for them to know whether its code of standards is anything more than a collection of piously held platitudes. Admittedly slimming preparations were probably an extreme case, but even so

43 per cent is a startlingly high percentage for infringements of a code which Sir Arnold Plant's Standards Authority could point to with such benign confidence.

And from one's own experiences of the advertising one sees, it is perfectly obvious that at present a great many more advertisements are getting through which a minimally strict enforcement of the code would rule out. Section 6 for instance, headed 'advertisements addressed to children', specifically rules out advertising 'which exploits their natural credulity', and yet a whole range of sweet, cereal and toy advertising continues to do just that. Section 4 (a) says that 'no advertisement should contain any reference calculated to lead the public to assume that the product advertised, or any ingredient, has some special quality or property which is incapable of being established', and yet a moment with almost any newspaper or magazine will show that our advertising is still full of what American advertising men call 'the operation of the uncheckable claim'.

Section Four (c) states that testimonials 'must be genuine and should not be used in a manner calculated to mislead', and yet the C A P committee has no regular machinery for checking whether testimonials are genuine or not.

At the same time it is noticeable that the code gives a minimum of guidance on the very topics which have been causing the greatest controversies over advertising recently. Except for the bland warning in section One (a) against anything 'offensive to public decency', there is not the slightest hint of how sex should or should not be used in advertising. And the code is similarly mute on such subjects as drink and cigarette advertising and about the age range at which the advertising for certain products like beer and cigarettes is aimed.

'The reason that such things as sex and age are not included specifically in our code,' says O'Connor of the I P A, giving an answer that echoes time and again within the industry, 'is that these happen to be matters of taste and taste is the one thing it is impossible to legislate about.'

Nevertheless, as far as the advertising industry itself is concerned, there is a great advantage in having this area of vagueness. The present situation already means that the work of correcting any abuses is kept firmly within the family, and with the discretion which the looseness of the code inevitably gives the different committees, it seems likely that advertising's attempts at self-discipline will continue to be as painless and decorous as they have invariably been in the past.

There is, however, one important exception to all this – one section of the industry which has been denied the gentle luxury of self-discipline, and which is compelled to conform to a rigidly enforced set of rules instead. When the 1954 Television Act made it mandatory for the different television companies to see that any advertising they carried conformed to the ITA's Principles of Television advertising, Parliament in effect was creating two quite separate standards of advertising. This double standard has continued ever since.

On the one hand is television advertising, every piece of which is scrutinized beforehand by a central committee and compelled to comply with an increasingly demanding set of rules, the infringement of which could lead to direct action by the Government. And on the other hand is the rest of advertising with no overall scrutiny of individual advertisements, an undemanding code and responsibility to an authority whose expenses the industry pays and whose members it appoints.

It should be emphasized that this double standard is not merely theoretical. In practice it appears even more clearly in the contrast between the leisurely operation of 'self-discipline' in advertising as a whole and the precise and often very tough way the programme companies' censoring committee deals with the commercials which are submitted to it. At first sight this censoring committee looks like yet another of those *ad hoc* creations which British media owners have been in the habit of setting up to enforce their own views of the standards of the advertising they accept. In itself it has no legal obligation to censor anything. (Under the Television Act it is the Independent Television Authority which is ultimately responsible for seeing that the legal minimum for commercials is actually imposed, just as each of the eleven independent television contracting companies in the country has an obligation to see that any commercials it broadcasts conform to it.)

But in practice it was found that the only way of making sure that they did conform was for the separate companies to join forces to vet all television commercials centrally and to impose a single standard of interpretation for the whole country. The copy committee of the Independent Television Companies Association was the organization set up to do it and at present deals with just over seven thousand separate television commercials a year.

The Independent Television Authority has the last word over any disputed or particularly difficult decisions, and also sees all projected commercials before they are finally accepted. This participation of the Authority in the work of scrutinizing commercials has recently been stepped up after criticisms that the programme companies were being left too much freedom in the work of censorship. But in fact the day-to-day work of scrutinizing commercials continues to be done by the ITCA, and however anomalous the idea may seem of having the bulk of the censoring done by the same people who are trying to sell television time to the advertisers, it is hard to fault the efficiency with which they have done their work over the last eight years.

The ITA's Code on Television Advertising which appeared in the summer of 1964 was based almost verbatim on the Notes of Guidance on Television Advertising which the I T C A had previously worked out to give advertisers a clearer idea of what was and was not acceptable than had been set out in the Television Act.

But the real significance of the work of the I T C A copy committee has been to show quite clearly that efficient scrutiny of advertisements is not only possible but is absolutely necessary if any real code of advertising practice is ever to be thoroughly enforced. It also shows that, however difficult it may be to legislate over matters of taste, it is perfectly possible to build up a body of 'case law' so that everyone involved knows, within narrow limits, where they stand.

The way the I T C A committee works is as follows. Once a fortnight the committee itself meets at Television House in the Kingsway under the chairmanship of Guy Paine, the sales director of Associated-Rediffusion. The other three members of the committee are selected sales directors chosen on a yearly basis (as the chairman is himself), from the fifteen television contracting companies. Their job is to deal with any disputed or complicated cases where the precise interpretation of the 'Principles of Television Advertising' is involved. Sometimes they may make a ruling on their own account, such as when they decided that although toilet cleansers could not be shown in action being poured into a lavatory pan, they might be shown against an unmistakable lavatory cistern. (Previously the I T C A's own 'Notes of Guidance on Television Advertising' had, on the grounds of good taste, banned any hint of where these cleansers were actually used. This had led to a number of complaints from manufacturers that members of the public had been using them as general cleaners on kitchen floors as a result of the vagueness of the commercials.)

At other times if more serious matters of principle are involved, the committee can decide to refer the case to the I T A itself.

In fact, such cases are comparatively rare for the simple reason that the majority of minor infringements of the rules are weeded out much earlier on. This is done, not at the level of the committee itself, but by the committee's secretariat, an organization of about ten people who every year check through the scripts and story-boards of the seven thousand or so commercials which ultimately appear on television.

An important feature of the way this secretariat works is that it does its checking not only before the commercials are actually broadcast (this is done every morning at ten, when all that evening's commercials are viewed on closed circuit television both at Television House and at the I T A's headquarters) but also before the advertiser has spent his money in making the film. For the secretariat usually insists on seeing the scripts and story-boards of the commercials, and it is here that the majority of the changes and amendments are made.

According to Reg Davies, the ITCA's chief copy executive and head of this secretariat, there are usually queries on about half of the scripts the agencies submit. At this stage the committee is very much open to argument over any disputed points, and claims that it is more of an adviser than a censor for the agencies. 'All the same,' says Davies, 'we do have an occasional punch-up with an agency. Only the other day I was told that I had obviously a middle-class, suburban mind. Perhaps I have, but in the end we usually get the amendments we want, and I suppose we actually have to reject less than 0.01 per cent of the commercials every year.'

The regulations Davies and his secretariat have to administer are wide and fairly complex, although as he says 'one soon gets to know whatever is contentious and highly charged'.

According to the Principles of Television Advertising, all commercials involving politics, religion and opinion-forming in the widest sense are firmly banned, and from the way the ITCA has interpreted this, a great deal of advertising which would have passed perfectly happily in other media has been ruled out. The medical code the ITCA imposes is much tougher than that used elsewhere – for instance, it is not allowed to refer to rheumatism in a commercial. They must be called rheumatic pains, just as the nearest an advertiser can get to a cold-cure commercial is to say that his product relieves cold symptoms.

The committee is very strict in checking on all testimonials – 'we insist in having a copy in writing on the file'. All technical claims have to be accompanied by a certificate from an accredited testing authority, and great care is taken to make sure that demonstrations of a product not only *are* genuine, but *appear* genuine. This is particularly important in television demonstrations of cleaners, where as Davies says, 'it is surprising what you can do with the lighting to make a perfectly genuine demonstration appear even better than it is'.

The ITCA's biggest headache before the total ban was placed on cigarette advertising on Television in February 1965, had been to work out its own rules for cigarette commercials. This is because it had had the virtually impossible task of ensuring that, while cigarette advertising was legal on television, it must not make any attempt to recruit new smokers. The most that was allowed in theory was to attempt to change the brand loyalties of people who already smoked. In practice, as Guy Paine himself admitted, 'it is probably true to say that if you do an effective cigarette ad at all these days for television, you're running into danger'.

For the rules the ITCA was even then enforcing for cigarette commercials were far stiffer than those imposed by any other medium for cigarette advertising.

The internal notes the ITCA prepared to guide its secretariat in censoring cigarette commercials listed the following 'areas of danger'

1. Hero appeals to manliness.
2. The appeal of social success or the suggestion that smoking is part of the modern, smart, sophisticated and fashionable way of life and that one should smoke to be in the swim.
3. Romantic appeal.
4. Emphasis on exaggerated satisfaction.
5. Young people unmistakably under 21.

Previously, a large proportion of cigarette advertising had seemed to stray into these 'areas of danger'. For instance, one copywriter gave us the following four reasons as his personal check-list when working on a cigarette advertisement.

'1. It's an initiation symbol – a proof that you are on your own in the tribe and have achieved independent manhood.
'2. A nipple substitute – something you still feel the urge to suck in times of stress.
'3. A proof of sociability, to show that you are liked and people like you in return.
'4. A virility symbol – a symbolic penis advertising the fact that in your estimation you can always have a woman anywhere and at any time you want one.'

Not everybody was prepared to go so far, but there had been frequent appeals to manliness – from associating cigarettes with a variety of rugged seafaring men to the advertisement for Guards in 1958 which asserted that the brand brought back 'that Forgotten Flavour' and set the claim oddly beneath the hairy legs of two Rugger players.

Equally, there had been a strong strain of snob-appeal in tobacco advertising. One advertisement for Churchman's No. 1 ran: 'Cigarettes can tell you quite a bit about a man. Men of judgement appreciate Churchman's No. 1'. And, of course, the classic campaign which revealed the romantic promise implicit in a puff of smoke (of the right brand) was the 'People Love Players' campaign, launched by Mather and Crowther in February 1960.

As one of the agency's television producers put it: 'Originally the one idea we had was to make our commercials as romantic and classless as possible – simple unsophisticated pretty girls, chaps without ties wearing raincoats or summer shirts'. All the shooting, the agency decided, would be outdoors because 'in a theatre club, for instance, the atmosphere's poisoned, whereas out in the open all the influences are towards fresh, uncontaminated young living'.

The newspaper advertisements pressed the theme home. 'She leant against a plane tree', said one. 'I against another. I passed her a Player's, and they made a bridge between us.'

The campaign appeared to be highly successful, but in March 1962 there appeared the Royal College of Physicians' report, which threw the tobacco world into a state of chaos.[4] Imperial Tobacco were about to launch a new brand – Wills' Embassy – in June, but the entire campaign was held back until the storm blew over. And, ultimately, the Players' campaign died the death, when the ITCA began to enforce its new rules.

There was also an increasingly strict scrutiny of the actual words the advertisers used for their cigarette commercials. 'Cool clean Consulate' was forced to become 'Cool Fresh Consulate'. 'It seemed to us,' Reg Davies explained, 'that the word "clean" was altogether unacceptable when applied to a cigarette.'

The banning from television of cigarette advertising provides an extreme case of Government stringency. But the fact is that ITCA is imposing a far stricter and a far more thorough-going control over all the advertising it gets than is demanded by any other media owner in the country.

People in advertising are always at pains to point out that television is something of a special case, and that this higher standard of code and enforcement has to do with the nature of the medium – the fact that television is seen by the family, that it enters the home, and that it is likely to be seen by young children. But this seems to ignore the fact that newspapers enter the home as well, that families can look at magazines, that young people can catch sight of hoardings, or even sit in cinemas when commercials are being shown. It is often argued that television must be censored more stringently than any other types of advertising because it has what advertisers like to call 'greater impact' than other media. Yet even this is open to doubt. Certainly, if there is something which is dangerous or controversial or offensive when it is flashed on a television screen for a few seconds there is no reason why it should be less dangerous or controversial or offensive if it is left lying in a newspaper where it can be studied and absorbed at far greater length.

The point is partly an academic one, and short of laboratory tests it is difficult to establish either way. But what is even more difficult to establish is that there is something inherently different in television advertising demanding that it should be controlled in such a totally different way from the rest of advertising.

[4] Another apparent result of this and subsequent medical reports on the connection between smoking and lung cancer was to increase the trend towards tipped smoking. Even in 1963, the country spent roughly £1100 million on cigarettes.

More than this, it seems that the way advertising is controlled on commercial television shows up the weaknesses of any other method being used at present, and suggests that if society is serious enough about the effect of advertising to impose this method of control on one medium, there is no reason at all why it should not be applied equally to the rest of advertising.

24. Final Thoughts

One of the strangest things about controversy over advertising is that the greater the fuss, the more of a mystery the industry itself seems to become. Advertising is a passionate area. It seems to affect those who attack it and those who defend it in remarkably similar ways. Before long both are exhibiting the same compulsive urge to overstate their case so that it is difficult to believe that the critics and the defenders of advertising are even arguing over the same thing.

But just as it seemed sensible to us to regard advertising without going to either extreme, so it also seemed logical to try and find out, as cold-bloodedly as we could, what advertising in the Britain of the 'sixties really was.

We knew that it consumed around £500 million a year, or roughly 2 per cent of the national income. We knew that it employed something over 200,000 individuals, the majority of whom were paid salaries considerably above the national average. And we knew that it was supposedly run in accordance with certain rather vague and often complex rules and 'professional' taboos.

But once we tried finding out exactly what all this money went on, what all these highly paid individuals did for it (and with it), and how the rules and taboos influenced them, a curious thing happened. This strange animal called advertising, so loathed by its critics and so beloved by its defenders, began to disappear. In its place were advertising men and advertising agencies – all working in different ways and to different rules and all showing quite startling differences of competence, taste and effectiveness.

We started by expecting to find a conspiracy of case-hardened persuaders. We ended by discovering groups of well paid, highly anxious individuals all trying, in their various ways, to accommodate a number of opposed and often contradictory forces within their work. Their success or failure in reconciling these forces results in the advertising we all must endure.

All this seemed of considerable importance. For unless society is willing to give advertising a complete *carte blanche* (which strikes us as lunacy) or to ban all advertising totally (which strikes us as absurdity) any future move to reform advertising, will have to make the mental effort to understand what it is about and why its practitioners behave as they do. To understand this the first necessity will be to understand these forces that shape their working lives.

The first of these forces lies in the very nature of the advertising agency itself. The artificial creation of the advertisers and the media owners, the agency is always in a particularly exposed and vulnerable position. It has maximum visibility with minimum responsibility. Existing on sufferance, living always on its wits, it is accountable for the image of companies over whose policies it has no ultimate control. It must do what it can while it can, for this is a frivolous as well as a competitive world. The easiest economy a company can make is to cut its advertising budget. The simplest decision a board can take is to change its agency.

The results of all this are those which we have seen. For the life of any successful agency is a sort of organizational high-wire act with only the most tenuous of nets to soften disaster. It must play safe and yet it must get results. It must flatter the client and yet not be so subservient that its advertising sinks into sycophantic mediocrity. It must make its own reputation through the face it puts on the products other men make.

Under such conditions the wonder is, not that advertising is as bad or as annoying or as tasteless as it often is, as that it emerges with any coherence at all. Certainly it is no coincidence that the men who have succeeded in putting their stamp on the work of a particular agency have inevitably been slightly larger than life. This is a world where a touch of megalomania does nobody's career any harm.

This chronic insecurity of the advertising business also accounts for many of the examples of silliness, assertiveness and anxiety which we have described in these pages. Again, the wonder is that so many advertising men manage to keep their sanity intact and their sense of humour in good repair. For advertising, despite the salaries and the expense accounts, is a nerve-racking way of making a living. Real success at it demands a scarifying amount of hard and often tedious work. The satisfactions of watching a sales curve flicker upwards after six months of solemn toil are not always sufficient to give the individual advertising man the sense of purpose most of us require out of life.

Because of this it is hardly surprising that only a smallish proportion of the people we talked to – and these mostly at the top end of the business – seemed happy at the idea of making advertising a lifetime's career. Even at the top, we got the idea that there was only a handful of men wholly committed to the advertising business, body and soul. Whole-hoggers like Patrick Dolan and Jack Wynne-Williams are exceedingly rare.

For despite the impassioned language with which the spokesmen of advertising defend their trade, and despite the earnest imprecations for belief in their calling which are a commonplace of any advertising conference, advertising can hardly help but be a fairly cynical business. One can only admire the people in it who, despite all this, do succeed in producing advertisements which are amusing or intelligent or stylish or straightforwardly effective. The odds against them are heavier than most of the advertising critics care to admit.

The other fact about the advertising business which struck us repeatedly was its surprising loneliness and isolation. Just as the agencies exist at the whim of their clients, so advertising men themselves seem to form a strange inner society of their own. More than in most careers, they form a sort of self-perpetuating clique, with its own gossip, its own brand of humour, its own distinct view of life. And as we have tried to show, it is remarkable how often the advertising they produce turns out to be a direct projection of this view.

Perhaps it is partly because of this that the final impression we got was not of how wicked most of their advertising was, but how incompetent. In these pages we have tended inevitably to single out the most original and usually the most successful advertising campaigns we discovered. But for every successful campaign, the death-rate among the unsuccessful is appallingly high. Instead of the steely-minded manipulators of public taste which some critics seem to be concerned about, we found a surprisingly high proportion of muddled, worried men who seemed disturbingly out of touch with the very people they were paid their high salaries to convince.

And just as the most successful advertising men seemed to be those who had a knack of picking out the essential thing about a product that people would want to know and then presenting this as simply and straightforwardly as possible, so the excesses and the failures of campaigns usually came when they began to reflect some part or other of the advertising world itself.

To say this is not to argue that there is no need for outside supervision and control over advertising. Rather the reverse. The sillier and the more out-of-touch advertising becomes, the more misleading and irresponsible it is likely to be. What would be incorrect, however, would be to suggest, as some critics have, that as a nation our buying preferences, our ideals, even our morals, are menaced by a sinister conspiracy of hidden persuaders in the advertising agencies.

Anyone who is seriously troubled by this can find comfort in the thought that the list of failed campaigns is reassuringly long. Hunch is all too often a substitute for brain-power. Research, except in remarkable cases, is usually pathetically sketchy. If advertising is ever to become the dangerous science of mental manipulation some people fear, that day is still a long way off.

One has only to observe the uncritical way the advertising industry adopted television as the great new medium to see just how little data they will actually work on. For at least five years after the introduction of commercial television, tens of millions of pounds were spent on television advertising by agencies which had literally no idea what they were getting for their (or rather their clients') money in terms of audience attention. Even today, they are still not sure precisely what they are buying.

And if it is the level of incompetence of the advertising industry which provides society at present with its surest defence against the wilder excesses dreamed up by certain critics, this seems to be even more so in the case of public relations.

For here, *par excellence*, is a case of an activity rendered impotent by its own excesses. The examples we have given must be judged on their own merits or lack of them, but it would be paying the majority of London's P RS too high a compliment to credit them with a fraction of the influence they would like to claim for themselves. Men who are often so inept can scarcely be considered sinister.